Improving the Quality of Child Custody Evaluations

Lauren Woodward Tolle • William T. O'Donohue

Improving the Quality of Child Custody Evaluations

A Systematic Model

Springer

Lauren Woodward Tolle
Aurora Research Institute
11059 East Bethany Drive
Suite 105
Aurora, CO 80014
USA

William T. O'Donohue
Department of Psychology
University of Nevada
Reno, NV 89557-0062
USA

ISBN 978-1-4614-3404-7 ISBN 978-1-4614-3405-4 (eBook)
DOI 10.1007/978-1-4614-3405-4
Springer New York Heidelberg Dordrecht London

Library of Congress Control Number: 2012934953

Printed on acid-free paper

Springer is part of Springer Science+Business Media (www.springer.com)

We dedicate this book to our spouses and children, Nate, Liam, Jane, Katie and Anna. We would also like to thank Ann Wilson for her editorial assistance.

Contents

List of Tables

Chapter 1
Introduction: Outlining the Problem

The phrase "valid custody evaluations" largely remains a paradox. There is no clear evidence that custody evaluators can conduct evaluations that are, in fact, in the "best interests of the child." This is a serious and important legal and societal problem. In dissolution of relationships, courts often rely on mental health professionals to aid them in making decisions so that harm to children is minimized and their best interests are served. But do mental health professionals know how to achieve these goals? (O'Donohue & Bradley, 1999). What is the scientific evidence that mental health professionals can actually meet the expectations and needs of the court, and produce an accurate account of arrangements that will serve the best interests of the child? What is the evidence that two evaluators will make similar recommendations in the same case (i.e., the inter-rater reliability of custody evaluations)? Is this a systemic problem, i.e., the knowledge of valid assessment protocols and decisions about custody dispositions based on these is simply not available? That is, has the science not progressed to this degree? Or, is it also in part that there is a range of competence of individual custody evaluators and that some can achieve this end better than others? If there is a quality crisis in custody evaluations, what should be done? Should there be a moratorium so that at least mental health professionals are following the Hippocratic ethical dictum of "at least doing no harm"? (O'Donohue & Bradley, 1999). How should professionals conducting custody evaluations be held accountable by the courts, by parents, and by professional ethical boards?

Children are affected in many ways, and for many years, by the recommendations that mental health professionals make in custody evaluations. These evaluations influence the amount of time children spend with each parent and under what conditions (i.e., supervised visitation, weeknights, weekends, overnights, etc.). Recommendations can influence whom the child spends important holiday and birthdays with; whether relocation on the part of one of the parents is allowed or disallowed and how this affects time with the remaining parent. These recommendations can last for a long period of time—in some cases 17 years, i.e., until the child comes of age (which of course makes the prediction task of the evaluator all that more difficult). Of course, these recommendations also affect parents, grandparents, and other relatives and friends.

L.W. Tolle and W.T. O'Donohue, *Improving the Quality of Child Custody Evaluations*,
DOI 10.1007/978-1-4614-3405-4_1, © Springer Science+Business Media, LLC 2012

Mistakes or errors in judgment made by an evaluator can be detrimental to the child's well-being in a number of ways. If child abuse or neglect is alleged by one parent and the evaluator erroneously determines that there is no sufficient evidence to support the allegation [e.g., no reports to Child Protective Services (CPS); child is not alleging this], the recommendations made by this evaluator might place a child in a harmful environment where further abuse could occur. In relocation cases, where the child moves with the primary parent, the child could suffer relational problems with the parent who does not move. Given the number of crucially important factors associated with a custody evaluation, one would hope that all precautionary measures are taken to ensure that the best interest of the child (BIC) is upheld. Disturbingly, however, there is little science guiding evaluators so that they can make valid, empirically driven recommendations for child custody (Emery, Otto, & O'Donohue, 2005; O'Donohue & Bradley, 1999).

The prominent philosopher of science Laudan (1977) has suggested that science has both conceptual and empirical problems. All too often psychologists have acted as if there are only empirical problems. Laudan points out that scientific progress also is made when progress is made in a science's conceptual problems. For example, psychologists have done more work trying to detect possible differences between ethnic groups in intelligence (an empirical problem) than in solving the conceptual problem of what is intelligence? This has led the eminent analytic philosopher Wittgenstein (1940) to comment.

The confusion and barrenness of psychology are not to be explained by calling it a "young science"; its state is not comparable with that of physics, for instance, in its beginnings. (Rather with that of certain branches of mathematics. Set theory.) For in psychology there are experimental methods and *conceptual confusion*. (As in the other case, conceptual confusion and methods of proof.) The existence of the experimental method makes us think we have the means of solving the problems that trouble us; though problem and method pass one another by (PI p. 232).

We think, similarly, custody evaluations and the child best interest standard "pass one another by" to use Wittgenstein's felicitous phrase. There is conceptual confusion regarding child custody evaluations and important conceptual problems to be solved. A key cause of this confusion, in our view, is the lack of clarity and explication of the key standard underlying these—the best interests of the child.

Rates of divorce have been reported to range from 40% to 60% in the USA (divorcerate.org). This is a slightly misleading statistic, however, as it combines first, second, and third marriages and divorce rates have been found to be higher in second and third marriages. Specifically, approximately 41% of first marriages, 60% of second marriages, and 73% of third marriages end in divorce (Baker, 2003).

Divorce rates have skyrocketed over the last 30 years. Many reasons have been purported to explain the dramatic increase seen in the late 1960s and 1970s, including a greater number of women entering the workforce, an increase in feminism and feministic attitudes, and the adoption of the "no-fault" divorce (divorce granted without having to establish wrongdoing by either party), making a divorce much easier to obtain (Powell, 2003). An estimated 660,000 divorces occurred between 2006 and 2008 in the USA, though this is likely an underestimate as not all states provide or keep track of divorce counts (i.e., California, Georgia, Hawaii, Indiana, Louisiana, and Minnesota) and monthly counts might be underreported (National Center for Health Statistics, 2008).

Divorce Rates in Families with Children

Along with the overall dramatic increase in divorce in the 1970s, the number of couples with children who divorced increased by 700% from 1900 to 1970 (Davis, 1977). Similarly, the 1998 Census Bureau reported that children under the age of 18 living with one parent increased from 12% in 1970 to 28% in 1996, and children living with both parents decreased from 85% to 68% during the same time span (U.S. Census Bureau, 1998). Despite these statistics, divorce rates have been found to be lower in couples who have children than in childless couples, with estimates of 40% of couples with children divorcing and 66% of childless couples divorcing (Heaton, 1990). In attempting to account for this discrepancy, researchers have reported that the attitude to "stay together for the sake of the family" (Thornton, 1985) may be an important reason that parents do not divorce. Another potential deterrent that has been reported is the financial expense related to both the cost of a divorce and the decrease from a dual-parent income to a single-parent income (Albrecht, Bahr, & Goodman, 1983). Finally, infertility in couples has been associated with an increase in risk for divorce (Myers, 1997). Despite the seemingly prophylactic effect children can have on marriage stability, there are still many cases for which this is an insufficient deterrent (Willats, 1993).

Annually, approximately one million children in America are involved in a divorce (American Academy for Child and Adolescent Psychiatry, 1997). In addition, close to one-half of children from divorced homes will also witness the dissolution of a parent's second marriage (Furstenberg, Peterson, Nord, & Zill, 1983). Additionally, approximately 100,000 custody evaluations occur annually in the USA. Despite the number of child custody evaluations completed every year, there is little research guiding how these evaluations should be conducted so that they actually describe the best interests of the child. Standards for establishing that child custody evaluation models are empirically supported should be comparable to standards for establishing that psychological treatments are empirically supported. In order for a treatment to be considered empirically supported (or validated) per the Division 12 Task Force (Chambless et al., 1998):

1. It must be supported by at least two randomized, controlled trials showing their superiority to placebo control conditions or another established treatment with appropriate sample sizes to detect significant differences.
   Or
   It must be supported by a number of single-case designs that involved good experimental design and comparison of one treatment to another.

2. The studies must be conducted with treatment (or in this case assessment) manuals or some equivalent.
3. Characteristics of the client samples must be clearly specified.

When applying these standards to models of custody evaluations, it is found that not only they meet none of these criteria—there is no outcome testing of the consequences of custody evaluations—but also no manualized models for conducting evaluations have been established. To be clear, currently there is no evidence that custody evaluations bring about superior outcomes for children involved in these. Put more pessimistically, there is also no evidence that custody evaluations do more good than harm. Longitudinal research is urgently needed which shows the predictive validity of custody evaluations.

In order to create some sort of floor for the quality of custody evaluations, there are some very vague standards regarding custody evaluations such as those promulgated by the American Psychological Association—and although these may decrease the likelihood of truly egregious evaluations (e.g., the standard's stipulation that multiple sources of information must be utilized would rule out a single source evaluation) but there is still too much room for unwanted variance. In addition, and partly because there are no existing manualized models, none have been tested or compared against anything else in order to determine their accuracy or error rates (i.e., no one model for conducting evaluations has been compared to another or any control group, mediation, etc.). What appears to exist instead of this more systematic process is: (1) custody evaluations with unwanted variability (i.e., evaluators use "clinical judgment" to interpret disparate collected data and use various measurement tools, each with its own error term, that they, for various reasons, have come to believe are relevant perhaps only because the tests seem face valid); (2) custody evaluations conducted in the context in which there is no research evaluating predictive validity of these (i.e., what is the long-term accuracy of what evaluators are predicting—to what extent are the predictions of best interests accurate?); (3) custody evaluations conducted in the context of no evidence of inter-rater reliability (i.e., if two evaluators were to conduct evaluations with the same family—would they come out with the same recommendations?); and (4) no evidence of construct validity (what data are important, what are not, and for what reasons?).

Thus, it might be said that there is a "quality crisis" with regard to custody evaluations. For decades these have been conducted in idiosyncratic ways, with substantial variance in the methods, and with no known accuracy. It is unclear, but quite discouraging to contemplate, how many lives have been affected by this quality problem. It might not be too much to say that the poor quality standards in this area have been a form of systematic child abuse.

There are also several important conceptual issues that O'Donohue and Bradley (1999) have argued need to be settled before higher quality custody evaluations can take place. First, there needs to be a model for what constructs ought to be measured. Ought parent–child relationships be measured, and if so, why? Ought parental psychopathology be measured, and if so, why? It is critical to enumerate the entire set of constructs that are relevant to the Best Interests of the Child. To date, this important—even foundational—task has not been done. Instead, to date evaluators have based their evaluations on inchoate, informal models of the child's best interests. For example, Stahl (2010) recently approvingly quoted the legal standard of one state—Michigan's—as if this state had adequately captured the standard. This unsystematic practice has several important negative consequences: (1) there will be unwanted variability in the models relied upon across clinicians resulting in poor inter-rater reliability, and (2) the full logic of the custody evaluation will remain hidden and thus there will be a kind of unaccountability. When the constructs are fully explicated, their measurement operations explicated and the logic of the decisions clearly stated, all parties can more clearly understand and critique the custody evaluations. Such feedback is important for quality improvement and for custody evaluations to become a more rational process. Without this they have a kind of Wizard of Oz aura in which a clinician picks constructs out of the air, measures these in unique ways, and synthesizes these mysteriously to produce custody evaluations. This is puzzling, and perhaps harmful, for the adults and children involved.

This absence of a firm conceptual foundation for custody evaluations is a distressing reality and has been the case for decades. As courts look to mental health professionals to conduct child custody evaluations, it is incumbent on clinical scientists to develop models and tools to begin to demonstrate consistency of process, and the reliability and validity of the inferences made from these evaluation processes. It is important to conceptualize what a solution to this complex problem would look like.

Purpose of This Book

A model of custody evaluations that is construct valid (i.e., the extent to which operationalization of the constructs actually measures what it purports to measure), that serves as a format to result in improved inter-rater reliability of custody evaluations and that has known and acceptable predictive validity would be an important first step. In looking at such a model, it would be necessary to first define predictive criteria. This book attempts to develop such a model, which would ultimately guide the assessment process in custody evaluations. The model will be informed by empirical literature that predicts best outcomes for children.

This book has four main aims: (1) to discuss the past and current state of science regarding child custody evaluations with a focus on the construct of the BIC, (2) to propose a preliminary model (the egregious/promotive factors model, EPFM) that is based on an extensive review of the empirical research related to factors that have been found to be predictive of poorer or positive outcomes in children in order to conduct improved child custody evaluations, (3) to identify and review existing psychological assessments that can reliably measure risk and promotive factors to support the EPFM, and (4) to gain feedback and preliminary support for the EPFM, a pilot study involving family court judges was conducted examining child custody decision making when provided either a EPFM-guided report or an unspecified constructs report.

Chapter 2
Past and Current State of the Field

Though estimates have been reported that 40% of marriages with children end in divorce in the USA, only 10% of divorces require the involvement of a child custody evaluation (Bow, 2006). The remaining 30% of families are able to come to agreements outside of court regarding placement of the child(ren) and visitation of the nonresidential parent (Bow, 2006). Though many attempts have been made to establish guidelines, little research guides what constitutes the best interest of the child (BIC) in the divorce. The first step in developing empirically supported child custody evaluation guidelines is to describe the history and controversies of child custody evaluations, and the problematic current state of science regarding how child custody evaluations are conducted.

Custody Arrangement Controversies

Over that last two centuries, there have been dramatic shifts in legal standards for determining custody. Most of these legal controversies continue. Pre-nineteenth century assumptions about custody were gender biased, with fathers initially being favored based on several assumptions including the belief that the father was better able to provide for the child financially, and the view that children were the property of the father (Kushner, 2006; Waller & Daniel, 2005).

The Tender Years Doctrine

This was followed by a complete reversal seen in the early nineteenth century—by a bias toward the mother largely due to the Tender Years Doctrine, which suggested that mothers should be the preferred guardian for children due to their natural role as caregiver and nurturer, especially in the infant and toddler years of the child's life (Kushner, 2006; Waller & Daniel, 2005). For more than a century, essentially all

L.W. Tolle and W.T. O'Donohue, *Improving the Quality of Child Custody Evaluations*, DOI 10.1007/978-1-4614-3405-4_2, © Springer Science+Business Media, LLC 2012

custody arrangements were awarded to the mother, with fathers given the burden to prove mothers as unfit (Kushner, 2006).

The Tender Years Doctrine continues to influence court decisions, with studies reporting that older judges, especially, are still more likely to award custody to the mother (Hellman, 1988 as cited in Kushner, 2006). Custody decisions were also heavily influenced by the general societal morals of the time, which resulted in discrimination against homosexual and cohabiting, but unmarried, parents (Waller & Daniel, 2005).

The Approximation Rule or Primary Parent

The American Law Institute (ALI) proposed in its *Principles of the Law of Family Dissolution* (1996) that parents in contested custody disputes be awarded custody of their children that most closely approximates the allocation of time parents had with children before the dissolution of the marriage. If, for example, the mother was primary caretaker and spent 80% of the time with the children and the father 20% before the divorce, the mother and father would be awarded the same proportion of time, and therefore promote some form of consistency in the child(ren)'s life pre to post-divorce. While the Approximation Rule attempts to overcome vague language related to the BIC construct and also attempts to mitigate parents' dispositions to viciously attack the integrity or parenting competence of their ex-spouse, it has received much criticism (Warshak, 2007). The Approximation Rule assumes that decisions made regarding primary caretaking roles in the home prior to the separation were permanent, and the primary caretaker, up until the time of the divorce, was the better parent, when this is frequently not the case (Warshak, 2007). An example would be when a couple agrees that a father will work outside the home and the mother will temporarily stay home and care for a young child, with the understanding that she is temporarily putting her career on hold. If the couple were to divorce before she returns to work, this should not freeze time allocations for visitation and prevent the father from having more time with the child, or the mother from re-entering the work force. Furthermore, it is often the case that a stay-at-home parent, due to changed financial circumstances, needs to reenter the workforce thus making time allocations prior to the divorce at least somewhat moot.

Shared Parenting

Shared parenting, joint custody or 50/50 shared custody, is another custody arrangement that describes a family arrangement in which parents have equal time, custody, and decision-making powers with their child(ren). The literature has generally supported joint custody or substantial contact with both parents as this arrangement has been associated with better child outcomes post-divorce (Emery, 1999).

While this seems like an important finding, it is interesting to note that joint custody is rarely recommended in cases that involve litigation, as it is uncommon in these situations that both parents agree to joint custody. That is, if one or both parents contest a shared parenting arrangement, it is unlikely that family courts will recommend this. It is estimated that only 5–10% of custody cases end in a joint custody arrangement (Emery, 1999). The definition of joint custody also appears to differ from state to state (i.e., primary physical residence with one parent but substantial time with another, versus completely equal time at both parents' homes, etc.).

The Least Detrimental Alternative or Psychological Parent

Though not adopted as a statute in any state, the psychological parent is an "all-or-nothing" custody arrangement, which gives sole legal and physical custody to only one parent, and has been an influential theory in the field (Melton et al., 1997). According to this theory, custody is recommended for the parent that has the strongest bond with the child, and that this parent should also have control over the child's amount of time available to the noncustodial parent. This theory has received much criticism regarding how much control it gives to one parent as well as to problems it raises for a custody evaluator to be able to accurately determine the one parent who is the "psychological parent," as frequently children are bonded to both parents (Buehler & Gerard, 1995). In addition, no assessment strategy has yet been established to accurately measure this construct.

Same Sex Custody

Though not frequently recommended as a custody arrangement, giving custody of sons to fathers and daughters to mothers has become a recent recommendation (Powell & Downey, 1997). This arrangement contends that children adjust better in situations in which they are with their same sex parent as opposed to the opposite (Powell & Downey, 1997). This is not to say that both parents are not important to children's adjustment, but that this model assumes that children should primarily reside with same gender parents. Research examining children's adjustment in same sex custody arrangements indicates positive adjustment in school performance and in relationships (Guttman et al., 1999). However, there is still a lot of missing data regarding outcomes, and no longitudinal studies involving direct comparisons of various custody arrangements have been conducted. It is also important to note that in families with children of both genders, this model would also involve separating the children from one another and the effects of this separation of siblings would also need to be carefully studied.

Father's Rights Movement

As a part of a backlash to the Tender Years Doctrine, which is alleged to still permeate family courts, father's rights groups have cropped up in the USA over the past decade (Crowley, 2003). The majority of father's rights groups contend that men are the victims in family law and are unfairly and unjustifiably discriminated against with regard to child custody and child support (Bertoia & Drakich, 1993). In the 1990s, groups such as the "Divorce Racquet Busters" were established with the purpose of protesting the courts' discriminatory actions against fathers that they felt caused men's financial and emotional devastation. The American Coalition for Fathers and Children (ACFC) was established in the 1990s to strive for a unified pro-fatherhood agenda. Local chapters such as Parents and Children for Equality (PACE) in Ohio and Fathers Are Parents, Too (FAPT) in Georgia were organized to attempt to influence state legislators and state courts to become more friendly to a pro-fatherhood agenda (Crowley, 2003).

BIC Doctrine

The doctrine that has received most attention in the past 30 years is the BIC Doctrine. The BIC Doctrine, conceptualized in the mid-1960s, was alleged to be a gender-neutral, child-centered model for custody decisions. The BIC Doctrine replaced parental preference, making room for a child to be awarded to a nonparent, as was seen in *Painter v. Bannister*, the first case in which custody of the child in question was awarded to the maternal grandparents. Though the first joint custody statute was passed in North Carolina in 1957, awarding joint custody was not a common practice until the 1980s (Waller & Daniel, 2005). Researchers have argued that the BIC Doctrine is problematic, suggesting that the "best interest" is a concrete solution that the courts must find, while the ambiguous nature of the definition often involves potential gray areas or disagreements as to what the "best interest" really is (Emery, Otto, & O'Donohue, 2005). The vagueness of this model has been noted for nearly a third of a century. Mnookin (1975) stated:

Deciding what is best for a child poses a question no less ultimate than the purposes and values of life itself. Should the judge be primarily concerned with the child's happiness? Or with the child's spiritual and religious training? Should the judge be concerned with the economic "productivity" of the child when he grows up? Are the primary values of life in warm, interpersonal relationships, or in discipline and self-sacrifice? Is stability and security for a child more desirable than intellectual stimulation? (pp. 260–261).

Controversies in State Law

In addition to the various models described above, states across the USA adopted what they consider to be important factors in deciding the best interests of the child. There is some homogeneity among states regarding important factors to consider; however, as is explained in more detail below, there is vast heterogeneity as well.

The fact that states use different factors for conducting custody evaluations has huge implications with regard to the reliability and validity of child custody evaluation methods.

Though states include their own BIC guidelines, most stem from the Uniform Marriage and Divorce Act (1979) which includes: (1) the wishes of the child's parent or parents involved; (2) the wishes of the children regarding their custody; (3) the interaction or relationship of the children and their parent or parents, siblings, or other individuals who may affect the BIC; (4) the children's adjustment (to their home, community, school, etc.); and (5) the physical and mental well-being of the parties involved. Though many states adhere to these, there is vast heterogeneity with regard to state law regarding BIC.

In addition to Uniform Marriage and Divorce Act (1979) guidelines, 48 states provide other factors to be considered in determining the best interests of the child. The number of additional factors included in state guidelines differ both in number and in content with the average number of factors to consider being 7, the highest being 17 factors (for both Maine and the District of Colombia) and the lowest being one other factor to consider.

Heterogeneity of the State Laws

Some states include having both parents construct a cooperative parenting plan, though states differ in their guidelines regarding specificity of the plan. Specifically, some states provide areas that they want each parent to cover, while others do not. Often the suggested guidelines differ from state to state. For example, Massachusetts' state law specifies, "If the issue of custody is contested and either party seeks shared legal or physical custody, the parties, jointly or individually, shall submit to the court at the trial a shared custody implementation plan setting forth the details of shared custody including, but not limited to, the child's education; the child's health care; procedures for resolving disputes between the parties with respect to child-raising decisions and duties; and the periods of time during which each party will have the child reside or visit with him, including holidays and vacations, or the procedure by which such periods of time shall be determined" (Massachusetts General Laws—Chapter 208—Sections: 28 and 31), whereas Washington state law specifies: "All custody cases must have a proposed parenting plan or agreement to be presented to the court for approval before the final order is put in place. The primary goals of the parenting plan are to: 1) Provide for the child's physical care; 2) Maintain the child's emotional stability; 3) Provide for the child's changing needs as the child grows and matures, in a way that minimizes the need for future modifications to the permanent parenting plan; 4) Set forth the authority and responsibilities of each parent with respect to the child; 5) Minimize the child's exposure to harmful parental conflict; 6) Encourage the parents to meet their responsibilities to their minor children through agreements in the permanent parenting plan, rather than by relying on judicial intervention; and 7) To otherwise protect the best interests of the child." (Revised Code of Washington—Title 26—Chapters: 26.09.181, 26.09.220). Washington's parenting plan guidelines go on to specify: "The plan shall allocate decision-making authority to one or both parties regarding the children's education, health care, and religious upbringing. The parties may incorporate an agreement related to the care and growth of the child in these specified areas, or in other areas, into their plan. Regardless of the allocation of decision making in the parenting plan, either parent may make emergency decisions affecting the health or safety of the child. a) Each parent may make decisions regarding the day-to-day care and control of the child while the child is residing with that parent; b) When mutual decision making is designated but cannot be achieved, the parties shall make a good-faith effort to resolve the issue through the dispute resolution process."

The following additional factors are included to demonstrate the vast heterogeneity of state guidelines regarding factors to consider in determining the BIC:

- The moral fitness of the parties involved (Michigan Compiled Laws—Sections: 552.16 and 722.23)
- The child's cultural background (Minnesota)
- Geographic distance between the parents' residences (Wyoming Statutes—Title 20—Chapters: 20-2-104, 20-2-107, and 20-2-201)
- The stability of the family unit (Tennessee Code—Volume 6A, Title 36, Sections 36-4-106)
- The age of the child (Maine Revised Statutes—Title 19A—Sections: 1501 and 1653)
- If the child is under 1 year of age, whether the child is being breast-fed (Maine Revised Statutes—Title 19A—Sections: 1501 and 1653)
- The existence of a parent's conviction for a sex offense or a sexually violent offense (Maine Revised Statutes—Title 19A—Sections: 1501 and 1653)
- The demands of parental employment (District of Colombia)
- The age and number of children (District of Colombia)
- The sincerity of each parent's request (District of Colombia)
- The parent's ability to financially support a joint custody arrangement (District of Colombia)
- The consideration of whether the party satisfactorily completed participation in a parenting education program established pursuant to section 46b-69b (Connecticut General Statutes—Title 46b—Chapters 56 and 84)
- The religious faith of the parents (Code of Laws for South Carolina—Chapter 3; Sections 20-3-160, 20-7-100, and 20-7-1520)

It is not difficult to see that the heterogeneity inherent in the differing state guidelines could be problematic. Is it actually the case that a child's best interest is a function of their state of residency? Or is this unfortunate state of affairs due to the fact that lawmakers are trying their best to respond to the problem addressed in this book: i.e., how to accurately explicate what constructs are components of the best interests of the child? In the absence of clear tested models in behavioral science, lawmakers have done their best to explicate this based on their common sense—but again, this has resulted in tremendous heterogeneity across states. A custody evaluator working in one state would be assessing vastly different issues in his or her custody evaluation from another evaluator in a different state. In addition, if evaluators change location and practice in different states, they will need to adhere to entirely different guidelines. Though it is impossible to know how differently any given custody evaluation might turn out if it were conducted in different states, the possibility for a different outcome (based solely on location) is very concerning. A further examination of these differing state guidelines is provided in Appendix A.

It is probably fair to say that no state systematically developed BIC criteria in consultation with expert input from mental health professionals. This could account for the wide degree of variability across states in their specification of the BIC standard. It might be the case that if this construct was more clearly explicated and found to produce better custody evaluations, states could adopt this and the unwanted variability across states could decrease.

Homogeneity of State Laws

Despite the varying numbers of factors set forth in different states' laws, there is some consensus across states regarding the most salient factors. However, even within the homogenous factors, there are still significant discrepancies.

Thirty-three states are in agreement that the wishes of the child should be taken into consideration, though differences are seen in determining when and under what conditions the child's wishes should be considered. Some states' statutes report that the child's wishes should be considered "if he or she is sufficiently mature to express reasoned and independent preferences as to the parenting time schedule" (Colorado Statutes—Article 10—Sections: 14-20-123, 14-20-124, and 14-20-129), or "if the child is of sufficient age and capable of forming an intelligent preference" (Connecticut General Statutes—Title 46b—Chapters 56 and 84) or a "meaningful preference" (Maine Revised Statutes—Title 19A—Sections: 1501 and 1653), though no specific age is provided leaving this as a source of heterogeneity in actual custody evaluations. Some states leave this discretion to the judge, such as "if the court considers the child to be of sufficient age to express preference" (Michigan Compiled Laws—Sections: 552.16 and 722.23).

Other states add age provisions, such as "the wishes of the child, with more consideration given to the child's wishes if the child is at least fourteen (14) years of age" (Indiana Code—Title 31—Article 15—Chapters: 17-2-8, 17-2-8.5, and 17-2-15), though these are inconsistent as well, as other states report, "the reasonable preference of a child over 12 years of age" should be considered (Tennessee Code—Volume 6A, Title 36, Section 36-4-106). Utah's state Code specifies, "The desires of a child 16 years of age or older shall be given added weight, but is not the single controlling factor" (Sections: 30-2-10, 30-3-5, and 30-3-10). Still other states report that "the desires and wishes of the minor child if of an age of comprehension regardless of chronological age, when such desires and wishes are based on sound reasoning" should be considered (Nebraska Statutes—Chapter 42—Section: 364).

Twenty-eight states are in agreement that the quality of the relationship the child has with the parent is important to consider, though states differ in how they define this. For example, some states report it is important to consider "the love, affection, and other emotional ties between each party and the child" (Louisiana Code of Civil Procedure—Article: 131, 132, 133, and 134), while other states report "the intimacy of the relationship between each parent and the child" should be considered (Minnesota), and the majority cite the Uniform Marriage and Divorce Act (1979) consideration stating "the interaction or relationship of the children and their parent or parents, siblings or other individuals who may affect the best interest of the child" should be considered.

Twenty-two states' laws include guidelines related to parents' abilities to co-parent. The way in which states define this differ somewhat from "the past and present ability of the parents to cooperate with each other and make decisions jointly" (Alabama State Divorce Code, Chapter 3, Sections 30-3-150 and 30-3-152), to "the willingness and ability of each parent to facilitate and encourage a close and continuing relationship between the other parent and the child" (Alaska State Divorce Code), to "the ability of parents to cooperate in the rearing of their children; and methods for resolving disputes regarding any major decision concerning the life of the child, and the parents' willingness to use those methods" (Minnesota State Divorce Code), and to "the ability and disposition of each parent to foster a positive relationship and frequent and continuing physical, written, and telephonic contact with the other parent, except where contact will result in harm to the child or to a parent. (a) The support of each parent for the child's contact with the other parent as shown by allowing and promoting such contact. (b) The support of each parent for the child's relationship with the other parent" (New Hampshire Statutes). Still other states' statutes discuss co-parenting in terms of negative behavior one or both parents have engaged in that would assume poor ability to co-parent (e.g., "Whether the residential parent or one of the parents subject to a shared parenting decree has continuously and willfully denied the other parent's right to parenting time in accordance with an order of the court"—Ohio Code).

Additional similarities that were found in the states' statutes on determining the BIC include:

- Twenty-six states report that the environmental stability of the home environment and the parent's ability to meet the needs of the child are important to consider.
- Twenty-five states report that domestic violence between spouses is an important factor to consider.
- Twenty-four states make explicit statements about considerations of child abuse or potential for child abuse.
- Twenty-one states statutes include the consideration of the parents' mental health, including considerations about substance abuse or dependence.

A more complete review of the state laws regarding child custody evaluations is provided in Appendix A. Though it is perhaps a step in the right direction to offer concrete factors that may determine the BIC, it is unknown what formula various states have used to determine their guidelines. The guidelines do not offer evaluators guidance regarding the relative weight and importance that should be given to various factors or how to assess these factors (or even more radically if there are any assessment strategies to validly measure these) or how to combine these to produce actual custody recommendations.

Controversies Regarding Existing Guidelines

In addition to common custody doctrines and statutes that have been provided from specific states, several organizations have published standards and guidelines for conducting child custody evaluations. These organizations include the American Psychiatric Association Task Force on Clinical Assessment in Child Custody (1988), the Association of Family and Conciliation Courts (1994), and the American Psychological Association (APA) (1994). We provided the APA guidelines to illustrate several points:

I. Orienting Guidelines

1. The primary purpose of the evaluation is to assess the best psychological interests of the child. (*Note*: *this is interesting and potentially problematic because not all states have adopted this standard*).
2. The child's interest and well-being are paramount.
3. The focus of the evaluation is on parenting capacity, the psychological and developmental needs of the child and the resulting fit. (*Note*: *again, the APA guidelines are mute on the variability across state laws regarding what these specify and how they should be measured*).

II. General Guidelines

4. The role of the psychologist is that of a professional expert who strives to maintain an objective, impartial stance.
5. The psychologist gains specialized competence. (*Note: but how, especially given the dearth of knowledge in this area?*).
6. The psychologist is aware of personal and societal biases and engages in nondiscriminatory practice. (*Note: what exactly are these biases and are there any specific to custody evaluations,* e.g., *there are allegations that these are biased against both genders—which is true*?).
7. The psychologist avoids multiple relationships.

III. Procedural Guidelines

8. The scope of the evaluation is determined by the evaluator, based on the nature of the referral question. (*But isn't there a commonality here—what arrangements are best for the child*?).
9. The psychologist obtains informed consent from all adult participants, and as appropriate informs child participants.

10. The psychologist informs participants about the limits of confidentiality and the disclosure of information.
11. The psychologist uses multiple methods of data gathering. (*Note*: *again, this only rules out single source evaluations—which isn't ruling out much*).
12. The psychologist neither overinterprets nor inappropriately interprets clinical or assessment data. (*Note*: *this is obvious; who would argue otherwise*?).
13. The psychologist does not give any opinion regarding the psychological functioning of any individual who has not been personally evaluated.
14. Recommendations, if any, are based on the psychological best interests of the child. (*Note*: *again, but what exactly does this mean exactly; what constructs are involved and how should these be measured and synthesized into custody recommendations*?).
15. The psychologist clarifies financial arrangements.
16. The psychologist maintains written records.

Though face valid, the APA guidelines have been considered "largely truisms" (O'Donohue & Bradley, 1999, p. 317) and read more as a collection of general ethical standards rather than providing the custody evaluator with a systematic model and concrete tools to conduct high quality, standardized evaluations. In addition, these guidelines make some practical sense, though the broad domains covered in the standards (i.e., interviews, testing, direct observation, record reviews, collateral contacts, etc.) leave too much room for subjective bias, uncontrolled variance, and inappropriate, overreliance on clinical judgment. In addition, recommended assessment tools used in custody evaluations have not been standardized, leaving room for the use of inappropriate testing either because of general validity problems of the test e.g., the Rorschach because these measure irrelevant constructs.

The standard practice in conducting child custody evaluations often includes an interview with both parents (either alone or together), an interview with the child or children, direct observation of child–parent interactions, conducting a home visit to each parent's home to assess the quality of the living environment, and an interview with collateral sources provided by both parents (i.e., teachers, primary care physicians, nannies, family members, etc.), a review of relevant records or materials provided by both parents, and psychological/intelligence testing of both parents and children (Mart, 2007).

In addition to organizations publishing guidelines for child custody evaluations, individual psychologists have suggested methods for the best way to conduct custody evaluations, with varying attention to the construct of the BIC. For example, Gould's (1998) *Conducting Scientifically Crafted Child Custody Evaluations* provided information regarding child custody guidelines, and what other researchers (i.e., Grisso's Objectives of Competency Evaluations) have purported to be useful in conducting custody evaluations. Gould discussed interviewing parents, children, and collateral sources; the limitations surrounding validity in evaluations and assessments [and mentions the ASPECT, Bricklin Perceptual Scales (BPS), Minnesota Mutliphasic Personality Inventory-2 (MMPI-2) and Millon Clinical Multiaxial Inventory-II (MCMI-II) as frequently used scales]; suggested variables to consider in child custody decision making; and finally discussed positive, as well as deficient, parenting behaviors to consider. Gould reported, "Now, the question becomes how to integrate the data; assign weights to the relative meaning of each factor; and make a responsible, fact-based decision about the lives of each person within this changing family system" (Grisso, 1998, p. 225). Gould reported that there are no rules to follow and that "any custodial determination is, after all, a judgment call" (p. 226). This unfortunately given the present state of affairs is correct. For example, interviews can focus on a number of constructs, e.g., job performance, substance use, sexual interests, presence of phobias, early childhood history, future plans, domestic violence, relationship with siblings, and so on. Which constructs ought to be covered in the interview and which ought not? There is insufficient specification of this key issue.

Additionally, Gould provided a list of 13 factors for the custody evaluator to consider. These factors include:

- Do not rely on memory (i.e., don't rely on recollection of interview data over other methods)
- Document (i.e., videotape, audiotape, or take thorough notes)
- Observe, Infer, and then Conclude (i.e., make a number of hypotheses regarding behavioral observations to minimize memory bias before assigning weight to any one hypothesis)
- Consider simple versus complex decision making (i.e., be aware of the issue of incremental validity in gathering data and consider your decision-making strategy and how you weigh each variable in making recommendations)
- Formulate specific psycholegal questions (i.e., ask the court what they want you to evaluate/if there are specific concerns to address)
- Good questions lead to well-chosen measurement tools (i.e., if the court is concerned about psychopathology of the father, choosing measures of adjustment or psychopathology should be used)
- Behavioral prevalence and base rates (i.e., having knowledge of the population and base rate behaviors in that population—e.g., behaviors related to depression can be commonly found in parents in contentious divorces)
- Confirmatory bias (i.e., tendency to look to information that supports evaluator's hypotheses rather than information that might be contradictory to expectations)
- Covariation and illusory correlations (i.e., whether variables have a true relationship between them or they may only appear to but in actuality are not related)
- Hindsight bias (i.e., a tendency to examine behavior retrospectively and draw conclusions from it rather than place it in context)
- Overconfidence (i.e., similar to confirmatory bias, it is important for evaluators to not become too confident in their assessments as this might cause them to overlook opposing ideas)
- Focus and use of unique data (i.e., using multiple sources to establish trends in a person's behavior rather than a single event)
- Correlated measures (i.e., be cautious when using measurements with high correlation as they may be redundant)

While these are useful factors to consider, these are also common heuristic errors that psychologists frequently make in all areas of practice (i.e., in individual therapy, case conceptualization, etc. These are important to be aware of when conducting child custody evaluations though, because of the generality of these there still may not be enough structure to provide adequate guidance that would lead to reliable and valid custody evaluations.

Rohrbaugh's *Comprehensive Guide to Child Custody Evaluations* (2008) provided extensive information regarding conducting evaluations. She reported that evaluators should assess: (1) the relationship between the child and parent/caregiver, (2) the relationship between parents/caregivers, (3) parenting abilities of each parent/caregiver, (4) psychological health of each parent/caregiver, (5) psychological health of each child, and (6) family dynamics including domestic violence or child abuse. She also attempted to explicate the primary caretaker's functions which she reported are:

1. Planning and preparing meals
2. Bathing, grooming, and dressing
3. Purchasing and care of clothes
4. Medical care, including nursing and trips to the doctor
5. Arranging and transporting children to afterschool activities and social engagements
6. Arranging alternative childcare such as babysitters and day care
7. Sleeping—bedtime, care during the night, waking in the morning
8. Disciplining, general manners, and toilet training
9. Education, including religious, cultural, and social information
10. Teaching elementary skills such as reading, writing, and arithmetic

Finally, Rohrbaugh identified what she termed "research-based criteria for identifying attachment figures" as (1) provision of physical care, (2) provision of emotional care, (3) quality of care provided, (4) time spent with the child, (5) continuity or consistency, and (6) emotional investment in the child. Taken together, Rohrbaugh reported that these make up what data should be collected in each custody evaluation. Rohrbaugh reported the use of testing, interviewing parents, interviewing children, interviewing collateral witnesses, conducting home visits, parent–child observations, and reviewing records as being important components of the evaluation (2008). She further provided structured questions to ask in the interviews, though she did not report specifically how these structured questions were selected (i.e., the use of incomplete sentences with child interviews such as "my favorite food is…"). Furthermore, it is not made clear as to how this information ultimately contributes to the formulation of custody recommendations. Rohrbaugh (2008) extended typical practices to attempt to increase the reliability of evaluations. She included numerous additional areas that increase the comprehensiveness of her approach (i.e., by including risk factors and their effects on children, by including nontraditional families and recommendations for them, and by including more specific, structured approaches to interviews).

Rohrbaugh's book is useful as it provides more specificity than APA's vague guidelines and more than other models. However, she still fails to present arguments that her model is directly attempting to explicate the construct of the best interests of the children, and, in fact, her model can be critiqued as not being well grounded in this legally relevant concept.

Stahl's *Conducting Child Custody Evaluations* (1994) also advocated the use of parent interviews, child interviews, collateral interviews, psychological testing, parent–child observations, and home visits in evaluations. Stahl provided sample questions, sample reports, and psychological tests and games for parents and children. The sample questions included "what was your marriage like before the problems began?"; however, he did not specifically explicate the key constructs that ought to be assessed. He also frequently provided examples that suggested he was basing decisions on clinical judgment by using numerous constructs with no clear valid measurement operations (e.g., "...He has a tendency to be defensive, deny common human frailties, and externalize responsibility for many of the problems in his life. He is easily overwhelmed by his emotions and works hard to control them as much as possible..." p. 86—how are any of these to be validly measured?). Because his reasoning is not always clearly explicated, evaluators may find his model difficult to replicate, which can decrease inter-rater reliability. And his model, like all others, has not been shown to have predictive validity, i.e., to actually produce custody arrangements that are in the BIC.

Taken together, the informal models provided by these authors appear to be roughly derived from some understanding of key legal concepts as well as from clinical judgment. However, it is important to note that although the models generally agree on the assessment methods that ought to be used, they are either silent or disagree on the specific constructs that the custody evaluator ought to be assessing. The models are not explicit about key issues such as how to synthesize these measurements into actual custody recommendations, and have not been shown to actually increase inter-rater reliability. They also confuse two distinct issues: what constructs ought to be measured in determining the BIC and what measurement operations (i.e., interviews, parent–child observations, home visits, etc.) ought to be used to assess these constructs. Too many models seem to think that it is sufficient to specify an assessment strategy without specifying the aim of that strategy. This is like telling someone who wants to find out something, to make observations. The key is to have a focus, i.e., to observe what, and when, where, and how?

This gap is helpful in explaining why some of the current evaluations lack reliability. Because of the problem and the absence of such a model, which explicates the key constructs that are components of the best interest standard, clinical scientists have called for a moratorium on conducting custody evaluations (O'Donohue & Bradley, 1999). It is clear that despite the BIC Doctrine being the predominant standard over the last 30 years, no clear model for operationalizing the construct has yet been developed. And though it is not known what evaluators have used to base their assessment models and their recommendations on, researchers have studied custody evaluator's common practices.

Custody Evaluator's Practices

Many researchers have suggested reasons as to why mental health professionals have come to be relied upon in conducting child custody evaluations. One possible reason for this may be the emphasis placed upon the psychological well-being of the child in custody arrangements (Bala & Saunders, 2003; Bolocofsky, 1989; Mason & Quirk, 1997). Melton et al. (1997) have found that since the adoption of the BIC Doctrine, courts have been depending more and more on expert parenting assessments. Melton et al. (1997) proposed that mental health professionals who specialize in family and child development are desirable professionals to conduct these assessments. It has also been proposed that the ambiguity inherent in the BIC Doctrine combined with the ambiguous and unexplicated psychological constructs which are thought to be important in custody decisions have led to the reliance on mental health professionals in child custody evaluations (Bolocofsky, 1989). Mason and Quirk (1997) have suggested that complex psychological factors (e.g., allegations of substance use, domestic violence, physical or sexual abuse, mental illness, etc.) often involved in custody evaluations make mental health professionals a natural choice for conducting custody evaluations. In addition, many mental health professionals have turned to forensic work to broaden their practices, because of practice and financial restrictions placed upon them by managed care companies (Gould, 2006). Finally, it has been proposed that judges often find custody cases stressful and outside the realm of their profession, and therefore turn to professionals who appear to be best able to conduct custody evaluations with the BIC criteria in mind (Kushner, 2006).

Several studies have examined the practices of child custody evaluators. Gourley and Stolberg (2000) received surveys from 21 psychologists who had been judged to be "highly credible" by attorneys in the area of child custody evaluations. Of the 21 psychologists, 90% indicated they had private practices and 42% described their theoretical orientation as being cognitive-behavioral (with 14% describing themselves as eclectic or interpersonal and 10% as psychodynamic). Over 90% of the psychologists reported that, in their evaluations, they assessed parental mental health, child mental health, parent–child conflict, parental conflict, parenting skills, sibling relationships, and the role of other extended family members. Psychologists also ranked the five most influential factors in making a recommendation as follows: parent mental health, parenting skills, child mental health, parent–child conflict, and parent conflict. However, there was still significant variability in the rankings of these constructs.

Keilin and Bloom (1986) surveyed 82 custody evaluators and discovered that 69% observed parent–child interactions, 50% had observed the parents interacting, 30% went to the children's schools, and finally approximately 30% contacted third parties, or collateral contacts, to gain more information about the parents and children. Keilin and Bloom asked psychologists to rank, in importance, factors that influenced their custody evaluation and found that the psychologists ranked preference of a 15-year old child as most important, followed by parental attempts to alienate the other parent, and the parent–child relationship (Keilin & Bloom, 1986).

In 1997, Ackerman and Ackerman replicated this study with 201 psychologists who conducted child custody evaluations. When asked to rank factors in order of importance in custody arrangements, psychologists in this study ranked parent substance abuse as the number one most important factor, followed by parenting skills, and parents' attempts to alienate the other parent (Ackerman & Ackerman, 1997). These surveys can be looked at as an attempt to explicate the informal models that custody evaluators are using to operationalize the BIC.

In a method that did not completely rely on self-report of the child custody evaluators, Bow and Quinnell (2002) reviewed 52 child custody reports of doctorate-level psychologists. Demographic information of the psychologists revealed that 62% of the sample were male, 78% Ph.D.s (as opposed to Ed.D.s or Psy.D.s) with average clinical experience of 21 years. Psychologists reported that the average time devoted to child custody cases was about 40% with an average of 22 custody evaluations conducted per year. Upon examining the reports of these evaluators, it was discovered that all evaluators interviewed parents individually, and with the exception of children under 5, almost all also conducted interviews with children (92%). Psychological testing of parents was conducted in almost all cases (90%), though only one-third of children were tested. The majority of cases included parent–child observations (83%) with approximately one-third taking place during a home visit. Significant others were interviewed 75% of the time, although they were tested only 33% of the time. Collateral contacts were therapists 78% of the time. When children were of school age, school personnel were contacted only 62% of the time. Sixty percent of the reports included detailed and specific information provided by collateral contacts, while 17% provided general information, 8% provided a list of collateral contacts but no information provided from them, and 15% did not report using collateral contacts. Less than half of the reports reviewed addressed the best interests of the child, with most instead addressing strengths and weaknesses of the parents, summary of findings, general and then explicit recommendations regarding custody. Physical custody recommendations were made 92% of the time, with legal custody and visitations being recommended less often (85% and 81%, respectively). Therapy was recommended for parents 64% of the time, and for children 40% of the time. Parenting classes were recommended only 11% of the time, and divorce groups for children and parents recommended only 2% and 5% of the time, respectively (Bow & Quinnell, 2002).

Horvath, Logar, and Walker (2002) also examined forensic child custody reports to establish how closely evaluators were adhering to child custody evaluation guidelines set forth by the APA (1994) and by psychologist Clark (1995). Nine guidelines that were taken into consideration in the study included: (1) the psychologist uses multiple methods of gathering data; (2) the focus of the evaluation is on parenting capacity, the psychological and developmental needs of the child and the resulting fit; (3) the same procedures are used for both parties; (4) the evaluator should conduct interviews with both parents, all children, any adults directly responsible for the care of the children, and any party living in the custodial or visiting home. If relevant, day care providers, medical, psychotherapy and school personnel should be interviewed; (5) interviews with parents should assess personal and legal history, drug and alcohol use, emotional problems, current living situation, health status, and employment status; (6) formal and psychological testing for adults is recommended; (7) parents and children should be observed interacting with each other; (8) children should be interviewed and assessed with psychological testing as is age appropriate; and (9) home or school visits may be conducted if further information is needed. Results indicated that of the 82 evaluations examined, 87% assessed parenting skills, 80% assessed psychological and developmental needs of the child, and 72% assessed parent's ability to meet those needs. Eighty-nine percent of the evaluations assessed the mother, and 90% the father, though only 65% assessed the mother's history and 71% the father's history. Approximately 60–62% assessed child–parent interactions while in only 9% of the cases, physicians or day care workers were interviewed. Thirty percent interviewed other counselors, and only 24% interviewed teachers. Psychological testing of the adults was used in only 19% of the reviewed cases and testing of children only 11% of the time. Children were assessed 68% of the time, with only 44% assessing the children's preference (Horvath et al., 2002).

It is clear from both this study and the Bow and Quinnell (2002) study that while child custody evaluators are using recommended guidelines in their evaluations, they are not using them consistently. This is problematic and speaks to the need for the implementation of more structured guidelines, which should be guided by empirical research on the negative impact of divorce on children. Some of this variability again may come from the fact that a conceptual model of the BIC standard has not been explicated. The research cited above emphasizes what assessment methods are being used, but it importantly misses the question of what constructs are being measured by these methods. Guidelines ought to follow such a model, rather than be developed independently of it. In addition, this is a self-report which raises two issues: are evaluators actually doing this (i.e., would their reports alone reflect that they followed guidelines) and second, the validity of their inferences are unknown and tell us nothing about the ultimate question—who gets the children and what guided their decision.

Controversies Concerning Assessments

It is difficult to justify the use of the MMPI-2, the Rorschach, the TAT or any intelligence tests, none of which were originally designed to be used in child custody evaluations, though many evaluators use them in evaluating parents (Emery et al., 2005; O'Donohue, Beitz, & Cummings, 2007). The lack of empirically established alternatives, or even agreed upon constructs for some of these factors (e.g., parent competence, quality of parent–child relationships) may cause custody evaluators to be reticent to stray from the conventional practice of psychological testing that is used in custody evaluations. Several alternative assessments have been developed for the purpose of establishing the BIC in custody evaluations; however, there are numerous problems with them (Emery et al., 2005; Grisso, 2003). Specifically, one of the most widely used tests is the BPS (Bricklin, 1990). The BPS is a projective measure that assesses children's "unconscious preferences" toward their parents by using a stylus to assess both parents across 32 activities thought to capture parents' competence, supportiveness, follow-up consistency, and possession of admirable traits. The problem with the BPS is that it has not been empirically validated, or normed, and there does not appear to be any evidence that it actually captures children's "unconscious preferences" (Emery et al., 2005; Otto & Edens, 2003). While projective tests may be problematic for conducting child custody evaluations, it is possible that they are used because of the problem that parents are highly motivated to present themselves in a positive light. This can distort test findings if parents minimize symptoms (Carr, Moretti, & Cue, 2005). Parents presenting themselves in a positive light can be especially difficult when observing parent–child interactions. Some researchers are even skeptical about the utility of observing parent–child interactions, because the process of being observed changes the authenticity of the interaction, especially in the context of child custody evaluations (Bricklin, 1995).

Similar to best interest guidelines, guidelines for the observation of child–parent interactions are highly face valid. Oftentimes, guidelines include observing parents interacting with each child individually, then together (if there is more than one child in the home), in a structured and then less structured environment (allowing the parent and child to pick a task to engage in or giving them a problem solving or cooperative task). The evaluator is encouraged to look for signs of attachment, communication, and expectations of the parent with the child's behavior (Ackerman, 1995; Gould, 1998; Schutz, Dixon, Lindenberger, & Ruther, 1989). The use of home visits is encouraged to observe the natural environment in which the majority of parent–child interactions take place so that more natural behaviors may be observed (Schutz et al., 1989). Some problems with these guidelines, which are similar to the problems of the BIC guidelines, are that they are not standardized and are too vague to be useful. They involve numerous threats to validity including reactivity, unrepresentative samples of behavior, unreliable coding systems, and no clear way to synthesize information gathered from them to make sense of how they relate to the BIC (Emery et al., 2005).

Custody Evaluators' Testing Practices

In examining custody evaluators' common practices regarding the use of psychological testing, virtually all psychologists reported the use of interviews to gather information, but again, without a formal model of constructs to guide the aims of these methods. They also report using psychological testing with regard to parent and child mental health. Gourley and Stolberg (2000) found that psychologists reported using the following psychological tests, in order of most frequently used: the MMPI, the Child Behaviors Checklist (CBCL), the Thematic Apperception Test (TAT), the Rorschach, intelligence tests, projective drawings and the Children's Depression Inventory (Gourley & Stolberg, 2000). The use of projective devices is particularly troubling given their psychometric inadequacies and the complete lack of validity data regarding inferences directly relevant to custody evaluations. In addition, when studied, projective testing has been found to have negative incremental validity, i.e., adding projectives has been shown to decrease the accuracy of clinician inferences in areas like predicting violence and suicide (Sechrest).

Keilin and Bloom (1986) surveyed 82 custody evaluators and discovered that 76% used psychological tests with adults (most commonly used in order were the MMPI, the Rorschach, and the TAT), and 74% with children (most commonly the TAT, followed by the Children's Apperception Test, projective drawings, and the Rorschach). Ackerman and Ackerman (1997) indicated that psychologists continued to use intelligence tests, the TAT and Rorschach when assessing children (92% of the sample reporting using psychological testing with children), and the MMPI, the Rorschach, and the TAT when assessing adults (98% reported using psychological testing with adults). In their study of custody reports, Bow and Quinnell (2002) found that with regard to psychological testing of the parent, the objective personality measures often used included the MMPI (93%) and the MCMI-III (44% of the time). Parenting inventories were used 45% of the time, followed by the Rorschach and other projective tests (40%) with child ratings scales and IQ tests being used most infrequently (30% and 22%, respectively). Only 17% of reports included actual test scores to substantiate conclusions made from them.

Based on the lack of standardization of practices or accountability for evaluators, it is not surprising that as many as 35% of a sample of 198 psychologists conducting custody evaluations have received at least one board or ethics complaint, and 10% have received a malpractice suit related to child custody work (Bow & Quinnell, 2002 as cited in Bow, 2006). Obviously the two major pathways for this kind of trouble can be actual problematic practice or disgruntled clients who did not like the outcome of sound practice. Clearly, there is a significant variability with regard to existing doctrines guiding custody arrangements, state statutes regarding important considerations, custody evaluation researchers' guidelines, organizational guidelines, and custody evaluators' practices. In addition, there are grounds to have deep concerns about the quality of these custody evaluations as no model has specified target constructs; there is evidence of problematic test use, and there is little to no information about how results from assessment are synthesized into actual custody recommendations.

Research examining children's adjustment post-divorce is conducted after the evaluation has been made and thus provides little information regarding how the recommendations of the custody arrangement might have influenced this adjustment. Furthermore, some potentially important research questions are impossible to answer as they would involve ethically questionable or impossible methodologies. For example, it would not be ethically permissible to randomly assign children to different custody arrangements and then follow their adjustment. One potential resource to guide evaluations, however, would be to examine longitudinal research that examines important factors that predict children's outcomes.

Chapter 3
Review of Post-divorce Child Outcome Literature

The ultimate question that a quality custody evaluation seeks to answer is somewhat similar to Gordon Paul's famous treatment matching question, "*what* treatment, by *whom*, is most effective for *this* individual with *that* specific problem and under *which* set of circumstances?" (Paul & Bernstein, 1976). When modifying this question to be used in child custody evaluations, it becomes: What custody arrangement is in the best interest of this particular child, with this particular history and set of needs, given this particular set of caregivers (i.e., biological parents, step-parent, adoptive parents, grandparents) who have their own particular histories and respective strengths and weaknesses, in this particular situation and its practical constraints, and why? This question also is based on an important assumption: that there are regularities among these classes of variables. This is inconsistent with a view of the radical idiographic of divorce contained in Tolstoy's quote "Happy families are all alike; every unhappy family is unhappy in its own way."

In order to begin answering this adaptation of Paul's question, a thorough assessment of what predicts poor and positive outcomes for children is necessary. Divorce research is largely limited to examining child outcomes after a significant event in the child's life (i.e., the divorce, separation, custody hearing, etc.) has already occurred, and not including random assignment and some sort of control group, thus obscuring possible differential outcomes that otherwise might have taken place. In addition, this research is correlational and causal inference is not possible.

While examining longitudinal data can be helpful in determining important predictive factors, there are problems in assigning causality to any specific factor. The identification of a specific causal agent in the development or progression of various infectious diseases is useful in medicine and has led to the advancement of medical breakthroughs in prevention and treatment. It is not often possible to use this in social research because of the underlying complexity of the phenomena (see Meehl, 1954 for a discussion). In identifying risk factors for psychopathology in individuals, for example, numerous factors from a variety of different domains (i.e., biological, environmental, social, behavioral) may play a role (including unique cohort effects) and the interaction of these.

L.W. Tolle and W.T. O'Donohue, *Improving the Quality of Child Custody Evaluations*, DOI 10.1007/978-1-4614-3405-4_3, © Springer Science+Business Media, LLC 2012

At the time that a custody evaluation occurs, various risk factors may already be in place due to the fact that the parents are divorcing. For example, studies have examined the negative effects that high family discord and divorce can have on children (Amato & Keith, 1991; Emery, 1999; Otto & Edens, 2003). It may be necessary to assume that because the custody arrangements of children in such divorces cannot be agreed upon amicably by parents (even through mediation) in cases in which a professional custody evaluator is asked to render a decision, high discord is present. It should be noted, however, that family risk influences such as marital conflict do not affect all children in the same way or to the same degree (Carbonneau et al., 2001; Carbonneau, Eaves, Silberg, Simonoff, & Rutter, 2002; Jenkins, Rabash, & O'Connor, 2003).

Psychological research has shown that the ongoing interplay between child risk and promotive factors makes attempts at predicting child outcomes difficult. However, the consistency of findings from a sizeable number of studies that have examined both risk and promotive factors for child outcomes provides a basis for an argument that these factors are important considerations for child custody evaluations. This literature around child outcomes and adjustment post-divorce is reviewed.

Outcomes for Children Post-divorce

Numerous studies have been conducted that have found that children from divorced homes exhibit more behavioral problems when compared to children from intact homes, and that these problems are often long-term. Specifically, meta-analyses that in total examined 104 studies reveal that children from divorced homes have more problems with psychological well-being (i.e., depression and low life satisfaction), family well-being (defined as presence of marriage dissatisfaction or divorce), socioeconomic well-being (low educational attainment, low income, and low occupational prestige), self-concept, social competence, and physical health problems than individuals from nondivorced families (Amato, 2000, 2001; Amato & Keith, 1991).

Several important longitudinal studies have been conducted that examined the long-term well-being of children from divorced families. Strengths and limitations of these studies are discussed elsewhere (e.g., Ahrons & Tanner, 2003). Results from these studies, all of which followed individuals from divorced families and intact families for at least 20 years, found that individuals from divorced families were more likely to engage in "acting out" behaviors as adolescents (e.g., engaging in their first sexual experience earlier; earlier onset of drug use; longer period of drug use at higher levels; more indicants of impulsivity, increased evidence of irresponsible behavior, more signs of antisocial behavior), less likely to experience academic accomplishments (e.g., fewer entered and completed college with a bachelor's degree; higher drop-out rate), were more likely to be pessimistic about marriage (e.g., less likely to marry; more difficulty in romantic relationships) and divorce (e.g., more likely to divorce), were more likely to experience depression, difficulty at work and reported feeling less close to their biological parents as compared to individuals from intact families (Amato, 2006; Hetherington & Kelly, 2002; Wallerstein & Lewis, 2004). It should be noted that Amato (2006) also found that offspring from intact, high-discord families experienced problems similar to individuals from divorced families, including greater discord in their own marriages, less social support, and lower levels of psychological well-being. However, they did not differ from intact, low-discord families in terms of educational attainment or relationship disruptions.

In addition to research that found poorer psychological adjustment of children from divorced homes, research has indicated which factors are associated with better adjustment post-divorce. In the context of the child–parent relationship, children who experienced a high-quality relationship with their father were found to have better adjustment post-divorce. However, if fathers were found to be a negative influence on the child (i.e., were absent or did not have a quality relationship with the child), this was associated with poorer outcomes in the child post-divorce (Amato & Gilbreth, 1999; Buchanan, Maccoby, & Dornbusch, 1996; Harper & Fine, 2006; Papp et al., 2005; Whiteside & Becker, 2000).

Thomson, Hanson, and McLanahan (1994) reviewed a number of studies that demonstrated that the impact of changes in family structure (i.e., divorce/separation) on children are attenuated by healthy parenting. Parental warmth, parallel parenting, age appropriate expectations, authoritative parenting, and supportive coparenting have all been found to be protective factors post-divorce (Gould, 1998; Hetherington, Cox, & Cox, 1982; Kelly & Emery, 2003; Lamborn, Mounts, Steinberg, & Dornbusch, 1991; Steinberg, 2001; Wallerstein & Kelly, 1980). Whereas, poorer adjustment (i.e., difficulties in cognitive, emotional and social areas of the child's life) was found to be associated with continuing disagreement and inconsistencies between parents, continued anger between parents, poor parental adjustment, and authoritarian or neglectful parenting (Wallerstein & Kelly, 1980; Whiteside & Becker, 2000).

One reason why divorce can be particularly stressful for children is that it is likely to be preceded, and often followed by a period of high parental conflict (Amato & Keith, 1991). It has been estimated that 25% of parents are in "high conflict" post-divorce (Maccoby & Mnookin, 1992). In addition, in general, the separation period is the most stressful period for parents and their children, followed by the first year post-divorce (Albrecht, 1980; Hetherington et al., 1982; Wallerstein & Kelly, 1980; White & Mika, 1983).

Economic stability is one of the most powerful predictors of post-divorce child functioning as unstable economic conditions tend to be associated with poorer housing, schools, neighborhoods, childcare, health care, and less supportive parenting (Hetherington, 1990; Lamb, Sternberg, & Thompson, 1997; Novak, 1996; Thomson et al., 1994). The lack of child monitoring following divorce [which could be attributed to motivational deficits of the parent or the parent's own environmental demands (e.g., work schedule)] (Hetherington, 1990, cited in Novak, 1996) has been associated with child behavior problems, including delinquency (Patterson, DeBaryshe, & Ramsey, 1989).

Custody Arrangement

Existing literature demonstrates a negative relationship between the father–child relationship quality and children's adjustment problems and depression (Buchanan et al., 1996; Harper & Fine, 2006; Papp et al., 2005). In their meta-analysis, Amato and Gilbreth (1999) confirmed this relation between quality father–child relationships and better child adjustment. Despite literature that suggests that children whose parents divorce during childhood have weakened emotional bonds with their parents later in life, 62% of adult children interviewed 20 years after their parents divorced reported that their relationship with their fathers improved or stayed the same (Ahrons & Tanner, 2003). In addition, empirical literature has suggested that better child outcomes post-divorce are associated with either joint custody or substantial contact with the noncustodial parent, with the child having frequent, positive interaction with both parents (Emery, 1999).

Wolchik, Braver, and Sandler (1985) assessed 133 children ages 8–15 whose parents, in the past 2½ years, had filed for separation or divorce. Thirty-three percent were in a joint custody situation with their parents with the remainder in maternal custody. Children were interviewed and measures of post-divorce experiences, psychological symptomatology (namely, depressive, anxiety, anger and hostility symptoms) as well as self-esteem were given. Parents were asked to complete the Child Behavior Checklist with respect to their child's behavior since the separation. Results indicated that children in joint custody reported a significantly greater number of positive experiences than did children in maternal custody. It was also reported that child symptomatology was not significantly different between the two groups; however, children in joint custody were found to have greater self-esteem than children in maternal custody. Children in joint custody also reported spending more time with the parent with whom they did not primarily reside. This study lends support for joint custody as being associated with a greater potential benefit to the child. It should be noted, however, that evidence has also suggested that in high-conflict couples, joint custody arrangements have led to poorer adjustment in children (Johnston, Kline, & Tschann, 1989).

In general, despite the overwhelming number of studies that have found associations between children from divorced families and poorer outcomes, when compared to children from intact families, the methodological problems inherent in this research render it impossible to conclude that these problems are solely due to divorce (Amato, 2000, 2001; Amato & Keith, 1991). Likewise, other studies have found that children from intact families as well as children from high-discord, but intact families, are quite similar in well-being to children from divorced families on a number of important outcomes (Amato, 2006; Hetherington & Kelly, 2002). In conclusion, while it appears that children from divorced families experience more long-term psychosocial problems than children from intact families, the definitive explanation for this has not yet found. Given that divorce effects are not likely to be eradicated, the pressing issue then becomes not whether or not it is bad for children, but which factors related to divorce are associated with better and poorer outcomes in children.

Risk Factors

Numerous longitudinal studies, including the Rochester Longitudinal Study (Seifer, Sameroff, & Jones, 1981), Garmezy's Project Competence (1973), the Philadelphia Project (Furstenberg, Cook, Eccles, Elder, & Sameroff, 1999), the National Longitudinal Study on Adolescent Health (Resnick et al., 1997), the Longitudinal Study of Australian Children (Zubrick, Smith, Nicholson, Sanson, & Jackiewicz, 2008), The British Cohort Study (Butler & Bynner, 1997, 2003; Butler et al., 1990; Chamberlain & Chamberlain, 1989), the National Institute of Child Health and Human Development (NICHD) Study of Early Child Care (1999), as well as other smaller studies have been conducted and have revealed relatively consistent findings regarding child outcomes. Risk factors have been defined as variables that "have proven or presumed effects that can directly increase the likelihood of a maladaptive outcome" (Rolf & Johnson, 1990, p. 387). Risk factors that consistently are revealed in this literature have been grouped into overarching meta-factors and include:

1. Poor parent–child relationship
2. Poor parenting skills (specifically, highly critical, harsh, inconsistent or permissive parenting)
3. Environmental instability (this factor subsumes low SES, low maternal education, disadvantaged minority status, as well as child maltreatment)
4. Parent mental health problems [poor emotional regulation/mental disorder of the parent (and particularly maternal disorders)]
5. Excessive interparental conflict

These factors have been identified as egregious parenting factors, or important factors to consider in custody evaluations (O'Donohue, Beitz, & Cummings, 2007; O'Donohue, Beitz, & Tolle, 2008). A review of literature for each factor is provided.

Poor Parent–Child Relationship

Healthy attachment to parents plays an important role in the functioning of children and adolescents (Taub, 1997). In attachment theory (Bowlby, 1969) and empirical research supporting this theory, the relationship formed between a child and their primary caregiver can influence learning, emotion regulation, and many other behaviors (Masten & Shaffer, 2006). Separation from a caregiver to whom the child is attached, as well as situations in which children are not able to form secure attachments are considered detrimental to development. Studies have indicated that poor attachment or insecure attachment is associated with problems forming later peer relationships, exhibiting aggression, poorer school performance, and low self-esteem (Ainsworth & Witting, 1969; Marcus & Betzer, 1996; O'Koon, 1997; Schneider & Younger, 1996, Shonkoff & Phillips, 2000; Suomi, 2000). In addition, data from the Minnesota Longitudinal Study of Parents and Children indicate that infant history of attachment disorganization/disorientation was correlated with mother–child relationship quality at 24 and 42 months, as well as subsequent child behavior problems in preschool, elementary and high school, and finally psychopathology and dissociation in adolescence (Carlson, 1998).

Poor Parenting Skills

Parenting styles tend to be relatively consistent over time (McNally, Eisenberg, & Harris, 1991), which is important to consider as inept parental discipline has been associated with child aggression, delinquency and an increased risk for child abuse (Novak, 1996). Research indicates that children of parents who are rejecting and unresponsive are more likely to demonstrate externalizing behaviors (i.e., anger, aggressiveness, hostility and noncompliant behavior) in their children (Shaffer, 1996). Poor parenting skills, including harsh, critical, or inconsistent parenting, which can be characteristic of both authoritarian and permissive parenting styles, lead to poorer outcomes in children (Baldwin, Baldwin, & Cole, 1990; Baumrind, 1967, 1971; Dodge et al., 2006; Dornbusch, Ritter, Leiderman, Roberts, & Fraleigh, 1987; Mann & MacKenzie, 1996; Masten & Coatsworth, 1995, 1998; Repetti et al., 2002; Steinberg et al., 1989). Rossman and Rea (2005) examined parenting styles and child outcomes of single-mother families where the mother had been a victim of domestic violence. It was determined that the parenting styles of the battered mothers were not significantly different in their endorsement of authoritative and authoritarian parenting practices than the nonbattered mothers. However, they did endorse significantly more permissive and inconsistent parenting practices. Higher endorsements of authoritarian parenting styles were significantly associated with higher levels of learning, conduct, and hyperactivity/impulsivity problems in children. In addition, endorsements of permissive parenting styles were associated significantly with higher levels of children's anxiety and poorer school performance. Children with the poorest outcomes (highest levels of externalizing and school problems) were in homes where inconsistent parenting (combination of permissive and authoritarian parenting practices) was practiced.

Environmental Instability

Recently there has been a shift from away from family preservation in recognition of the fact that children who remain in unstable homes are at risk (Ballou et al., 2000). Environmental stability is important for promoting child security (Bray, 1991, cited in Gould, 1998). An "instable environment" may include factors such as inconsistent living arrangements, extreme poverty, inadequate supervision, substance abuse, violence and physical and/or sexual abuse. LeVine (1974) places economic goals second in the hierarchy of universal functions of parenting, which includes things like providing basic education. Factors including Socioeconomic Status (SES), maternal education, income and occupational status have been found to have significant effects on a number of academic factors including achievement test scores, course failures, and children's completed years of education (McLoyd, 1998). In addition, SES and the functional competence of parents have been associated with child competence or achievement—in that less affluent or competent parents may increase exposure of children to dangers, deviant peers, or other negative influences in the environment due to environmental circumstances, choices or behaviors (Collins et al., 2000; Masten & Coatsworth, 1998; McLoyd, 1998; Repetti et al., 2002).

Gutman, Sameroff, and Eccles (2002) examined the effects of multiple risk and promotive factors on academic achievement in African-American adolescents. Risk factors included: maternal depression, low family income, low occupational status in the household, low maternal education, unmarried, higher number of children living in the household, higher number of family stressful events, higher percent neighborhood poverty, higher percent neighborhood female headed households, and higher percent neighborhood welfare recipients. Promotive factors included: consistent parenting, democratic decision making, higher parental school involvement and higher social support from peers as well as teachers. Results from this study indicated that when multiple risk factors were present, these children tended to have lower GPAs, more school absences, and lower math achievement test scores. Although the effects of poverty can be mitigated by various factors (i.e., accepting, stimulating, and organized environment) (Novak, 1996), economic hardship in its extreme (i.e., homelessness) is likely to severely impact child functioning. Finally, substance abuse, violence, and physical abuse are factors that cause family disruptions and negatively affect the well-being of children (Lamb et al., 1997; Sun, 2001). Specifically, excessive parental drug and alcohol abuse have been shown to be detrimental to the development of socialization and a variety of internalization and externalization problems in children (Otto & Edens, 2003). In addition, alcohol abuse has a significant impact on families. Estimates have suggested that as many as 25% of children are affected by alcohol abuse in their families (Grant, 2000). Families with parental alcohol abuse are more likely to experience increased family hostility, poor parenting, and decreased child monitoring (Chassin, Pillow, Curran, Molina, & Barrera, 1993; Sher et al., 1991). Miller, Smyth, and Mudar (1999) found that mothers with alcohol and other drug problems were more punitive toward their children, and that this parenting behavior continued even after the substance abuse problem was treated. Children of parents who abused alcohol were at increased risk for early alcohol use themselves in addition to more externalizing behavior (Chassin, Pitts, DeLucia, & Todd, 1999).

Parent Mental Health Problems

Emery (1999) suggested that four mental health problems among adults are of special concern to understanding the outcomes of children: (1) depression,

(2) antisocial behavior, (3) serious mental illness (i.e., schizophrenia and bipolar disorder), and (4) personality disorders. Specifically, research suggests that parental depression, schizophrenia, and display of antisocial behaviors or display of other problematic behaviors that are indicative of other personality disorders have been associated with a number of negative child outcomes. These outcomes have been found to include: adjustment problems, psychopathology, aggression, delinquency, conduct disorder, attention deficit disorder, and other externalizing problems (Emery, 1999; Hammen et al., 1987; Johnston, 1995; Orvaschel et al., 1988; for a review, see Otto & Edens, 2003).

Studies of the offspring of clinically depressed parents show that having a depressed parent is one of the strongest predictors of depression in children and adolescents. Estimates suggest that approximately half or more of the children raised in homes with depressed mothers experience depressive, anxiety and substance use disorders (Beardslee, Versage, & Gladstone, 1998; Downey & Coyne, 1990). Studies have found that these problems extend into adulthood as well (Hamilton & Hango, 2008). For example, Weissman et al. (1997, 2006) followed offspring of a depressed and nondepressed sample of parents and found that depression was much more common in the offspring of depressed parents than the offspring of nondepressed parents at 10- and 20-year follow-ups. Findings from several other studies suggest that maternal depression in early childhood is predictive of behavior problems in early childhood (i.e., poorer cognitive functioning, lower feelings of self-worth, conduct problems) (Morrell & Murray, 2003; Murray, Fiori-Cowley, Hooper, & Cooper, 1996; Murray, Woolgar, Hipwell, & Cooper, 2001).

Seifer et al. (1981) examined data from the Rochester study and concluded that offspring of Schizophrenic, depressive or otherwise seriously mentally ill parents were less cooperative, more timid, more fearful, more depressed, and more likely to engage in bizarre behavior than their comparison groups. Other researchers have noted that the relationship between psychopathology and children's functioning might not be causal (Jenuwine & Cohler, 1999). When this link can be demonstrated, measurement of parental emotional stability is clinically relevant for determining child custody or placement.

Another important consideration when examining psychological problems in parents, and its risk on outcomes in children, is the specific nature of these disorders. For example, in maternal depressive disorders, an area that has been consistently associated with risk in children, it is important to consider the severity and chronicity of depression, its degree of functional impairment, and the ways in which it impacts child development. Relatively few studies have attempted to tease out these factors. Studies have reported that chronically depressed mothers have more negative interactions with their children than those with acute or intermittent depressive symptoms (NICHD Early Child Care Research Network, 1999).

Brennan et al. (2000) examined the relationship between chronicity, severity, and timing of maternal depressive symptoms on the longitudinal outcomes of children (N=4,953) at 5 years of age. Specifically, mothers reported their depressive symptoms during pregnancy, immediately postpartum, again when infants were 6 months and finally at age 5. The interaction of the chronicity and severity of depressive symptoms were found to be significantly related to higher levels of child behavior problems, as were chronicity and severity when analyzed alone. Moderate levels of depression were defined by a score of 11 or higher on the Beck Depression Inventory (Beck, Ward, Mendelson, Mock, & Erbaugh, 1961) while severe levels of depression were defined by a score of 19 or higher, which were consistent with scoring guidelines for the BDI (Beck, Steer, & Garbin, 1988). Chronicity was defined as the mother reporting either moderate or severe symptoms across time points.

In another study examining varying factors associated with depressive symptoms and its impact on children's adjustment, Hammen and Brennan (2003) studied mothers ($N=816$) with varying degrees, durations, and timing of depressive symptoms. An overall evaluation of the chronicity and severity was conducted, in addition to the effects of duration of mild-only and severe-only maternal depression in predicting depressive and nondepressive disorders in the mothers' 15-year-old children. Analyses of timing exposure were also conducted in mothers who experienced depression only during one time period of the child's life: from birth to 2, 3–5, and 6–10 years of age. Results of this study reflected that overall, depression in children was found to be twice as likely in children of depressed, as opposed to never-depressed mothers. Severity of depression was found to be a stronger predictor of children's risk for depression than was chronicity. Children who were exposed to 1–2 months of major maternal depression or to more than 12 months of mild depression were found to be at higher risk for depression themselves.

Excessive Interparental Conflict

Parental conflict [i.e., hostility, violence and other acts of marital aggression, acting deliberately subversive and using the child in ways to harm the other parent (e.g., telling the child to not obey the other parent, using the child as a conduit for punishing the other parent, etc.)] is associated with deleterious effects on child and adolescent functioning (Cummings & Davies, 2002; Emery, 1999; Gould, 1998; Hetherington et al., 1982; Otto & Edens, 2003; Wallerstein & Kelly, 1980; Whiteside & Becker, 2000) and has been shown to be a stronger predictor of adjustment than family structure (Kot & Shoemaker, 1999). In their book, *Children in Violent Families: The Impact of Exposure*, Rossman, Hughes, and Rosenberg (2000) report that children who are exposed to interparental violence (IPV) have lower self-esteem, lower levels of social and academic competence, higher attentional difficulties, greater trauma symptomatology, and higher levels of internalizing and externalizing behavior problems. Also, when conflict is encapsulated (i.e., children are not placed in the middle) or mediated by paternal involvement and the parent–child relationship, children appear to function as well as those from no- or low-conflict families (Hetherington, 1999; Pruett, Williams, Insabella, & Little, 2003). This is similar to findings from Grych and Fincham (2001) and Grych, Seid, and Finchman (1992), which indicate that severe marital conflict that focuses on children is predictive of adjustment problems and much more so than conflict that is not focused on the children. Buehler et al. (1998) studied parental conflict styles and frequency of conflict. They found that overtly hostile conflict styles were associated more with both externalizing and internalizing behavioral problems in children, whereas covert conflict styles (i.e., passive–aggressive behavior and triangulation) were associated more with internalizing problems in children.

Fortunately for the validity of custody evaluations, these factors overlap with what many states have included in their statutes as being important considerations for determining the best interest of the child (BIC). It appears that a standardized model, which includes these important factors, guided by empirical literature, would be an important first step in minimizing variability of evaluations.

Longitudinal research has established that it is not any one risk factor that will lead to poorer outcomes in children, but rather that the cumulative effect of multiple risk factors dramatically increases the chance of later psychiatric disorders in children entering into adolescence or adulthood (Gutman et al., 2002; Rutter, Maughan, Mortimore, Ouston, & Smith, 1979; Sameroff, Seifer, Baldwin, & Baldwin, 1993; Sameroff, Seifer, Barocas, Zax, & Greenspan, 1987). In Rutter's longitudinal findings, it was established that among 10-year olds who were part of families with zero or one risk factor, their psychiatric risk was 2%, as compared to 20% in children of families where four or more risk factors were present.

Promotive Factors

Promotive factors are the obverse of risk factors in that they are associated with leading to adaptive or positive outcomes. They are found in both high- and low-risk populations (as opposed to protective factors, which have been related to factors found in high-risk groups that protect individuals from risk factors) (Sameroff et al., 1999). Similarly to risk factors, these promotive factors have been consistently identified in longitudinal studies as predicting adaptive or positive outcomes in individuals. Some of them appear to be the converse of an identified risk factor; however, these are distinct from the absence of a risk in that additional components are present that not only mitigate the risk of poorer outcomes but also enhance positive outcomes. Several variables have also been identified as being important not only to positive child outcomes, but also predictive of improved outcomes in children of divorced families. Promotive factors that have consistently been identified in research include:

1. Positive parenting—which includes parental warmth, acceptance, consistency and encouragement while also communicating realistic expectations for the child.
2. Parental school involvement—which includes providing an environment conducive to learning and educational opportunities through help with school work, providing books in the home, and communicating regularly with school personnel.
3. Promotion of interpersonal development—which includes provision of opportunities to engage with other positive figures and school-age peers and modeling effective social skills to enhance the child's potential for social competence and peer acceptance.

4. Promotion of mental health—which includes supporting the child's self-esteem, self-efficacy, and autonomy at appropriate developmental stages.
5. Promotion of community involvement—which includes involvement in community resources, church, extracurricular activities, or other team opportunities that enhance the child's capacity for empathy, moral development, sense of interpersonal connectiveness and support.
6. Effective coparenting—which includes parents' specific attempts to collaborate and cooperate with one another in terms of child-rearing behaviors in a nonconfrontational, low conflict manner.

Positive Parenting

In their meta-analysis of 47 studies examining the relationship between parenting behavior and child externalizing behavior, Rothbaum and Weisz (1994) reported that parental approval, guidance, use of motivational strategies, synchrony, and absence of coercive control were significantly negatively associated with child externalizing behavior. They further asserted that when a pattern of all variables was present in parenting it was found to be especially predictive of low child externalizing behavior. In fact, effective parenting has pervasively been associated with positive adjustment in children from both high-risk and low-risk families (Damon & Eisenberg, 1998; Maccoby & Mnookin, 1992; Masten & Coatsworth, 1998). Specifically, in studies related to children of parents who have divorced, children receiving effective parenting were found to be better adjusted than children receiving less appropriate parenting (Hetherington, 1999; Kelly & Lamb, 2000; Maccoby & Mnookin, 1992). Consistent parenting, consistent discipline, parental warmth, scaffolding and consistent praise have been found to be associated with positive achievement-related and other positive outcomes in children and adolescents (Baldwin et al., 1990; Clark, 1983; Damon & Eisenberg, 1998; Gutman et al., 2002; Katz & Gottman, 1997; Walker, Stieber, Ramsey, & O'Neill, 1991). In Garmezy's Project Competence, it was found that parenting quality was a better predictor for girls rather than boys for disruptive classroom behavior (Garmezy & Devine, 1985). These parenting practices, most aligned with the authoritative parenting style, have been found to promote child adjustment, and are associated with self-acceptance, psychological autonomy and better behavioral control in children (Rossman & Rea, 2005; Steinberg, Elmen, & Mounts, 1989). An additional objective measure that has been cited in research as being associated with better outcomes in children is that of eating dinner together as a family. After accounting for sex, race and family household income, eating dinner together as a family was the strongest predictor of positive adolescent development and related to higher levels of positive youth development and community contribution as well as lower levels of depression and at-risk behavior (Zarrett et al., 2008).

Schofield and Beek (2005) broke positive parenting into four dimensions that they found to be in line with both attachment theory as well as with theories on resiliency in children (Gilligan, 2000; Rutter, 1999; Sroufe, 1997): (1) promoting trust in availability, (2) promoting reflective function, (3) promoting self-esteem, and (4) promoting autonomy. Schofield and Beek report that this trust in availability is important for children's healthy emotional involvement in that all children need caregivers who are "accessible but not intrusive, dependable, and alert to signals of need, ready to provide whatever nurture and protection is needed" (p. 10).

In a longitudinal study that evaluated how these positive parenting dimensions were expressed, Schofield and Beek (2005) found that the anticipated concern and availability in addition to anticipated enjoyment into the future was important for providing a perceived sense of security in foster children. Verbal and nonverbal expressions were seen in showing availability (i.e., physical affection, bedtime rituals, being met reliably from school, etc.) reflecting that the children are in caregiver's minds even while apart.

Parental School Involvement

Parental involvement in the child's education focuses on the cognitive, behavioral, and motivational aspects of children's learning (Seginer & Vermulst, 2002). Involvement often consists of the following activities: volunteering at school, communicating with teachers or other school personnel, assisting in academic activities at home, and attending school events, meetings of parent–teacher associations, and parent–teacher conferences. For middle and high school students, discussions between parents and adolescents about school and plans for the future are often also included in definitions of parental academic involvement (Hill & Taylor, 2004). At-home academic involvement has been described as contact between parent and child that is focused on the child's schooling (Shumow & Miller, 2001).

Home-based involvement includes activities such as direct help with schoolwork, guidance on course selection, and advice on career planning. At-school involvement requires parents to initiate, or be available for contact with school personnel, including activities like attending conferences and school events (such as sporting events), participating in parent–teacher organizations, or by serving in decision-making roles (such as on school boards) (Shumow & Miller, 2001).

Studies reflect that parental involvement in their children's academics, as well as other extracurricular activities, is related to positive outcomes in children. These types of positive interactions begin with initial literacy. Studies have found that children's success in learning to read early or at the average level of same-aged peers is predicted by both shared reading activities (in which parents and children regularly read together) (Scarborough & Dobrich, 1994) and the provision of books or accessibility to books in the home (Scarborough, 1998). In addition, a parent's positive attitude toward their child learning to read and school in general is predictive of reading skills acquisition in their children (Scarborough & Dobrich, 1994). This positive trend has been followed in adolescence as well, with research reflecting that parents who encourage their children by attending school functions or monitoring homework have children who display higher achievement and more advanced educational or vocational aspirations (Brown & Haung, 1995). Nord, Brimhall, and West (1997) found that fathers' attentiveness, specifically, to their children's scholastic activities is associated with academic success.

Good parent–child problem solving interactions and parental school involvement (support for school based activities) have been positively associated with school achievement, better adjustment, and peer relationships (Estrada, Arsenio, Hess, & Halloway, 1987; Gutman & McLoyd, 2000). Guttman, Sameroff, and Eccles (2002) determined that parental school involvement had positive effects on adolescents' grade point average and number of absences from school. In addition, families that encourage children and adolescents in decision making have children who have more positive school adjustment, higher self-esteem and greater satisfaction with school and peer relations (Lord, Eccles, & McCarthy, 1994). In their National Longitudinal Study on Adolescent Health, Resnick et al. (1997) found that protective factors, including a feeling of connectedness with their school, largely guided by peers as well as parental school involvement, were associated with lower levels of emotional distress, suicidality, involvement in violence, substance use, and sexual behaviors.

Several studies have found that divorce increases the risk for academic difficulties in children (Emery, 1999; Hetherington, 1999). When examining what specific factors are associated with a decline in academic functioning, several factors have been identified. Furstenberg and Teitler (1994) reported that the decline in academic achievement in children of divorce is associated with high marital discord prior to divorce and that this accounts for the decline in post-divorce functioning. Other factors that have been identified include increased poverty post-separation (Pong & Ju, 2000) and lessened parental supervision (McLanahan & Sandefur, 1994). McLanahan (1999) reported that an increase in school absences, an increase in television viewing, less attention to homework and an overall decrease in monitoring were all consequences found in children post-divorce. It is important to note that other studies have found that children of divorced homes have been found to fall within the average range for academic competence and very similar to academic outcomes of children from nondivorced families (Amato & Rezac, 1994).

Promotion of Interpersonal Development

Social support and the importance of having multiple positive relationships with competent and caring adults have been shown to be associated with positive outcomes in children and adolescents (Wright & Masten, 2005). The presence of external social support systems that encourage and reinforce a child's coping efforts through secure and supportive personal relationships, outside of parental relationships, are promotive of adaptive outcomes in children (Garmezy & Devine, 1985; Masten & Garmezy, 1985; Rutter, 1990; Luthar, 2003; Masten, Best, & Garmezy, 1990; Rutter, 1999, 2000 as cited in Rutter, 2006). In addition, social self-efficacy and social support have been found to be negatively associated with depression in children and adolescents (McFarlane, Bellissimo, & Norman, 1995). Friendship has also been found to be positively associated with psychological well-being as well as physical health in individuals (Rareshide & Kern, 1991). Friendships are a source of emotional security and intimacy and allow a child to identify as worthwhile and competent (Furman & Buhrmester, 1985). In addition, close friendships can be helpful in providing significant support to even young children in stressful situations (Hartup, 1999; Ladd, Kochenderfer, & Coleman, 1996). Specifically, as a part of the Avon Longitudinal Study of Pregnancy and Childhood (ALSPAC), which examined over 13,000 families, Dunn, Davies, O'Connor, and Sturgess (2001) examined the importance of friendships during stressful family changes (i.e., parental separation or divorce). Results indicated that children with higher quality friendships had positive relationships with their mothers and confided more in them. In addition, children who felt more positive about moving between parents' homes (in a joint custody arrangement) were also found more likely to have close friendships. Finally, children who reported being frequently involved in parental conflict reported fewer close and affectionate friendships (Dunn et al., 2001).

Knickmeyer, Sexton, and Nishimura (2002) reported that the presence of friendships may serve as a buffer against stress, which in turn lowers one's risk for cardiovascular disease and other physical problems. In contrast, poor peer acceptance or peer rejection has been related to poorer self-esteem and poorer outcomes in children's interpersonal development. Specifically, peer rejection has been associated with higher rates of depression and anxiety (Ladd, 2006), delinquency, substance abuse, risky sexual behaviors, and lower school achievement (Prinstein & La Greca, 2004; Romano, Hubbard, McAuliffe, & Morrow, 2009).

Research has focused on a number of pathways in which parents influence their children's social relationships. Specifically, strong parent–child relationships as well as positive parenting are related to quality peer relationships in children. In contrast, children from highly authoritarian parents (i.e., parents who utilize harsh discipline practices) are likely to show less adaptive interpersonal behaviors (i.e., are more aggressive with peers) and are at an increased risk for peer rejection (Conger, Neppl, Kim, & Scaramella, 2003; Romano et al., 2009). Another way in which parents contribute to children's peer relationships is the degree to which parents are involved. Parents' initiation, facilitation, and monitoring of children's social activities have been found to be related positively to peer acceptance, pro-social behavior, friendship quality, and social competence (Simpkins & Parke, 2002). Simpkins and Parke examined the relationship of parental rules and children's social adjustment. Eighty-eight sixth graders and their mothers were included in the study. Mothers were asked to disclose rules that they used with their children regarding social situations and these responses were ultimately grouped into three categories: (1) rules for the need for adult supervision of activities (i.e., need to ask permission for specific activities; need to tell parents their whereabouts; and have adult present, etc.), (2) rules concerning social interactions with peers (i.e., prohibition of aggressive behavior or other unwanted behavior; prohibition of interaction with aggressive peers; encouragement of pro-social engagement with peers; and guidelines regarding conflict resolution with peers), and (3) rules concerning other restrictions (i.e., guidelines concerning allowable places and activities for play; timelines for play and other behaviors such as finishing chores first or cleaning up messes). Findings indicated that closer monitoring was associated with less peer conflict in children as well as positive friendship quality in girls (Simpkins & Parke, 2002).

In addition to parenting behaviors, parents' own social adjustment and peer relationships have implications for their children's social adjustment. Specifically, Marshall, Noonan, McCartney, Marx, and Keefe (2001) found that mothers who endorsed more emotional support were more warm and responsive to their children, and they, in turn, showed fewer behavioral problems and more social competence. In addition, the size of parents' friendship networks has been found to be positively associated with that of their child's friendship network, as well as children's social acceptance and social skills (Romano et al., 2009). Romano et al., 2009 investigated this relationship by comparing parents' reported friendship network size, satisfaction, quality and conflict with that of their children's. Results indicated that parents' friendship conflict and dissatisfaction both negatively predicted children's peer rejection and aggression. These results may indicate that parents who have satisfactory friendships model pro-social skills and encourage or facilitate friendships for their child leading to more peer acceptance. In addition, parents who report conflict with friends may also model appropriate conflict resolution and therefore their children show fewer aggressive behaviors in peer relationships.

Promotion of Mental Health

The promotion of mental health has been found to be negatively associated with depression (McFarlane et al., 1995). The promotion of mental health has been conceptualized as the promotion of self-esteem, self-efficacy, and autonomy. The development of problem-solving skills and a flexible, adaptive approach to new situations has also been associated with resiliency in children (Luthar, 2003; Garmezy & Devine, 1985; Masten & Garmezy, 1985; Masten et al., 1990; Rutter, 1990, 1999, 2000 as cited in Rutter, 2006). The promotion of self-esteem has been identified as a process that begins in infancy and involves parents showing full and unconditional acceptance toward their child. This may be expressed through the use of loving words, tone of voice, and gestures that indicate to the child that she or he is loveable, valuable, and a source of joy and interest to others (Schofield & Beek, 2005). Schofield and Beek reported that as children develop, parents who promote self-esteem create environments in which children can continue to feel a sense of accomplishment or achievement while being cognizant of their own child's strengths and limitations. This is important in that it allows children to tolerate some failure in order to recognize that they are accepted and loved for who they are.

Likewise, the promotion of self-efficacy and autonomy comes as a natural consequence of improved confidence and parents who promote this create an environment where children have continual opportunities to feel effective or influential (Schofield & Beek, 2005). Parents who promote self-efficacy and autonomy present choices to children to allow them to learn that their own behavior contributes to their feelings of pleasure or sociability. Through this, children learn that they can rely on their own resources to meet their needs and can contribute to controlling their own environment. Parents who provide security for children to explore and support this behavior and reinforce successes (i.e., "You did it all by yourself! Great job! I'm so proud of you!"), assist in promoting self-efficacy. Children of parents who promote this have been shown to be more resilient in the face of adversity (Rutter, 1999; Sroufe, 1997).

Promotion of Community Involvement

In addition to the promotion of social skills, involvement in activities outside of school is associated with positive outcomes in children (Denault & Poulin, 2009; Zarrett et al., 2008). This is especially important to examine in the context of divorce as studies have found that involvement in extracurricular activities may decline post-divorce. Some of this may be accounted for by a decrease in financial resources that is often found in families post-divorce (McLanahan, 1999). Additionally, however, high parent conflict, poor cooperation, and limited resources prior to separation have also been identified as factors associated with a decrease in extracurricular activities (Kelly & Emery, 2003).

Organized activities have been characterized as those that occur at school or in the community that involve an adult identified as a group leader or coach, consistent participation in meetings and activities, and an emphasis on skill-building (Larson, 2000). Outside school activities include anything from youth development programs such as 4-H or the boys and girls club, after-school clubs, individual and team sports, performing arts, arts and crafts, religious activities, and service activities.

Results from numerous studies reflect that the involvement in activities outside of school is associated with higher academic achievement (Darling, Caldwell, & Smith, 2005; Eccles & Barber, 1999; Jordan & Nettles, 1999; Mahoney & Cairns, 1997; Mahoney, Cairns, & Farmer, 2003), a lower risk of engaging in risky behavior (i.e., risky sexual behavior, substance use, antisocial behavior) (Darling et al., 2005; Linville & Huebner, 2005), lower levels of internalizing problems (i.e., depression) (Bohnert, Kane, & Garber, 2008; Fredricks & Eccles, 2005; Mahoney et al., 2003), higher self-esteem (Barber, Eccles, & Stone, 2001), and more investment in the community (Denault & Poulin, 2009). Research has also reported that involvement in organized activities may protect against the development of psychopathology (Mahoney & Cairns, 1997; McHale et al., 2001). Researchers posit that involvement in these activities promote pro-social behavior in children and adolescents because they are provided with opportunities to create a sense of identity, opportunities to learn from social experiences and increased involvement with peers and leaders. These experiences help children to negotiate effective behavior in these relationships, set and achieve goals, compete fairly, and learn from defeats or successes (Carnegie Corporation of New York, 1992; Denault & Poulin, 2009; Lerner & Lerner, 2006; Mahoney et al., 2005a, 2005b).

Results from a longitudinal study analyzing positive adolescent development indicated that, after accounting for sex, race, and household income, more outside school activity was predictive of positive outcomes. These adolescents scored higher on scales of positive youth development and contribution to family, school, and the community at large (Zarrett et al., 2008). Furthermore, results from prospective studies controlling for prior symptoms have found positive effects of participation in outside school activities. Specifically, Darling et al. (2005) found that more years of participation in school-sponsored activities during high school was associated with less marijuana and other substance use, after controlling for prior use. In a study examining free-time activities of 10-year-olds, participation in sports predicted fewer internalizing problems 2 years later (McHale et al., 2001).

Bohnert et al. (2008) examined prospectively the effects of organized activity involvement on externalizing and internalizing problems in children who were either at risk or not at risk for psychopathology (i.e., came from families in which maternal depression was present). Results indicated that of the 240 adolescents involved, higher levels of activity involvement in tenth grade significantly predicted lower levels of internalizing problems in 11th grade. In addition, higher levels of internalizing problems in 11th grade predicted less activity involvement in 12th grade, controlling for prior involvement as well as risk.

Similarly, Mahoney and Cairns (1997) found that early drop-out rates were much lower among high-risk youth who had participated in at least one extracurricular activity in middle school or early high school than those who had not. Studies have also shown that adolescents who participate in school-based extracurricular activities tend to be from a higher socioeconomic status, are of European-American descent, are more positively inclined toward school, are more oriented toward adult standards and are more likely to come from authoritative families (Darling et al., 2005; Durbin et al., 1993; McNeal, 1998). In spite of this, several studies have found similar outcomes of children from lower socioeconomic status, who are at-risk for psychopathology, or are ethnic minorities. For example, in a predominantly African-American sample, Fredricks and Eccles (2005) found that participation in school clubs and sports participation predicted fewer externalizing problems in boys. In fact, it has been shown that the benefits of activity participation in reducing problem behaviors are especially strong for at-risk youth (Mahoney, 2000; Mahoney & Cairns, 1997). Huebner and Mancini (2003) reported that African-American youth are more likely than youth from other racial or ethnic backgrounds to participate in religious activities. In addition to the types of activity involvement in disadvantaged, at-risk youth, the behavior of parents is an especially important component for their success in children's extracurricular activities. Couton and Irwin (2009) examined the degree to which parental community involvement, neighborhood safety, and disadvantage affected participation in out-of-school activities. Results indicated that children whose parents participated in community volunteering and action were more likely to participate in out-of-school activities.

Finally, Denault and Poulin (2009) followed 299 youth for 5 years beginning in the seventh grade to examine involvement in extracurricular activities and resulting outcomes over time. Activities that the youth participated in at the outset of the study were grouped into seven categories: (1) individual sports (i.e., swimming, karate, gymnastics, etc.), (2) group sports (i.e., soccer, volleyball, basketball, etc.), (3) performance and fine arts (i.e., band, drama, dance, art, etc.), (4) academic clubs and organizations (i.e., math club, chess club, student government, etc.), (5) community-oriented activities (i.e., boys' and girls' scouts, 4-H, etc.), (6) service activities, and (7) faith-based youth groups. Outcome measures that were examined included: (1) academic orientation (i.e., grades, educational aspirations, self-perceptions of academic competence, and skipping class), (2) risky behaviors (i.e., antisocial behaviors, substance use, and unsafe sex), (3) internalizing problems (i.e., depressive symptoms, self-worth, and loneliness), and (4) civic development. Civic development was conceptualized as commitments to civil society (i.e., helping those who are less fortunate), environmental sustainability (i.e., doing something to help the environment) and altruism (i.e., being willing to work fewer hours for less pay if it helped unemployed people get jobs). Results indicated that family income was associated with youth participation intensity (i.e., number of activities) and breadth (i.e., varying types of activities). In addition, though both intensity and breadth of activities declined over time, academic orientation and civic development were positively associated with involvement, reflecting that extracurricular activities predict positive outcomes in youth.

Effective Coparenting

The quality of the relationship between former partners has been identified as a very important predictor of children's well-being post-divorce, with cooperative and nonconflictual coparenting associated with improved social competence in children (Camara & Resnick, 1988; Demo & Acock, 1988; Emery, 1982; Hess & Camera, 1979; Hetherington et al., 1982; Jacobson, 1978; Kurdek & Blisk, 1983; Wallerstein & Kelly, 1980). Feinberg (2003) defined coparenting as consisting of four elements: (1) childrearing agreement, (2) division of labor, (3) support-undermining, and (4) joint family management. Frequently following divorce, families involved in custody evaluations have difficulty defining new coparenting roles. The attempt on parents' parts to make this transition smooth for children can play an important role in ensuring better outcomes for these children. Effective coparenting has been conceptualized as working together to support each other's parenting decisions while also remaining flexible and maintaining healthy boundaries (Adamsons & Pasley, 2006). Effective coparenting behaviors including respect, communication, forgiveness, and cooperation have been shown to be protective for children's adjustment among divorced families (Bonach, 2005; Bonach & Sales, 2002; Gasper, Stolberg, Macie, & Williams, 2009; Macie, 2002). Not only do children of cooperating parents show fewer behavior problems (Hess & Camera, 1979; Kurdek & Berg, 1983; Jacobson, 1978; Luepnitz, 1986), but they also enjoy more harmonious sibling relationships (MacKinnon, 1989) and experience fewer problems in dating during adolescence (Booth, Brinkerhoff, & White, 1984). Cooperative coparenting not only has implications for children's adjustment directly, but also has indirect implications in the way that it impacts parents' adjustment, which, in turn, has implications for children's adjustment. Cooperative coparenting has been found to be associated with father's well-being (Baum, 2003) in addition to a decreased risk of mother's depression (Whiteside & Becker, 2000).

Outcome studies have revealed that cooperative parents engage in a full range of custody arrangements, with no one type proving superior in benefiting children's adjustment or in protecting children from interparental conflict (Glover & Steele, 1989; Kline, Tschann, Johnston, & Wallerstein, 1989; Pearson & Thoennes, 1990; Wolchik et al., 1985). In a later study, Markham, Ganong, and Coleman (2007) posited that because mothers frequently act as the primary parent prior to separation or divorce and frequently have primary physical custody following divorce, their attitude toward shifting to a role of a coparent can predict how cooperative of a coparenting relationship ex-spouses will have. Furthermore, mothers can behave as "gatekeepers" in coparenting relationships, restricting the amount of time fathers are allowed with their children. Post-divorce, this restriction of a father's time may be intensified as conflict in the relationship increases and parents inhabit separate homes (Fagan & Barnett, 2003; Markham et al., 2007).

Bronstein, Stoll, Clauson, Abrams, and Briones (1994) examined the ways in which the presence of a father figure following biological parents' divorce is related to preadolescent children's adjustment. The sample included 136 children ages 9–12 and parents from a variety of households (i.e., single mother, mother and step-father, shared parenting households). Results indicated that there was a trend in single-mother households for more cooperative coparenting between ex-partners to be associated with children's popularity with peers. In step-parent situations in which noncustodial fathers still had direct contact with children (i.e., mothers had remarried), the coparenting relationship between ex-partners was a direct predictor of children's adjustment. In cases where the relationship was cooperative, children were more likely to have a positive self-concept, higher grades, and fewer psychological problems.

Developmental Considerations

With the exception of a few states' statutes that take into consideration the age of the child, developmental needs are discussed as being important and something that parents should meet, though they often are not explicated, and not discussed in anything other than a general, vague fashion. Some divorce researchers have addressed the fact that children have different needs at different developmental periods and that these should factor into the custody recommendations (Bray, 1991; Wallerstein & Kelly, 1980).

Table 3.1 Diagnostic classification of mental health and developmental disorders of infancy and early childhood (DC: 0-3 R)

Axis I	Infant's primary diagnosis. Examples include post-traumatic stress disorder, affective disorder, and eating behavior disorder
Axis II	Disorders related to the caregiver–child relationship. Examples include angry/hostile, over-/under-involved, and physically or sexually abusive relationship problems
Axis III	Medical and/or developmental conditions including developmental language disorder, failure to thrive, and cerebral palsy
Axis IV	Acute and chronic stressors in the child's environment. Examples are parental psychopathology and parent conflict
Axis V	The young child's current functional and emotional level of adaptation

In his book, Conducting *Scientifically Crafted Child Custody Evaluations*, Gould (1998) explicated the developmental needs of children throughout different developmental periods. In order to assess the BIC Gould argued that it is necessary to consider the age and developmental stage of the child, although this becomes fairly complex as all future developmental stages/needs also need to be considered.

With the explosion of research examining the importance of early development and promotion of health in infancy through toddlerhood, it is important to determine how these factors impact child custody determinations. Although each stage in development is important, particularly complex stages for child development occur from birth to 3 years of age. Meeting the needs of children at these critical stages is very important to the social and emotional, as well as physical, health of children. Assessing the capacity and knowledge parents have to meet these needs is important to the child custody evaluation. More recognition is now being given to the early origins of mental health disorders that are later diagnosed in adolescents and adults. In an effort to recognize and treat early symptoms, the Revised Diagnostic Classification of Mental Health and Developmental Disorders of Infancy and Early Childhood (DC: 0-3 R) (Zero to Three, 2005) was developed. It uses a multiaxial system with five major classifications of disorders similar to the Diagnostic and Statistical Manual for Mental Disorders (DSM-IV TR); however, the DC: 0-3 R focuses on various factors that relate to social and emotional well-being (Table 3.1).

The DC: 0-3 R axes overlap with the egregious and promotive factors noted above in literature as factors that are associated with maladaptive or improved outcomes in children. In addition, the DC: 0-3 R attempts to outline the needs of infants and children in the prevention of psychopathology. Good parenting skills and a strong parent–child relationship that is characterized by: warmth, consistency, stability and promotion of health, and minimizing exposure to parental conflict and traumatic situations (i.e., risky, unstable or abusive environments), are important factors to consider in a developmentally focused child custody evaluation. In addition, if there is reason to believe that a child may be experiencing developmental and/or social/emotional difficulties, formal testing should be considered. Many standardized, norm-referenced and empirically supported evaluation measures exist and include: The Bayley Scales of Infant Development (BSID-III; Black & Matula,

1999), The Ages and Stages Questionnaires (ASQ-3/ASQ-SE; Squires, Bricker, & Twombly, 2002; Squires, Potter, & Bricker, 1995), The Child Behavior Checklist (CBCL; Achenbach & Edelbrock, 1983), the Child Depression Inventory (CDI; Kovacs, 1981), the Behavior Assessment System for Children (BASC; Reynolds & Kamphaus, 1992), the Multidimensional Anxiety Scale for Children (MASC; March, Parker, Sullivan, Stallings, & Connors, 1997), the Modified Checklist for Autism in Toddlers (M-CHAT; Robins, Fein, Barton, & Green, 2001), and the Vanderbilt ADHD Parent Rating Scale (VADPRS; Wolraich, Hannah, Baumgaertel, & Feurer, 1998) as well as the Vanderbilt ADHD Teacher Rating Scale (VADTRS; Wolraich, Feurer, Hannah, Pinnock, & Baumgaertel, 1998). These assessments have extensive research supporting their psychometric properties and have been frequently used to assist in the diagnosis of common childhood disorders.

It is possible that specialists have already screened or diagnosed children by the time they are involved in a child custody evaluation. The American Academy of Pediatrics (AAP) recommends that pediatricians screen all children for developmental disorders at every pediatric visit in addition to formal developmental screening at 9-, 18- and 30-month visits (American Academy of Pediatrics, Council on Children with Disabilities, 2006). When developmental concerns are identified, health care providers should administer developmental screening tools and make referrals for further evaluation as necessary. It is important for the child custody evaluator to be aware of emotional and developmental problems that are present in a child involved in a custody evaluation. The custody evaluator will need to determine whether the parent has the capacity to access the special supports and services that are needed in order to promote the optimal health and development of the child (i.e., taking children to medical/other appointments, or early interventions such as language/speech therapy, occupational therapy, etc.).

Chapter 4
Development of the Egregious/Promotive Factors Model to Guide Custody Evaluations

In outlining the scope of the problem and examining the vast amount of literature regarding child outcomes, it is not difficult to see why few organizations or researchers have attempted to develop more specific guidelines for child custody evaluators. The numbers of indicators and factors that can potentially influence child custody decisions are so vast that it can be paralyzing. However, an attempt to outline the most salient factors, supported by empirical research, into a model in order to add to the body of knowledge and move the science of child custody evaluations forward is necessary. Without this map of relevant factors, custody evaluations will continue to have too much heterogeneity and thus to have problematic validity.

The Egregious/Promotive Factors Model

The egregious/promotive factors model (EPFM) was guided by extant research that has identified important constructs that have been shown to be predictive of outcomes in children and thus the development of the EPFM was not based strictly on an a top down deductive process. This literature has been summarized above in Chap. 3. In addition to this research, the EPFM expands on the egregious five-factor model purported by O'Donohue, Beitz, and Cummings (2007). The five egregious parenting factors that O'Donohue and colleagues developed include: (1) poor parent–child attachment, (2) poor parenting skills that are developmentally sensitive, (3) emotional instability or mental disorder of the parent, (4) environmental instability, and (5) exaggerated conflict (2007). The fundamental idea was that, to the degree these factors are present, a child's best interests are not being served. These factors were based on empirical literature of children's adjustment post-divorce and were recommended as important constructs to assess in child custody evaluations. These factors have also been identified in the literature as being predictive of poorer outcomes for children in general. The same egregious factors found in O'Donohue et al.'s (2007) five-factor model are included in the EPFM.

L.W. Tolle and W.T. O'Donohue, *Improving the Quality of Child Custody Evaluations*,
DOI 10.1007/978-1-4614-3405-4_4, © Springer Science+Business Media, LLC 2012

Table 4.1 The egregious/promotive factors model of the best interests of the child

	Factors					
Egregious factors	Parent–child relationship	Parenting skills	Environmental instability	Parent mental health	Excessive interparental conflict	
Promotive factors	Positive parenting	Parental school involvement	Promotion of interpersonal development	Promotion of mental health	Promotion of community involvement	Effective coparenting

What is particularly unique about the EPFM model described in this chapter is the inclusion of promotive factors that have been shown to enhance mental health and developmental outcomes. By combining both risk and promotive factors into an explicit model—the EPFM was created (see Table 4.1).

The EPFM includes both factors that have been shown to be predictive of poorer outcomes in children and factors found to be predictive of positive post-divorce outcomes. By including both detrimental factors and promotive factors it is thought to be a more comprehensive model which will more fully explicate that child's best interests. While, admittedly, it is not an exhaustive list of factors, it covers those variables found most consistently in the literature as being important to child outcomes post divorce and hence important to examine in a custody evaluation. The flexibility of this model will also allow for the addition or subtraction of factors as continued research evaluates the utility of this model. We do not view this as an ossified model but one that can be subject to research to continue to improve it.

Important Considerations of the EPFM

The EPFM initially assumes joint custody as the default parenting plan. This default value is often embodied in state law and is based on the assumption that *ceteris paribus* contact with both parents is in the child's best interest. The factors described in the EPFM that are present in either parent then further influence and weigh the balance of time with one or the other parent. For example, if neither parent has egregious factors and both have similar promotive factors, joint custody would be the final recommendation. This is in line with past research regarding resilient children from divorced homes, as it is apparent that *ceteris paribus* involvement of both parents (i.e., involvement and regular contact with the nonresidential parent, or joint custody and adequate time with both parents) is related to better adjustment in children (Amato & Gilbreth, 1999; Bausermann, 2002; Lee, 2002; Menning, 2002). Of course, it is necessary to qualify that shared parenting involves low levels of conflict between parents, which is also involved in improved adjustment (Buchanan, Maccoby, & Dornbusch, 1991; Hetherington, 1999).

When reviewing the factors that comprise the EPFM, there are some general considerations that should be kept in mind. Consistent with literature on risk and overall outcomes, the EPFM seeks to evaluate both parents along the various dimensions on both risk and promotion. As studies have indicated, the more risk factors that are present in a particular parent, the higher the risk for poorer outcomes in a child placed with that parent (Gutman, Sameroff, & Eccles, 2002; Rutter et al., 1979; Sameroff, Seifer, Baldwin, & Baldwin, 1993; Sameroff, Seifer, Barocas, Zax, & Greenspan, 1987). This should be considered when making ultimate conclusions regarding what compromise would best serve the child's welfare. In addition, as is consistent with the existing literature, a parental mental health diagnosis is not the primary concern; but rather the impact of problematic parental psychological functioning on child development is paramount to consider (Herman et al., 1997; Otto & Edens, 2003).

Another consideration relevant to these risk factors is the acute or chronic nature of these factors in each parent. For example, certainly, some degree of psychological distress is to be expected when a parent is involved in a custody battle. The parents' current psychological distress should be placed in the context of the legal situation and the stress of divorce before determining that this factor is present in this parent. Evidence suggesting a long history of severe and chronic mental health problems that existed before the present situation would be more impactful than current disturbances related to the transient stressful situation (Brennan et al., 2000; Hammen & Brennan, 2003). Custody evaluations are inherently predictive tasks and thus a model of future changes needs to condition the evaluation.

In examining each risk factor, the stability of the particular construct should also be considered. For example, the parent–child relationship may be under stress in the midst of a separation, changes in the residence, changes in the living arrangements, changes in financial conditions, and changes of time each parent has with their child. These factors should be considered when predicting the future state of the relationship.

When conducting interviews, it is important to remember that interviews with parents and friends of parents can be less constructive and objective than interviews with independent and rather objective professionals involved in the child or parent's life (i.e., pediatricians, psychologists, teachers, babysitters, or other regular caregivers). An examination of the child's history of care (i.e., activities engaged in with the child, history of involvement with child protective services) should also be assessed in this determination as these are relevant to the parent–child relationship factor as well as environmental stability factor. Other sources of information also should be sought out, such as police or other professionals' reports, and used in conjunction with the custody evaluator's assessments. This ensures that clinicians' opinions about parents' competencies are not based solely on test scores but on a convergence of results with data from many sources (APA, 1994; Heinze & Grisso, 1996).

When taking into consideration any of the factors, it is important also to consider the extent to which the factor is amenable to change. For instance, it has been shown that the parent–child relationship and parenting skills can be improved through intervention and motivation to change (Harnett, 2007). Research indicates that these factors have the capacity to improve and should therefore be distinguished from stable characteristics. A recent meta-analysis of 23 studies examining the impact of parent training on reducing or preventing physical and emotional abuse or neglect have reflected efficacy in promoting improvement in child rearing attitudes, child rearing behavior, and parental emotional adjustment (Lundahl, Nimer, & Parsons, 2006). In addition, Parent–Child Interaction Therapy (PCIT), an intervention originally developed by Hanf (1969), modified by Forehand and McMahon (1981) and finally adapted by Eyberg and Robinson (1982) has been shown to be effective. PCIT is designed to use parent behavior strategies including limit-setting, time-out, positive attention which promotes positive behavior and improved parent–child relationships (see also Eyberg, in press). PCIT has been found to be efficacious in improving parent–child relationships in physically abusive families, though parental substance abuse, psychopathology, severe inter-parental conflict, and parental lack of motivation limited effectiveness (Urquiza & McNeil, 1996). In addition, parenting interventions designed for parents who abuse substances, which has been found to increase risk for child maltreatment (Dawe et al., 2007), have been successful in improving family functioning (Catalano, Gainey, Fleming, Haggerty, & Johnson, 1999; Luthar & Suchman, 2000).

Operationalizing the EPFM

Another necessary component is ensuring that the factors of the EPFM can be reliably and validly assessed. Existing measures have been developed and tested by researchers that assess these constructs. Though not all have been used in the context of child custody evaluations, it is an important first step to look at what is currently available. Another important consideration of using these assessments in a custody evaluation is that several of them are self-report, as self-report may introduce invalidities. Because demand characteristics, or the tendency to want to present oneself in a positive light, can be common in child custody evaluations, and parents are likely to under-report problematic behaviors, it is important to try to include measures that use validity checks. Additionally, it is necessary to note that not all assessments would be recommended for every custody case, as this would involve an overly extensive and exhaustive evaluation. Rather, findings from brief screens should guide where further assessments would be warranted. These brief screens could involve an investigation into areas of concern for either parent. For example, having each parent note the concerns regarding the other parent and respond specifically to the presence of any egregious factors in the other parent may be helpful in focusing on areas that need further attention in the evaluation. If neither parent asserts that substance abuse is a concern of the other parent, for example, it would not make sense to conduct extensive assessments focusing on substance abuse. Because the presence of egregious factors in each parent is a more serious concern, as opposed to providing evidence that promotive factors are present or absent, screens should be conducted mainly for the egregious factors. An example of a brief screen is provided in Appendix B. In addition to information provided from both parents about the potential presence of egregious factors, evaluators should examine data from other sources to help in determining areas that would need to be assessed more carefully in parents. These sources might include legal documents (e.g., police reports, CPS investigation reports, past legal records, mental health records, etc.), professional collateral sources, information gleaned from the home observation or the parent–child observation, and information from the interviews and assessments of the child(ren). If information gathered from these sources indicates the presence of a given egregious factor, a further in-depth assessment of this factor would be warranted. Provided is a review of assessment tools for each of the factors presented in the EPFM with a discussion of other information to consider in seeking to assist in ruling in or out each factor.

Assessing Egregious Factors

Many measures have been developed that assess common risk factors, which are conceptualized as egregious factors in this model. Though they have not been normed for parents in the context of a child custody evaluation, a number of the measures reviewed here are considered the "gold standard" for assessing these constructs.

Parent–Child Relationship

Multiple measures exist that are meant to measure the quality of the parent–child relationship. Several existing assessments that aim to examine the quality of the parent–child relationship utilize observations of parents and children interacting. Though these are frequently used in assessing the quality of parent–child relationships, observations often rely on subjective evaluation of parent–child interactions and may be less useful in detecting problematic relationships as brief observations are not representative of typical behavior (occasionally they involve giving the parent and child a task to carry out together) and insensitive to demand characteristics. The Parent–Child Early Relational Assessment (PC-ERA; Clark, 1985) is used with parents and children from birth to 5-years old. It utilizes parent–child observations and examines parent positive affect and behavior, involvement and verbalization, in addition to looking for infant positive affect, social skills, interest and intentional skills. Parent–child dyads are videotaped and then a replay of the video for the parent is done followed by an interview to discuss the child's behavior as well as the parent's perception of self in the parenting role. The PC-ERA has been found to have high inter-rater reliability, good face, and construct validity, and has been useful in discriminating between high-risk and normative dyads (Clark, Tluczek, & Gallagher, 2004).

In addition, the Dyadic Parent–child Interaction Coding System (DPICS; Eyberg, Nelson, Duke, & Boggs, 2005) is a behavioral observation system designed to assess the quality of parent–child interactions. Based on the original edition of the

DPICS (Eyberg & Robinson, 1982), the third edition of the DPICS utilizes overt verbal and physical behaviors during social interactions that vary in degree of control required by the parent (i.e., child-led play, parent-led play, and clean up). For child-led and parent-led play, parents are given instructions and then interact with their child for 10 min. The second 5 min of the interaction are coded. For clean up, the first 5 min are coded. In each situation, verbalization, vocalization, and physical behavior are coded for both parent and child. The behaviors for parents include direct or nondirect commands, which are coded by compliance, noncompliance, or no opportunity to observe with regard to the child's behavior. In addition, information questions, reflection/description questions, labeled or unlabeled praise, neutral, positive and negative talk, and finally position and negative touch are coded for parents. For children, negative talk, pro-social talk, question command, whine, yell, positive touch, and negative touch are coded. Child behaviors that are coded reflect social reciprocity and cooperation in dyadic interaction. Parent behaviors of interest include reciprocity, nurturance, and parental control. Parent behaviors represent Baumrind's conceptualization of Authoritative, Authoritarian, and Permissive parenting styles (Baumrind, 1967, 1991). Though many of the behaviors are coded with regard to frequency of behavior, others have a specific sequence (i.e., indirect command followed by compliance/noncompliance).

Normative data for the DPICS have been presented for use with children aged 3–6 years; however, validation studies have been conducted with older children aged 7–12 years (Deskins, 2005). Recently, the DPICS was used with low-income Mexican–American families and was able to discriminate between referred and nonreferred families (i.e., referred parents demonstrated more negative behaviors in both nondirective and directive situations) (McCabe, Yeh, Lau, Argote, & Liang, 2010). Studies examining the DPICS inter-observer reliability have yielded fairly adequate reliability with kappa estimates for parent categories ranging from 0.038 to 1.00 and 0.29 to 0.88 for child categories (Bessmer, Brestan, & Eyberg, 2005; Brestan, Foote, & Eyberg, 2005). With regard to validity, numerous studies have established discriminative validity, convergent validity, and construct validity (Bessmer et al., 2005; Brestan et al., 2005; Deskins, 2005; Foote, 2000).

The Parent–Child Relationship Inventory

The Parent–Child Relationship Inventory (PCRI) (Gerard, 1994) is a 78-item, self-report inventory intended to assess parents' attitudes toward their children and their parenting. Responses are along a 4-point Likert scale from "strongly disagree" to "strongly agree." The PCRI is made up of seven content scales: Parental Support (level of emotional and social support a parent receives), Satisfaction with Parenting, Involvement (level of interaction with a child and knowledge of this child), Communication (effectiveness of communication with the child), Limit-Setting (parenting discipline practices with the child), Autonomy (the ability of the parent to promote autonomy in the child), and the Role orientation scale (concerning gender roles in parenting). The measure also contains two validity indicators: Social

Desirability as well as Response Inconsistency. The test is written at the fourth grade level, takes approximately 15 min to complete and is meant to be completed with one child in a family in mind (i.e., for multiple children, parents would need to complete a second PCRI for that child). Separate norms were developed for mothers and fathers. Higher scores on the PCRI are indicative of positive parenting characteristics and good parenting skills and low scores indicate poor parenting skills (Heinze & Grisso, 1996).

Internal consistency and test–retest reliability estimates were generated from normative samples and reveal individual scale alphas ranging from 0.70 to 0.88, with a median alpha of 0.80 (Gerard, 1994). The initial development of the PCRI involved a large pool of items that were rated by expert judges, assessed by qualitative feedback from professionals and respondents, and then evaluated with a pilot-test study. The final items included were selected by eliminating high and low frequency items, eliminating items that had low-scale correlations, and retaining items that were highly rated by judges. This yielded an inventory with high content validity. Additionally, analyses of interscale relationships and cross validation confirmatory factor analyses are encouraging for construct validity. Finally, a number of studies have evaluated the predictive validity of the PCRI. In one study examining 71 parents involved in court-ordered custody mediation, significant correlations were found between the PCRI and the Personality Inventory in Children (Gerard, 1994). In addition, it was found that PCRI subscale scores were related to parental discipline practices. Parents who scored lower on the PCRI were more likely to use harsh discipline and perceive their child as more difficult (MacPhee, Fritz, & Miller-Heyl, 1996). Using the Fullerton Longitudinal Study, Coffman, Guerin, and Gottfried (2006) examined the psychometric properties of the PCRI. Results revealed acceptable internal consistency coefficients for most subscales and moderate to high stability over a year for all subscales. Maternal PCRI scores were highly convergent with adolescents' perceptions of the parent–child relationship as well as the family climate. This relationship was not found between fathers' PCRI scores and adolescents' perceptions. Overall, the PCRI has received favorable attention and researchers report that it shows promise with additional research on validity needed (Coffman et al., 2006; Heinze & Grisso, 1996).

The Parenting Stress Index

The Parenting Stress Index (PSI; Abidin, 1990) is a 120-item measure developed to identify stress levels in the parent–child relationship and can be used for children aged 1 month to 12 years. Specifically, the PSI is intended to identify potentially dysfunctional parent–child relationships that may place a child at risk for poor outcomes. Items in the PSI are in two domains: child domains and parent domains. The child domain is comprised of 47 items and 6 subscales: Adaptability, Demandingness, Mood, Distractibility/Hyperactivity, Acceptability (match between child characteristics and parental expectations), and Reinforces Parent (the degree to which parents perceive their child as being positively reinforcing). The Parent Domain consists of

54 items and 7 subscales: Depression, Competence (parent's sense of competence with their parenting skills), Attachment (level of motivation the parent has to fulfill their role as a parent), support of the Spouse, the parent's Health, the level of Role Restriction (with regard to their role as a parent), and Social Isolation (level of social isolation parent is experiencing). The remaining 19 items measure Life Stress, which may be indicative of a level of stress a parent may be experiencing outside of the parent–child relationship which can negatively impact the parent–child relationship. High total stress scores are indicative of high stress, though low scores are related to low stress, defensiveness, or dysfunctional parent–child relationships (i.e., low investment parenting) (Heinze & Grisso, 1996). A Defensive Responding Scale, which identifies unusually low scores, was developed to identify parents trying to present themselves in an overly positive light.

The PSI has adequate to good internal consistency with reliability for child domains found at 0.90, 0.93 for the parent domain, and 0.95 for the total score and with subscale alphas ranging from 0.70 to 0.83 for child domain subscales, and 0.70 to 0.84 for parent domain subscales. Numerous studies have supported concurrent, predictive, and divergent validity for the PSI, reflecting that it has been found to be quite strong among diverse populations (Abidin, 1990; Bigras, LaFreniere, & Dumas, 1996; Heinze & Grisso, 1996; Hutchison & Black, 1996; Solis & Abidin, 1991).

The PSI Short Form (PSI-SF) has also been found to have good psychometric properties. Haskett, Ahern, Ward, and Allaire (2006) examined the PSI-SF with 185 mothers and fathers and found through factor analysis two distinct factors involving parental distress and dysfunctional parent–child interactions. Both factors were found to be internally consistent and to correlate with measures of parental psychopathology, parental perceptions of child adjustment, and observation of parent–child interactions. In addition, the child-rearing stress scale was found to significantly predict a parental history of abuse.

The Parenting Relationship Questionnaire

The Parenting Relationship Questionnaire (PRQ; Kamphaus & Reynolds, 2006) is a 4-point (Never, Sometimes, Often, and Almost Always), self-report scale completed by parents or caregivers to reflect the nature of the parent/child relationship. The questionnaire has two forms: a 45-item preschool scale for children aged 2–5 years (PRQ-P), and a 71-item child and adolescent scale for children aged 6–18 years (PRQ-CA). The PRQ-CA has seven scaled scores describing the parent/child relationship relative to empirically established dimensions of Attachment, Communication, Discipline Practices, Involvement, Parenting Confidence, Satisfaction with School, and Relational Frustration. The PRQ-P involves five of the seven scores from the PRQ-CA with the exception of the Communication and Satisfaction with School scores. Four indices are also included in the scales to discern the validity of the responses and include defensiveness, unusual negativity, response consistency across items, and invalidating response patterns.

Median internal consistency coefficients of subscales across age groups have been reported as being above 0.80 (Kamphaus & Reynolds, 2006). Test–retest reliabilities have ranged from 0.78 (Parenting Confidence scale) to 0.89 (Discipline Practices scale) for the PRQ-P level, and from 0.72 (Discipline Practice scale) to 0.84 (Communications scale) for the PRQ-CA level. The test authors report strong evidence to support the content, convergent, discriminant and criterion-related validity of the PRQ (Kamphaus & Reynolds, 2006). Though the PRQ is a fairly new assessment tool and has not accumulated as much research using this instrument, the developers appear to have taken rigorous steps to create a tool that was psychometrically sound, which is why it is being included here.

Taken together, the PCRI, the PSI, and the PRQ are examples of assessment tools designed to assist in the identification of problematic parent–child relationships. Both have promising or solid psychometric properties and assess domains related to the parent–child relationship. In addition, multiple behavioral observation rating systems including the DPICS and the PC-ERA create additional data to be included regarding information for the parent–child relationship. Of course, behavioral observations are subject to reactivity effects which affect behavior (Haynes & Horn, 1982). Additionally, there is the potential to overgeneralize or misinterpret findings from clinical observations (Budd & Holdsworth, 1996). It would not be recommended that any assessment tool be used in isolation, and it would be necessary to correlate findings from multiple sources of data, including information gained from professional collateral sources, as well as objective legal documents (i.e., CPS investigations or findings, etc.) related to factors that impact a parent–child relationship (i.e., most seriously evidence of physical or sexual abuse). In addition, self-report assessments and observations provide different perspectives on parenting behavior. Some researchers have recommended the use of both to give a more complete picture of parenting (Ramey, 2002; Zaslow et al., 2006). Finally, measuring the quality of the parent–child relationship is very important to the custody evaluation because it has been reported to moderate or mediate the effects of other stressors such as poverty (McLoyd, 1998) and parental depression (Cicchetti & Toth, 1998).

Parenting Skills

The skills of parents involved in custody disputes are an important factor to consider as it has been found to predict poorer adjustment (i.e., difficulties in cognitive, emotional, and social areas) in children. Specifically, harsh, hostile, or neglectful parenting has been consistently documented as being associated with more problems in children (Wallerstein and Kelly, 1980; Whiteside & Becker, 2000). Several of the parenting measures already described, including the PRQ and the PCRI, have subscales that measure parent discipline practices and could be used to assess parenting skills as well. One questionnaire that specifically measures parents' parenting style is the Parental Authority Questionnaire.

Parental Authority Questionnaire

The Parental Authority Questionnaire Revised (PAQ-R) was developed by Buri (1989, 1991). The 30-item instrument consisted of three 10-item scales representing authoritative, authoritarian, and permissive parenting styles. Items are rated on a 5-point Likert scale ranging from 1 (strongly disagree) to 5 (strongly agree). The PAQ-R was designed for use with parents and children aged 3–8 years. In validation studies (Buri, 1989, 1991), items were constructed based on Baumrind's descriptions of the parenting style prototypes and then subjected to multidisciplinary expert review. The PAQ appeared to have good internal consistency (range = 0.74–0.87) and test–retest reliability ranged from 0.77 to 0.92.

Reitman, Rhode, Hupp, and Altobello (2002) conducted a study analyzing the psychometric properties of the PAQ-R in a diverse sample of parents and children of pre-school and elementary school age. Internal consistency of the PAR-Q was found to range from 0.56 to 0.77 in this study. Modest convergent validity was found with correlations of the PAQ-R to the PCRI as well as the Parenting Scale (PS; Arnold, O'Leary, Wolff, & Acker, 1993). The Authoritativeness subscale was found to have poorer psychometric properties with lower SES, African-American populations. African-American mothers were found to report more Authoritarian attitudes after controlling for income and maternal education. This has been found to be consistent with extant literature reporting Authoritarian parenting styles are more adaptive of positive outcomes in children of low SES African-American backgrounds (Steinberg, Lamborn, Dornbusch, & Darling, 1992).

Environmental Instability

Environmental stability is important for promoting child security (Bray, 1991, cited in Gould, 1998). An "instable environment" may include factors such as inconsistency, extreme poverty, inadequate supervision, substance abuse, violence, and physical abuse. LeVine (1974) places economic goals second in the hierarchy of universal functions of parenting, which includes things like basic education. Economic stability is one of the most powerful predictors of post-divorce child functioning as instable economic conditions tend to be associated with poorer housing, schools, neighborhoods, childcare, health care, and less supportive parenting (Hetherington, 1990; Lamb, Sternberg, & Thompson, 1997; Novak, 1996; Thomson et al., 1994). Although the effects of poverty can be mitigated by various factors (i.e., accepting, stimulating, and organized environment) (Novak, 1996), economic hardship in its extreme (i.e., homelessness) is likely to adversely impact child functioning. The lack of child monitoring following divorce [which could be attributed to motivational deficits of the parent or the parent's own environmental demands (e.g., work schedule)] (Hetherington, 1990, cited in Novak, 1996) has been associated with child behavior problems, including delinquency (Patterson, DeBaryshe, & Ramsey, 1989). Finally, substance abuse, violence, and physical abuse are factors that cause family disruptions and negatively affect the well-being of children (Lamb et al., 1997; Sun, 2001). Specifically, excessive parental drug and alcohol abuse has been shown to be detrimental to the development of socialization and a variety of internalization and externalization problems (Otto & Edens, 2003). While some assessments are described here that attempt to measure environmental stability, important questions as a part of a thorough clinical interview can assess additional key aspects of this factor (i.e., parent's income, occupational status, living arrangements for themselves and their child/children) as well as information gleaned from visits to the home and information gathered from collateral sources who have access to this information. Additional assessments, including the HOME, provide a semi-structured way of assessing the home environment.

The Home Observation for Measurement of the Environment

The Home Observation for Measurement of the Environment (HOME, preschool, and school-age editions; Caldwell & Bradley, 1984) is designed to measure the quality and extent of stimulation available to a child in the home environment. HOME has different versions for infants and toddlers (birth to 3), early childhood (aged 3–6 years), and middle childhood (aged 6–10 years). The infant and toddler version is a 45-item inventory involving six subscales including: (1) responsiveness to parent, (2) avoidance of restriction and punishment, (3) organization of the environment, (4) appropriate play materials, (5) parental environment, and (6) variety in daily stimulation. The HOME for preschool age children consists of eight subscales. The HOME takes approximately 45–90 min to administer and involves both observation and parent interview.

Internal consistency for HOME has been found to be good with Cronbach's alphas of 0.84 and subscale alphas ranging from 0.49 to 0.78. Test–retest reliability has also been found to be adequate with Pearson correlation coefficients of 0.62 for the inventory and subscales ranging from 0.29 to 0.62 administered to children at ages 6 and 12 months, 0.64 for the inventory and ranged from 0.27 to 0.64 when administered at ages 6 and 24 months, and 0.77 for the inventory and ranged from 0.30 to 0.77 when administered at ages 12 and 24 months. The intra-class correlation, which measures stability by comparing the similarity of paired scores relative to the total variation of all scores, resulted in slightly lower values. The intra-class correlation coefficients were 0.57 for the inventory and ranged from 0.23 to 0.57 for the subscales when administered at ages 6 and 12 months, 0.58 for the inventory and ranged from 0.25 to 0.58 for the subscales at ages 6 and 24 months, and 0.76 for the inventory and ranged from 0.30 to 0.76 at ages 12 and 24 months (Caldwell & Bradley, 1984).

With regard to validity, concurrent and predictive validity was demonstrated for HOME when the child was 6, 12, and 24 months old were compared to the child's scores on the Bayley Scales of Infant Development Mental Development Index (MDI) at 6 and 12 months, the Stanford-Binet at 36 and 54 months, and the Illinois Test of Psycholinguistic Abilities (ITPA) at 37 months. The HOME was found to be a better predictor of intelligence than socioeconomic measures (Caldwell & Bradley, 1984).

The Child Abuse Potential Inventory

The Child Abuse Potential Inventory (CAP Inventory; Milner, 1986) was designed primarily as a screening tool for the detection of child physical abuse. The CAP inventory contains ten scales and three validity scales (Lie, Random Response, and Inconsistency). The CAP is a 160-item self-report instrument that takes approximately 12–20 min to complete. Respondents answer "Agree" or "Disagree" to statements. The primary clinical scale (Abuse) can be divided into six-factor scales: Distress, Rigidity, Unhappiness, Problems with Child and Self, Problems with Family and Problems with Others. The CAP Inventory has high internal consistency reliabilities with coefficient alphas ranging from 0.92 to 0.96 for nonabusive parents, and 0.95 to 0.98 for abusive parents. Test–retest reliabilities have also been found to be adequate, with 0.91 coefficients for 1-day intervals and 0.75 for 3 months. Content validity has been reported as being established through the creation of items expressing child abuse correlates identified in an extensive literature review, expert review, and evidence of good internal consistency. The ability to distinguish between "abusive" and control participants using the CAP has been demonstrated across cultures (Diareme et al., 1997; Haz & Ramirez, 1998). In a study examining the predictive validity of the CAP with at-risk parents, Milner, Gold, Ayoub, and Jacewitz (1984) found a significant correlation between elevated abuse scores and subsequent confirmed reports of child abuse. In this sample, all parents who later abused were identified on the CAP, though a number of false positives were also identified.

Milner and Crouch (1997) also assessed the impact of instructional conditions (participants were told to fake good, be honest, fake bad and respond randomly) on completing the CAP Inventory along with two other parenting measures. The CAP Inventory validity indexes correctly identified 94.7% and 91.1% of the invalid protocols among parents in the general population and at-risk parents, respectively. In addition, the labeling rates of the CAP Inventory validity indexes for each of the response-distortion conditions in both groups was found to range from 82.4% to 100%.

Ultimately, the CAP Inventory can be a useful tool in assessing factors that are associated with risk or potential for child physical abuse. Of course, with any assessment used in predicting violence, risk assessments like the CAP should not be used in isolation, as elevations in the CAP are also associated with other factors (i.e., elevated scores on the Beck Depression Inventory, BDI) (Nealer, 1992). Therefore, multiple assessments taken from multiple sources should also be considered.

The Substance Abuse Subtle Screening Inventory

The Substance Abuse Subtle Screening Inventory (SASSI-3; Miller & Lazowski, 1999) is an empirically derived inventory designed to indicate the risk of substance dependence using items that are less likely to elicit suspicion and untruthful answers. The SASSI-3 consists of two parts that are printed on either side of a single sheet of paper. The first part represents the subtle portion of the inventory and consists of 67 true/false statements. Nine subscales are embedded in the instrument: Face Valid Alcohol, Face Valid Other Drugs, Symptoms (assesses the presence of behavioral, emotional, and social correlates of substance abuse), Obvious Attributes (assesses the social effects of substance abuse including legal problems), Subtle Attributes (which includes statements endorsed by substance dependent individuals attempting to hide their dependence as well as others answering honestly), Defensiveness (assesses attempts to deliberately deny substance dependence as well as a personality trait or reaction to stressful personal circumstances), Supplemental Addiction Measure (differentiates between defensive respondents hiding substance abuse and other defensive individuals), Family vs. Controls (identifies individuals who may live with or have a significant relationship with a substance abuser), and Correctional (assesses respondents involvement with legal/criminal problems). In addition, The Random Answer Pattern is a scale to detect random responding.

Feldstein and Miller (2007) reviewed the empirical evidence of 36 peer-reviewed reports yielding data regarding the SASSI's internal consistency, test–retest reliability, psychometric structure, convergent and divergent validity, and predictive validity. The total sample size for the studies reviewed equaled 22, 110. Results of their review indicated high internal consistency for the overall SASSI, as well as for the direct subscales with alpha coefficients ranging from 0.59 to 0.83. In addition, SASSI classifications converged with other direct screening instruments and were also correlated with ethnicity, general distress and social deviance. Laux, Salyers, and Kotova (2005) compared the SASSI to the CAGE, the MAST and MAC-R and found moderate correlations ranging from 0.29 to 0.52. Sensitivity of the SASSI was found to be equivalent to other screening instruments, though specificity was found to yield a number of false positives. For example, in a study of the SASSI-2, Svanum and McGrew (1995) found a sensitivity of 33% and 87% specificity in their college student population. Using an incarcerated population, Peters et al. (2000) found an overall accuracy rate for the SASSI-2 of 69.4% with a sensitivity of 73.3% and a specificity of 62.2%. Finally, little evidence was found to indicate that the SASSI effective in circumnavigating respondents' propensity for denial or dishonesty (Feldstein & Miller, 2007). Other studies have examined psychometric properties of the SASSI-3. Lazowski, Miller, Boye, and Miller (1998) utilized a 2-week test–retest to explore reliability and found score stability of 1.0 for the face valid scales and between 0.92 and 0.97 for the subtle scales. More research appears to be necessary in further developing tools that have reliable and useful validity indexes as a part of substance abuse assessment. Certainly there are a number of face valid assessments including the Alcohol Use and Disorders Identification Test (AUDIT; Saunders, Aasland, Babor, de la Fuente, & Grant, 1993), the Michigan Alcoholism Screening Test (MAST; Selzer, 1971) and the CAGE (Ewing, 1984), that directly assess substance or alcohol use/abuse though these also have the same difficulties in relying on self-report and are unable to detect dishonesty in responding. When using a specific substance abuse measure as a part of the custody evaluation, it is necessary to also gather multiple methods of assessment from multiple sources.

Parent Mental Health Problems

Emery (1999) suggests that four mental health problems among adults are of special concern to understanding the consequences of divorce: (1) depression, (2) antisocial behavior, (3) major mental illness (i.e., schizophrenia and bipolar disorder), and (4) personality disorders. Specifically, research suggests that parental depression, schizophrenia, display of antisocial behaviors or problematic behaviors indicative of other personality disorders has been associated with a number of negative child outcomes including adjustment problems, psychopathology, aggression, delinquency, and other externalizing problems (Emery, 1999; for a review, see Otto & Edens, 2003). Measures provided here are examples of assessments for these four mental health problems, though other additional assessments with good psychometric properties are available as well, including the Millon Clinical Multiaxial Inventory III (MCMI-III; Millon, Millon, Davis, & Grossman, 2009), the Personality Assessment Inventory (PAI; Morey, 1996), the Hare Psychopathy Checklist-Revised (PCL-R; Hare, 1991), and the Hamilton Depression Rating Scale (HAM-D; Hamilton, 1960). In addition to using these empirical tools in assessing emotional instability, it is important to review, when available, previous mental health records, consult with current or past treating psychologists or psychiatrists who may be involved with the family (i.e., either parent or children) and conduct clinical interviews to gather other points of data regarding emotional stability.

The Minnesota Multiphasic Personality Inventory-2

The Minnesota Multiphasic Personality Inventory (MMPI-2; Butcher, Dahlstrom, Graham, Tellegen, & Kaemmer, 1989; Hathaway & McKinley, 1989) is one of the most frequently used and researched psychological tests in existence. It has been estimated that over 10,000 articles and books have documented the use of the MMPI (Butcher et al., 1989). The MMPI-2 contains 567 items and takes approximately 60–90 min to complete. The MMPI contains 10 clinical scales that are used to indicate different psychiatric conditions. Though the labels of the different scales capture some of what they are meant to measure, there is much overlap and as such, professionals often refer to them by the number of their scales. Scale 1, Hypochondriasis, was designed to assess concern over somatic symptoms and physical well-being. Scale 2, Depression, was designed to assess symptoms of depression including lack of hope in the future and general dissatisfaction with life. Scale 3, Hysteria, was originally designed to measure one's reaction to stressful situations, specifically hysterical reactions. Scale 4, Psychopathic Deviate, was developed to identify psychopathic characteristics including social deviation, lack of acceptance of authority and amorality. High scorers on this scale tend to be indicative of rebelliousness whereas low scorers tend to be more accepting of authority. High scorers are more likely to be diagnosed with a personality disorder than a psychotic disorder. Scale 5, Masculinity/Femininity, assesses stereotypical gender role behaviors and the degree to which an individual relates to either of these. High scores are related to factors including intelligence, socioeconomic status, and education. Scale 6, Paranoia, was developed to identify paranoid symptoms including suspiciousness, feelings of grandiosity, persecution, sensitive or rigid attitudes. Scale 7, Psychasthenia, which is an outdated term, was developed to assess symptoms similar to Obsessive–Compulsive Disorder including excessive worry, compulsions, obsessions or unreasonable fears. Scale 8, Schizophrenia, was developed to assess symptoms related to schizophrenia, including bizarre or unusual ideations, perceptions, relational problems, difficulty in concentration or impulse control, low self-worth, and sexual difficulties. Scale 9, Hypomania, was developed to assess symptoms related to hypomania including accelerated speech or motor activity, flight of ideas, irritability and periods of depression. Finally, Scale 0, Social Introversion, was developed to assess an individual's tendency to withdraw from others socially as well as other responsibilities.

The MMPI-2 has numerous validity scales as part of its assessment. The L Scale, or the "lie scale," was developed to identify respondents attempting to present themselves in an overly positive light, rejecting shortcomings or unfavorable characteristics. The F Scale was developed to identify respondents' attempts to "fake good" or "fake bad," responding in ways that attempt to present either a better or worse profile than how they actually are. The K Scale was designed to detect respondents' attempts to present themselves in an overly positive light. The K Scale has also been called the "defensiveness scale" and was meant to detect this in a less obvious, more subtle way than the L Scale. In addition, the number of responses left unanswered was another measure assessed as part of the MMPI-2's validity scales. More than 30 items left unanswered was reported to be an invalid profile. The TRIN Scale, or the true response inconsistency scale, was developed to detect respondents who answered inconsistently to 23 paired questions that are opposite to each other. The VRIN Scale, or the Variable Response Inconsistency Scale was another validity scale designed to assess inconsistent responding. Finally, the Fb Scale is composed of 40 items that less than 10% of normal respondents support. High scores may indicate that respondents answered randomly. In addition to the Clinical scales and Validity scales, there are 15 Content Scales that include Anxiety, Depression, Anger, Cynicism, Antisocial practices, Family Problems, Work Interference and Low Self-Esteem.

Extensive research has examined the psychometric properties of the MMPI-2. Test–retest reliabilities on the clinical scales for men and women have been found to range from 0.67 to 0.92 (Butcher et al., 1989). Internal consistencies for the clinical scales have been found with alpha coefficients that range from 0.37 to 0.87 (Butcher et al., 1989). Studies have demonstrated convergent validity of scores from Clinical scales among a wide variety of samples as evidenced by their correlations with related measures (Graham, Ben-Porath, & McNulty, 1999). Ben-Porath, Butcher, and Graham (1991) found that MMPI-2 validity, clinical and content scales were able to differentiate accurately between schizophrenic patients and individuals with depression. Discriminant, convergent, and construct validity of the supplemental and content scales has also been demonstrated through research with a number of populations including outpatient and inpatient mental health patients (Archer, Aiduk, Griffin, & Elkins, 1996; Dwyer, Graham, & Ott, 1992; Graham et al., 1999; Green, Handel, & Archer, 2006).

The BDI-II

The BDI-II (Beck, Steer, & Brown, 1996) is a 21-item, self-report measure of depression. Responses to each item range from not present to severe and item content includes: sadness, pessimism, past failure, loss of pleasure, guilty feelings, punishment feelings, self-dislike, self-criticalness, suicidal thoughts or wishes, crying, agitation, loss of interest, indecisiveness, worthlessness, loss of energy, changes in sleeping pattern, irritability, changes in appetite, concentration difficulty, tiredness or fatigue, and loss of interest in sex. These changes reflect the DSM-IV-TR (American Psychiatric Association, 2000) diagnostic criteria for depression. The BDI-II is a straightforward and relatively efficient assessment tool, however, it also lacks a validity indicator and thus would not be sensitive to respondents' attempts to deliberately distort results.

The psychometric properties of the BDI-II are quite good, with coefficient alpha estimates for psychiatric samples found to be 0.92 and for nonclinical samples 0.93. Test–retest reliability over the course of a week has been high with a reliability coefficient of 0.93. Concurrent validity evidence appears good with high correlations between scores on the BDI-II and the Hamilton Psychiatric Rating Scale for Depression-Revised ($r = 0.71$) and evidence for discriminative validity found with low correlations between BDI-II scores and scores on the Hamilton Rating Scale for Anxiety-Revised ($r = 0.47$). Storch, Roberti, and Roth (2004) examined the psychometric properties of the BDI-II with a sample of 414 college students. A confirmatory factor analysis confirmed a two-factor structure measuring cognitive-affective and somatic depressive symptoms. Internal consistency was found to be high and concurrent validity of the BDI-II was also supported by correlates with self-reported depressive and anxious symptomatology. The BDI-II has been found to be valid and reliable with a number of specific populations, including African-American, low-income populations, older adults, chronic pain and substance abuse populations (Grothe et al., 2005; Harris & D'Eon, 2008; Jefferson, Powers, & Pope, 2000; Segal, Coolidge, Cahill, & O'Riley, 2008; Seignourel, Green, & Schmitz, 2008).

Structured Interview for DSM-IV Axis I and Axis II Disorders

The Structured Interview for DSM-IV for Axis I Disorders (SCID-I; Spitzer, Williams, Gibbon, & First, 1992) is a clinician-administered semi-structured interview aimed to assist in the diagnosis or assessment of Axis I Disorders according to the Diagnostic and Statistical Manual for Mental Disorders (DSM-IV-TR; American Psychiatric Association, 2000). The SCID-I has a Research Version and a Clinical Version. The SCID-I Research Version is distinguished from the Clinical Version in that it is much longer and it contains more disorders, subtypes, severity, and course specifiers, in addition to coding for specific details of past mood episodes. The SCID-I Research Version examines nine diagnostic categories: Mood Episodes, Psychotic Symptoms, Psychotic Disorders, Mood Disorders, Substance Use Disorders, Anxiety Disorders, Somatoform Disorders, Eating Disorders, and Adjustment Disorder. There are some disorders that are in the Research Version that are not in the Clinical Version including Acute Stress Disorder, Minor Depressive Disorder, Mixed Anxiety Depressive Disorder, and Binge Eating Disorder.

Multiple studies have examined the psychometric properties of the SCID-I. Studies have reported on the test–retest reliability of the SCID-I for Major Depressive Disorder (kappas ranging from 0.61 to 0.73) (Zanarini et al., 2000; Zanarini & Frankenburg, 2001), Dysthymic Disorder (kappas ranging from 0.35 to 0.60) (Zanarini et al., 2000; Zanarini & Frankenburg, 2001), Bipolar Disorder (κ=0.84) (Williams et al., 1992), Schizophrenia (κ=0.65) (Williams et al., 1992), Alcohol Dependence or Abuse (kappas ranging from 0.75 to 0.77) (Williams et al., 1992; Zanarini et al., 2000), Other Substance Abuse (kappas ranging from 0.76 to 0.84) (Williams et al., 1992; Zanarini et al., 2000), Panic Disorder (kappas ranging from 0. 65 to 0.82) (Zanarini et al., 2000; Zanarini & Frankenburg, 2001), Social Phobia (kappas ranging from 0.47 to 0.59) (Williams et al., 1992; Zanarini et al., 2000), Obsessive–Compulsive Disorder (kappas ranging from 0.42 to 0.60) (Zanarini et al., 2000; Zanarini & Frankenburg, 2001), Generalized Anxiety Disorder (kappas ranging from 0.44 to 0.63) (Zanarini et al., 2000; Zanarini & Frankenburg, 2001), Posttraumatic Stress Disorder (kappas ranging from 0.78 to 1.0) (Zanarini et al., 2000; Zanarini & Frankenburg, 2001), and Eating Disorder (κ=0.64) (Zanarini et al., 2000). Inter-rater reliability has been found to be fairly high with reliability coefficients for these disorders ranging from 0.57 (for Obsessive–Compulsive Disorder) to 1.0 (Substance Abuse/Dependence Disorders) (Zanarini et al., 2000). A number of studies have examined the validity of the SCID-I, reporting it to be superior to other structured interviews, and in fact, the SCID has frequently been used as the "Gold Standard" in determining the accuracy of clinical diagnoses (Basco et al., 2000; Phillips, Charles, Sharpe, & Matthey, 2009; Preuss, Watzke, Zimmermann, Wong, & Schmidt, 2010; Sanchez-Villegas et al., 2008; Shear et al., 2000).

The Structured Clinical Interview for DSM-IV-TR Axis II Personality Disorders (SCID-II; Spitzer et al., 1992) is a semi-structured interview for the assessment of personality disorders. Unlike the SCID-I, there is only one version of the SCID-II. The SCID-II interview itself covers the 11 DSM-IV-TR Personality Disorders: (Paranoid Personality Disorder, Schizoid Personality Disorder, Schizotypal Personality Disorder, Antisocial Personality Disorder, Borderline Personality Disorder, Histrionic Personality Disorder, Narcissistic Personality Disorder, Avoidant Personality Disorder, Dependent Personality Disorder, Obsessive–Compulsive Personality Disorder, and Personality Disorder Not Otherwise Specified) as well as the Appendix categories Depressive Personality Disorder and Passive–Aggressive Personality Disorder (APA, 2000). The SCID-II consists of eight open-ended questions regarding the respondent's general behavior, interpersonal relationships, and self-reflective abilities, followed by 140 structured questions.

A questionnaire (the SCID-II Personality Questionnaire) was designed as a first step in administering the semi-structured portion of the assessment to cut down on time taken to conduct the interview. Following completion of the questionnaire by the respondent, items endorsed on the questionnaire are circled for the clinician to inquire about further. The test authors report that respondents would conceivably answer "no" aloud to the same items that they respond "no" to on the questionnaire. Answers to the structured questions in addition to other verbal or nonverbal information gathered from open-ended questioning are then scored as 1 (*absent*), 2 (*subthreshold*), or 3 (*threshold*). Personality disorders are established when the number of symptoms endorsed as threshold meets diagnostic criteria according to the DSM-IV-TR.

Numerous studies have examined the psychometric properties of the SCID-II, which, similar to the SCID-I, is considered the "gold standard" in validating diagnoses (Ball, Rounsaville, Tennen, & Kranzler, 2001; Jacobo, Blais, Baity, & Harley, 2007). Inter-rater reliability coefficients have been reported to range from 0.48 to 0.98 for categorical diagnosis and 0.90 to 0.98 for dimensional judgments (Maffei et al., 1997). In examining the psychometric properties of the SCID-II with a sample of inpatients and outpatients ($N=231$), Maffei et al. (1997) demonstrated good internal consistency with alpha coefficients ranging from 0.71 to 0.94. Ullrich et al. (2008) examined the cross-instrument validity of the SCID-II questionnaire and the SCID-II structured clinical interview with male and female prisoners ($N=496$). Specifically, participants completed the questionnaire and were then interviewed 2 weeks later. The questionnaire was found to have good internal consistency with alpha coefficients ranging from 0.53 (Antisocial Personality Disorder) to 0.81 (Borderline Personality Disorder). In addition, following adjustment of the algorithms to establish diagnoses, the questionnaire discriminated between personality disorders (Axis II) and Axis I disorders. Test authors report strong reliability and validity of the SCID-II (First, Gibbons, Spitzer, & Williams, 1995).

Excessive Interparental Conflict

Parental conflict [i.e., hostility, violence and other acts of marital aggression, acting deliberately subversive and using the child in ways to harm the other parent (e.g., telling the child to not obey the other parent, using the child as a conduit for punishing the other parent, etc.)] is associated with deleterious effects on child and adolescent functioning (Emery, 1999; Gould, 1998; Hetherington, Cox, & Cox, 1982; Otto & Edens, 2003; Wallerstein & Kelly, 1980; Whiteside & Becker, 2000) and has been shown to be a stronger predictor of adjustment than family structure (Kot & Shoemaker, 1999). Allegations of domestic violence or marital aggression may come up in the context of a child custody evaluation without documentation from other professional sources (i.e., law enforcement was never called to the house to mediate, no assault charges or temporary protection orders have been filed) or collateral sources (i.e., parents did not share with professionals, relatives or friends). It is not the evaluator's role to determine whether domestic violence has or has not occurred, but to assess the safety of the child and the degree to which parents currently are able to coparent without excessive interparental conflict. Some assessments are available that are meant to measure conflict, however, these are largely self-report and therefore insensitive to parents' attempts to present information in a biased or misleading fashion. It is important to look to other sources of data that would be expected to correlate with the presence of significant violence in the home to assist in providing evidence to support the child's safety or exposure to conflict (i.e., problems with the parent–child relationship, adjustment problems with the child) (Drozd, Kuehnle, & Walker, 2004).

Revised Conflict Tactics Scale

The Conflict Tactics Scales (CTS; Straus, 1979) are the most commonly used self-report measures of marital and courtship violence. They were designed to assess the various types of behaviors used to solve conflicts between intimate partners. A modified form of the CTS, the Revised Conflict Tactics Scales (CTS2; Straus, Hamby, Boney-McCoy, & Sugarman, 1996) now consists of 39 item pairs, asking respondents to report how many times in a given time period the respondent or their partner has engaged in a list of behaviors that sometimes occur during relationship conflicts, ranging from showing concern and respect to severe physical assaults. This revised version includes four subscales that assess different types of tactics used (negotiation, psychological aggression, physical assault, and sexual coercion), as well as the injury subscale that addresses the impact of violence.

Vega and O'Leary (2007) examined the test–retest reliability of the Revised Conflict Tactics Scale with 82 men who were court-ordered to attend a batterer intervention program over a 2-month interval, and found strong stability for psychological aggression ($r=0.69$), physical assault ($r=0.76$), injury ($r=0.70$), and negotiation ($r=0.60$) but weaker for sexual coercion ($r=0.30$). Internal consistency coefficients for the subscales of the CTS2 have been reported to range from 0.79 (psychological aggression) to 0.95 (injury) (Straus et al., 1996). Straus (2004) examined the reliability and validity of the CTS2 with 7,179 college students at 33 universities in 17 countries. The results show high alpha coefficients of internal consistency and low confounding with social desirability response set. This study also provided evidence for cross-cultural construct validity with correlations to similar measures reported at 0.77.

The Children's Perception of Interparental Conflict Scale

The Children's Perception of Interparental Conflict Scale (CPIC; Grych, Seid, & Fincham, 1992) is a 49-item measure designed to assess children's exposure to interparental conflict. The CPIC is comprised of nine subscales: Interparental conflict Intensity, Frequency, Resolution, Threat, Coping Efficacy, Blame, Content, Stability and Triangulation. Items are on a 3-point Likert scale, indicating responses of "true," "sometimes true" and "false." Higher scores on the CPIC are indicative of higher levels of conflict and lower levels of resolution. Internal consistency for the CPIC has been reported with Cronbach alphas ranging from 0.62 to 0.88 (Grych et al., 1992; O'Donnell, Moreau, Cardemil, & Pollastri, 2010).

Test authors conducted investigations of the CPIC's reliability and factor structure of the CPIC with two samples of elementary school-aged children. The validity of the CPIC was also investigated by examining its relationship to parent-report of conflict, measures of child adjustment, and children's responses to conflict vignettes (Grych et al., 1992). Through factor structure analyses, three scales (Conflict Properties, Threat, and Self-Blame) were formed through unit weighting and summing scores on the dimensions loading on each of the three factors. Coefficient alphas for the three scales ranged from 0.79 to 0.90 across the two independent samples of elementary school-aged children ($N=222$ for the first study and $N=114$ for the second) (Grych et al., 1992). Test–retest reliability over a 2-week time interval indicated the CPIC had adequate reliability for the three scales (Conflict Properties=0.70, Threat=0.68 and Self-blame=0.76). In comparing the CPIC to parent-report measures of conflict, the Conflict Properties subscale was significantly correlated to parents' report on the Conflict Tactics Scale ($r=0.39$) in addition to another conflict scale, the O'Leary Porter Scale (Porter & O'Leary, 1980) ($r=0.30$). Children's adjustment as measured by the Child Behavior Checklist (CBCL; Achenbach & Edelbrock, 1983), the Childhood Depression Inventory (CDI; Kovacs, 1981) were significantly correlated to children's responses to the CPIC. This is consistent with extant literature reporting the association between higher levels of frequent, intense, and poorly resolved conflict between parents and higher levels of externalizing and internalizing problems in children.

Cummings, Davies, and Simpson (1994) found good reliability and a significant relationship between children's scores on the CPIC and their adjustment with a sample of 9–12-year-old children. Bickham and Fiese (1997) examined the utility of the CPIC with older adolescents aged 17–21 years ($N=215$) and found the same three subscale factor structure, in addition to good reliability and external validity. Specifically, the CPIC was found to have good internal consistency with Cronbach alphas of 0.95 for the Conflict Properties scale, 0.88 for the Perceived Threat subscale and 0.85 for the Self-Blame subscale. Test–retest reliabilities over a 2-week period were 0.95 for the Conflict Properties scale, 0.86 for Perceived Threat, and 0.81 for Self-Blame subscales. Scores on the CPIC were also found to be significantly related to measures of participants' self-esteem, competence, and identity integration as assessed by the Multidimensional Self-Esteem Inventory (MSEI; O'Brien & Epstein, 1988).

Multidimensional Assessment of Interparental Conflict Scale

The Multidimensional Assessment of Interparental Conflict Scale (MAIC; Tschann, Flores, Pasch, & Marin, 1999) was developed as an attempt to assess both parents' and children's perceptions of interparental conflict. The MAIC was developed based on six dimensions identified in the literature as having the greatest potential for negative impact on children and adolescents: frequency of conflict, child-related content, intensity, conflict behavior, child involvement, and resolution. The MAIC was developed as part of a study examining health-risk behaviors and interparental conflict among European–American and Mexican–American adolescents ($N=304$; adolescents' ages ranged from 12 to 15 years) (Tschann et al., 1999). The MAIC for Parents (MAIC-P) and Adolescents (MAIC-A) contained five subscales: frequency, content, conflict behavior, child involvement, and resolution. The MAIC-P also contains intensity and conflict avoidance subscales. The validity of the MAIC was also assessed by having parents complete marital satisfaction measures and a social desirability scale while adolescents completed measures related to self-perceptions in the domains of school, behavior and global self-worth.

Cronbach's alpha coefficients for the subscales were found to range from 0.53 to 0.89 for European Americans and Mexican Americans. Inter-rater agreements between parents were significantly higher in European–American parents ($r=0.53$) than in Mexican–American parents ($r=0.24$) on mothers' verbal aggression as well as fathers' verbal aggression ($r=0.48$ and 0.26 for European–American and Mexican–American parents, respectively). All dimensions were found to be significantly correlated between adolescents and parents across ethnic groups. When examining the validity of the MAIC, all but one dimension of interparental conflict was found to be associated with marital satisfaction (mothers' expression of feelings was unrelated to marital satisfaction for fathers). Parents reporting poor conflict resolution reported low marital satisfaction. For adolescents, mothers' and fathers' withdrawal were related to more behavioral problems in European–American adolescents but not for Mexican–American adolescents, whereas mothers' expression of feelings was related to better behavioral conduct in Mexican–American adolescents but not for European–American adolescents (Tschann et al., 1999). Because of the relatively recent construction of the MAIC, additional research to test its psychometric properties is warranted, however, it appears to be a promising tool that assesses both parents' and adolescents' perceptions of interparental conflict.

Taken together, assessments appear to exist that cover the egregious factors associated with poorer outcomes in children. Although the majority of these questionnaires were not developed for specific use in child custody evaluations, they offer important information to relevant constructs highly important to children's welfare in custody arrangements. Additionally, several of the instruments have validity indexes that are important to custody evaluations, an arena that has problems in relying on parent self-report to be objective and unbiased. As has been consistently mentioned with each factor, as well as established in the APA guideline regarding child custody evaluations in addition to a variety of other establishments that have put forth guidelines for conducting evaluations, it is necessary to use a variety of sources of data to investigate each of these factors and no instrument should be used alone in determining the presence or absence of an egregious factor for a given parent. A further review of existing assessments that measure constructs associated with the promotive factors discussed previously is provided.

Assessing Promotive Factors

Assessment of the egregious factors differs in several respects from the assessment of the promotive factors. One specific contrast is that the egregious factors largely pertain to characteristics that are inherent in the parent: the parent's parenting skills, the parent's ability to provide a stable environment, the parent's mental health, and the parent's difficulty in minimizing interparental conflict. The parent–child relationship greatly involves the child and the assessment of the health of this dyad, though with the exception of this factor, most egregious factors assessments discussed above can be done irrespective of the child's developmental level. In addition, perhaps because of the emphasis placed on assessing pathology and minimizing potential for harm, extensive research has been conducted examining the utility of assessments associated with egregious factors. The promotive factors, however, have different implications for children at different developmental stages and ages. For example, parental school involvement would be a relevant factor for school-aged children in divorcing families and less so for infants or younger children. The same could be said for the promotion of interpersonal development, where parents have both direct and indirect pathways for impacting their child's development. In addition, the promotion of community involvement is also relevant for school-aged children and less so for infants or young children.

To date, instruments have not been developed that assess a parent's potential for promoting some of these domains. Rather, instruments that directly assess children along these dimensions (i.e., pro-social behavior, social competence, self-esteem, self-efficacy) are included. One advantage of this, however, is that additional professionals who have access to the child are able to comment on the child's adjustment in each of these areas, and several teacher-report instruments have been created and empirically tested. Additional research is necessary to further develop tools that assess parent's ability to promote future skills, however, until then, it is necessary to utilize direct methods for obtaining this information, as well as utilizing existing tools to attempt to make relationships between positive parenting skills and the provision of opportunities for future promotive factors when they come into play.

Positive Parenting

Several measures that are included in the parent–child relationship factor have subscales that relate to positive parenting skills (i.e., the PRQ, the PRCI, and the PAQ-R) and these are also recommended for use in assessing attributes of positive parenting. Other assessments that measure positive parenting (i.e., warmth, acceptance, and supporting autonomy) are the Alabama Parenting Questionnaire (APQ) and the Parent Behavior Inventory (PBI).

The APQ

The APQ (Shelton, Frick, & Wooton, 1996) consists of 42 self-report items designed to measure five constructs associated with parenting behaviors: Parental Involvement, Positive Parenting, Poor Monitoring/Supervision, Inconsistent Discipline and Corporal Punishment. Parenting behavior is assessed on a 5-point frequency scale (1 = Never to 5 = Always). The APQ has parent-report forms and child-report forms (for children aged 6–17 years) in addition to a telephone interview format in which respondents are asked to recall the frequency with which a specified behavior has occurred for the previous 3 days. The child-report form includes repeated items related to parent involvement to be answered regarding both parents. By standardizing the scores (i.e., to *z* scores) and combining like scales, the APQ allows for composite scores of a Positive Parenting Composite Score (by combining the Parental Involvement and Positive Parenting subscales), and a Negative Parenting Composite Score (by combining the Poor Monitoring/Supervision, Inconsistent Discipline and Corporal Punishment subscale scores).

Shelton et al. (1996) tested the psychometric properties of the APQ with clinically referred and nonreferred children aged 6–13 years and their families ($N = 124$) and found adequate internal consistency with the exception of the 3-item subscale for Corporal Punishment across all formats and the Poor Monitoring/Supervision subscale with the telephone interview format. These findings were replicated in a larger community study ($N = 802$) of 4–9-year-old children and their families with Cronbach alpha coefficients being lower for Corporal Punishment and Poor Monitoring/Supervision subscales at 0.55 and 0.59, respectively. Alpha coefficients for the remaining subscales were significantly higher, ranging from 0.73 to 0.77 (Dadds, Maujean, & Fraser, 2003). Multiple studies have been conducted which support the validity of the APQ. An association between the APQ and conduct problems has been reported across multiple populations including in the community (Dadds et al., 2003; Frick, Kimonis, Dandreaux, & Farrell, 2003), among clinic-referred families (Frick, Christian, & Wootton, 1999; Hawes & Dadds, 2006; Hinshaw, 2002) as well as families of deaf or hearing impaired children (Brubaker & Szakowski, 2000) and families with substance-abusing parents (Stanger, Dumenci, Kamon, & Burstein, 2004). Essau, Sasagawa, and Frick (2006) also found support for the five-factor model of the children's global report version for the German translation of the APQ through exploratory and confirmatory factor analysis among a large sample of German children ($N = 1{,}219$) aged 10–14 years.

Parent Behavior Inventory

The PBI (Lovejoy, Weis, O'Hare, & Rubin, 1999) was developed to be a multimethod, multi-informant measure assessing parent behavior in parents of preschool and young-age children. The measure focuses on two main areas of parenting behavior: support/engagement and hostility/coercion. The authors report that the support/engagement dimension corresponds closely to the construct of parental warmth (Maccoby & Martin, 1983), which is conceptualized as "behavior which demonstrates the parent's acceptance of the child through affection, shared activities, and emotional and instrumental support" (Lovejoy et al., 1999, p. 535). The hostility/coercion dimension represents more maladaptive control strategies and was defined by Lovejoy et al. as "behavior which expresses negative affect or indifference toward the child and may involve the use of coercion, threat or physical punishment to influence the child's behavior" (p. 535). Items for the PBI were taken from existing self-report inventories as well as observational measures of parenting behavior. Items were chosen for the PBI based on how well they mapped on to the support/engagement and hostility/coercion dimensions. The items were then subjected to principal-component analyses to identify groups of items that are indicative of behavior of parents of young children. Items were then rated by 234 undergraduate students, 25 graduate students and professors with expertise in child development on a 7-point Likert scale regarding the degree to which items were found to be indicative of support or hostility. Based on additional analyses following results of these ratings, items were eliminated, yielding a total of 31 items.

Lovejoy et al. (1999) conducted a series of eight studies to establish psychometric properties for the PBI. A series of confirmatory factor analyses were conducted that specified the two-factor structure of the scale. Finally, the instrument was tested with 86 mothers and preschool children. Analyses were conducted to reduce the scale to 20 items that maintained the two-factor structure. The 20-item version was assessed by experts in the field of child development to gain content validity. The inventory was tested with a second group of parents ($N = 107$) to examine its internal consistency, factorial validity, and construct validity (Lovejoy et al., 1999). Cronbach alpha was 0.81 for Hostility/Coercion and 0.83 for the Supportive/Engaged scale. Inter-item correlations ranged from 0.09 to 0.58 for the two scales. In an additional study using the CBI, Cronbach alphas of 0.85 and 0.75 were found for the Supportive/Engaged factor and Hostility/Coercion factor, respectively (Dallaire et al., 2006). Lovejoy et al. (1999) tested the test–retest reliability and convergent validity of the PBI. Specifically, they assessed this using 45 mothers from the previous study and asked them and their spouses to complete the PBI in addition to the PSI, the Eyberg Child Behavior Inventory and the Positive and Negative Affect Schedule and again a week later. Spouses were asked to complete the PBI with regard to their child's mother's parenting behavior. Results indicated that test–retest reliability was adequate with reliability coefficients of 0.69 for the Hostility/Coercion scale and 0.74 for the Supportive/Engaged scale. Spouse responses on the PBI were significantly correlated with the parent-report of the PBI with coefficients of 0.26 for the Supportive/Engaged scale and 0.42 for the Hostility/Coercion scale. Furthermore, the Supportive/Engaged scale was significantly negatively correlated with all of the other measures with reliabilities ranging from −0.57 to −0.40. The exception of the Positive Affect scale of the PANAS which was significantly positively correlated (0.59). Furthermore, the Hostility/Coercion scale was significantly negatively correlated with the Positive Affect scale of the PANAS (−0.23) and significantly positively correlated with the Eyberg Child Behavior Inventory and the PSI with reliabilities ranging from 0.28 to 0.61 (Lovejoy et al., 1999). Additional studies examined inter-rater reliability, which was found to be $r=0.90$ for the Supportive/Engaged subscale and $r=0.87$ for the Hostility/Coercion subscale (Lovejoy et al., 1999). Though a relatively new inventory, the PBI has been used in multiple studies as an assessment of parental warmth (Skopp, McDonald, Jouriles, & Rosenfield, 2007), physical aggression toward one's child (Minze, McDonald, Rosentraub, & Jouriles, 2010) and both positive parenting and negative parenting (Cole et al., 2007).

Parental School Involvement

Relatively few assessments have been constructed to measure the degree to which parents are involved in their children's academic activities. Preliminary measures that have examined this factor are provided. This factor offers an important opportunity for collateral input from the teachers, as well as school personnel. Custody evaluators can access information related to child academic success as well as classroom behavioral problems from school records. In addition, collateral contacts with teachers provide invaluable information.

The Family Involvement Questionnaire

The Family Involvement Questionnaire (FIQ; Fantuzzo, Tighe, & Childs, 2000) is a 42-item rating scale that assesses primary caregivers of young children and their involvement in the educational experiences of their children. The FIQ was developed as a part of a large-scale project and partnership with a large urban school district. A research committee, composed of university researchers, school administrators, teachers and parent representatives from Head Start, Comprehensive Daycare, kindergarten and first grade programs were involved in the development of the FIQ. Epstein's (1995) model was used to examine the six important categories of parental involvement: (1) ways in which parents provide basic needs, (2) ways in which parents create a home environment that is conducive to learning, (3) communication with school personnel, (4) active participation in class or school activities, (5) parent participation in decision-making processes related to school governance, and (6) participation in political issues that affect children. Next, focus groups were formed examining parent behaviors in these categories that led to the development of questionnaire items. These items were then field tested with several groups of parents yielding an ultimate 42-item measure assessing the frequency of parent behaviors on a 4-point Likert scale.

The test authors (Fantuzzo et al., 2000) conducted a large-scale study ($N=641$) to assess the psychometric properties of the FIQ with an urban, diverse sample. An exploratory factor analysis was conducted and yielded a three-factor solution defined by: School-based involvement (i.e., activities and behaviors that parents engage in with their children at school, including volunteering in the classroom, going on school trips, meeting with other parents to organize or participate in school events, fundraisers, etc.), home-based involvement (i.e., behaviors that assist in promoting a learning environment for children at home including initiating or participating in learning activities with children at home, creating learning experiences at home or in the community and providing a place in the home for learning materials), and home–school conferencing (i.e., behaviors related to communicating with school personnel regarding their children's educational experience including discussing the child's progress or difficulties, the child's learning behavior, and work to practice at home). Each construct was found to be highly reliable, with Cronbach alpha coefficients of 0.85, 0.85 and 0.81, respectively. Studies have used the FIQ for use in assessing ethnic minority parents' involvement (Fantuzzo, McWayne, Perry, & Childs, 2004; Mendez, 2010; Mendez, Carpenter, LaForett, & Cohen, 2009; Rockhill, Stoep, McCauley, & Katon, 2009).

Manz, Fantuzzo, and Power (2004) further developed the FIQ to be used with parents or caregivers of older elementary children from first to fifth grade. Through additional expert review and focus groups, the FIQ was slightly modified to 46 items, 39 of which were the same items from the original instrument to create the FIQ-E (Elementary). An additional seven items were added as being especially relevant to elementary school-aged children. A study with primary caregivers of elementary school-aged children ($N=444$) was conducted to evaluate the psychometric properties of the FIQ-E. Analyses confirmed the three-factor structure found from the original FIQ: Home-based Involvement, School-based Involvement, and Home–school communication. The internal consistency was found to be high, with Cronbach alpha coefficients of 0.88, 0.84, and 0.91, respectively.

More research is needed to establish additional psychometric properties of the FIQ. Currently, research has established strong internal consistency, good content and construct validity through the use of empirical evidence and focus groups. Additional studies need to be conducted to further support for this measure, though it is potentially a good measure to assess parent's involvement in academic experiences for their children. With all measures, it is important to gain corresponding evidence from collateral sources, specifically, ones who would have converging data regarding parents' involvement. Teachers and other professionals who are involved in the children's academic achievements (i.e., tutors, paraprofessionals) would provide additional information regarding parent's school involvement. Home observations would allow for the opportunity to observe environments that are conducive to facilitating learning in children (i.e., an area set up for learning materials as well as books and educational materials or opportunities), in addition to interviews with parents around how they support children's educational needs or endeavors.

Promotion of Interpersonal Development

Social support and the importance of having multiple positive relationships with competent and caring adults have been associated with positive outcomes in children and adolescents (Wright & Masten, 2005). Parents' initiation, facilitation, and monitoring of children's social activities have been found to be related positively to peer acceptance, prosocial behavior, friendship quality, and social competence (Simpkins & Parke, 2002). In addition to parenting behaviors, parents' own social adjustment and peer relationships have implications for their children's social adjustment. Specifically, Marshall, Noonan, McCartney, Marx, and Keefe (2001) found that mothers who endorsed more emotional support were more warm and responsive to their children, who in turn showed less behavioral problems and more social competence.

The Child Behavior Scale

The Child Behavior Scale (CBS; Ladd & Profilet, 1996) was developed to provide an efficient, teacher-report instrument that reliably and validly assesses children's behaviors and relations with peers at school. The CBS includes measures for two forms of externalizing behavior (i.e., aggressiveness with peers, hyperactive–distractible), two forms of internalizing behavior (i.e., asocial with peers, anxious–fearful) one form of behavioral/social competence (i.e., prosocial with peers), and one indicator of peer rejection (i.e., excluded by peers). The CBS is composed of 59 items, 35 of which related to the six specific subscales: Aggressive with Peers, Hyperactive–Distractible, Asocial with Peers, Anxious–Fearful, Prosocial with Peers and Excluded by Peers. The additional 24 items were created as "filler" questions and relate to interpersonal or other classroom behaviors. These were included with the intent of attenuating potential for response bias. Items are on a 3-point scale and respondents are asked to respond according to the applicability of the behavior to the child they are completing it for (i.e., 1 = doesn't apply, or child seldom displays this behavior; 2 = applies sometimes; 3 = certainly applies, or child frequently engages in this behavior). Teachers are instructed to consider peer context when rating CBS items, and most items pertain to peers or peer relations. When first constructed, the CBS was validated with samples of Kindergarteners (aged 5 and 6 years) (Ladd & Profilet, 1996), however it has since been used with children up to age 12 (Ladd, 2006; Miles & Stipek, 2006; Xu, Farver, Chang, Zhang, & Yu, 2007).

Ladd, Herald-Brown, and Andrews (2009) assessed the psychometric properties of the CBS longitudinally and across age groups (children were followed from first to eighth grade, aged 5–13 years) (N=496). Validity for the CBS was obtained through Peer's reports of children's behavior and peer relations, Peer Nominations (Coie, Dodge, & Coppotelli, 1982), in which the class confidentially and separately ranks three children in the class who represent each subscale most, the CBCL (Achenbach, 1991a), the Teacher Report Form (Achenbach, 1991b), and finally additional ratings by peers regarding peer group acceptance and number of mutual friends. The internal consistency of the CBS was found to be high, with Cronbach alpha coefficients ranging from 0.71 to 0.92 (Ladd et al., 2009). Convergent validity was obtained through cross-informant measures of aggressive behavior, attention problems, withdrawn behavior, anxiety and depression, prosocial behavior, and social problems or peer rejection. Criterion-related validity was examined by evaluating gender differences and found significant differences between boys and girls, with boys' aggressive and hyperactive ratings higher than girls' across time periods, and girls' prosocial with peers ratings higher than boys' across time periods. Additionally, scores for earlier ratings were found to significantly predict social competence ratings for future time points, indicating predictive validity of the CBS (Ladd et al., 2009). Overall, the CBS was found to be a highly reliable and a valid indicator of social competence in school-aged children aged 5–13 years and it has the additional advantage that it is a measure that relies not on parent-report but report of the child's teacher.

Multidimensional Scale of Perceived Social Support

The Multidimensional Scale of Perceived Social Support (MSPSS; Zimet, Dahlem, Zimet, & Farley, 1988) is a 12-item, 7-point Likert scale (1 = very strongly disagree; 7 = very strongly agree) measure of perceived social support with regard to three social areas: family, significant other, and friends. Zimet et al. (1988) investigated and found internal reliability estimates of 0.88 for total score and 0.87, 0.85, and 0.91 for the Family, Friends, and Significant Other subscales. The MSPSS' three-factor structure, in addition to its reliability and validity, has been demonstrated in a number of studies across a number of different populations including college students (Dahlem, Zimet, & Walker, 1991), pregnant women (Zimet, Powell, Farley, Werkman, & Berkoff, 1990), and adolescents (Kazarian & McCabe, 1991; Zimet et al., 1988). Total and subscale scores range from 1 to 7, with higher scores suggesting greater levels of perceived social support. Canty-Mitchell and Zimet (2000) assessed the psychometric properties of the MSPSS with adolescents from diverse ethnic backgrounds ($N = 222$) and found high internal consistency, with Cronbach alpha coefficients of 0.91 for the Family subscale, 0.89 for the Friends subscale, and 0.91 for Significant Others. Additionally, evidence supporting the discriminant validity was found for the family subscale, which was significantly correlated to a family support scale. Additionally, the readability of the MSPSS items was assessed and found to be at a fourth-grade reading level. It appears that although the MSPSS items are written at the fourth-grade level, items may not be appropriate to fourth graders. Specifically, the Significant Other subscale assesses items that would be more relevant to adolescents and parents.

The Survey of Children's Social Support

The Survey of Children's Social Support (SOCSS; Dubow & Ullman, 1989) is a child self-report measure of three aspects of social support: specific behaviors of support provided to the child (Scale of Available Behaviors or SAB), the child's appraisal of support received from family, peers, or teachers (APP) and the size and identity of the child's support network (NET). Items selected for inclusion in the SOCSS involved instances of emotional, informational, and tangible support as is consistent with extant literature on social support. Item analyses led to the 38-item

SAB measure, and the 31-item APP measure, which requires children to rate how frequently they receive each type of support, feel a certain way (i.e., left out by friends) on a 5-point Likert scale from never (1) to always (5). Items for the APP were generated to reflect literature on social support that it assesses whether the child feels loved, cared for and valued by his social network. Finally, for the NET, children are asked to list, in order of importance, the network members who provide each of the three types of support: emotional ("Who helps you when you need to talk about your feelings?"), tangible ("Who gives you things you need or like but don't have?") and informational ("Who helps you when you need to know something that you're not sure of?"). Scores for the NET are the summed number of people for each type of support that is identified. A pilot study of the SAB yielded good internal consistency (Cronbach alpha = 0.91) and test–retest reliability for total scale scores (0.74) were reported by the test authors (Dubow & Ullman, 1987). Additionally, children who rated themselves as very high or very low on the SAB were similarly rated by parents, teachers, and peers. Pilot tests were similarly done for the APP and NET subscales.

Dubow and Ullman (1989) conducted a study of third, fourth, and fifth graders ($N = 361$) to further assess the psychometric properties of the SOCSS. Cronbach's alpha for the SAB was 0.94, and 0.88 for the APP. Test–retest reliabilities for the APP was 0.75 with subscale reliabilities ranging from 0.66 to 0.73. Test–retest reliability for the NET was 0.54 for emotional support, 0.54 for tangible support and 0.52 for informational support. It was found that 85% of the children responding listed their mother in the top three support providers for emotional support either both times or neither time, and the range of such figures across emotional supporters was 67–96%; across tangible support 65–97% and across informational support 70–96%, indicating consistency in children's choices of specific network members. Correlations were found to be high among the SAB subscales, ranging from 0.59 to 0.74, moderate among the APP subscales (range = 0.31–0.47) and moderate for the NET (range = 0.43–0.63) indicating that children who endorsed receiving one type of support were likely to endorse receiving others as well. APP subscales were found to highly correlate with corresponding subscales on the Harter Social Support Scale (Harter, 1985), Peer support on the APP correlated with the Loneliness Scale as well as the Peer Social Preference (French & Waas, 1985), indicating support for its construct validity. Finally, scores on the APP and SAB were positively correlated with global self-worth. Multiple studies have used the SOCSS with children to assess dimensions of social support including children with emotional and behavioral difficulties (Kolko, Dorn, Bukstein, & Burke, 2008; Popliger, Toste, & Heath, 2009); children from low-income, minority backgrounds (Elias & Haynes, 2008); children in Big Brothers Big Sisters (De Wit et al., 2007); and children of drug-abusing parents (Pilowsky, Zybert, & Vlahov, 2005) among others.

Friendship Quality Questionnaire

The Friendship Quality Questionnaire (FQQ; Parker & Asher, 1993) was designed for use with children third to sixth grade and is intended to measure the quality of a child-identified friendship. Parker and Asher (1993) initially examined the distinction between friendship adjustment and acceptance by the peer group with third through sixth graders ($N=881$) by having children complete sociometric measures of peer acceptance and friendship, a measure of loneliness, a questionnaire on the features of their very best friendships, and a measure of their friendship satisfaction. Results indicated that many low-accepted children had best friends and were satisfied with these relationships, however, these relationships were lower than those of other children on most dimensions of quality. The FQQ consists of 40 statements that characterize a friend or a friendship. Children are asked to rate on a 5-point Likert scale (0 = not at all true to 4 = really true) the degree to which each statement is true concerning his or her friendship with a specific friend. The FQQ contains six subscales: Companionship and Recreation, Validation and Caring, Help and Guidance, Intimate Disclosure, Conflict Resolution, and Conflict and Betrayal. Cronbach's alphas for these subscales have been found to range from 0.85 to 0.90 (Parker & Asher, 1993).

Promotion of Mental Health

The promotion of mental health has been conceptualized as the promotion of self-esteem, self-efficacy and autonomy. The development of problem solving skills and a flexible, adaptive approach to new situations has also been associated with resiliency in children (Luthar, 2003; Garmezy, 1985; Masten & Garmezy, 1985; Masten, Best, & Garmezy, 1990; Rutter, 1990, 1999, 2000 as cited in Rutter, 2006). Both the Parent Behavior Inventory and the Alabama Parenting Questionnaire contain subscales related to the promotion of autonomy, and these should also be taken into consideration for the promotion of health factor. There are additional measures that also are available to examine this factor and are discussed further below.

The Child's Report of Parental Behavior Inventory

The Child's Report of Parental Behavior Inventory (CRPBI; Schludermann & Schludermann, 1970) includes 30 items on mother and father parenting behaviors that are grouped into three subscales: (1) acceptance/rejection, which measures the degree to which parents are close to and are accepting of the child; (2) psychological autonomy/control, which measures the extent to which parents use aversive strategies as a means of discipline; and (3) firm/lax behavioral control, which measures the extent to which parents monitor children's direct behavior. Higher scores are indicative of more maladaptive parenting. The CRPBI is a widely used inventory of parenting behavior that is well established. Previous research has established cross-ethnic equivalence of the CRPBI among diverse groups (Knight, Virdin, Ocampo, & Roosa, 1994). Internal consistency has been found to be high, with Cronbach alpha coefficients ranging from 0.68 to 0.93 (O'Donnell et al., 2010). Test–retest reliability has been reported for subscales from 0.66 to 0.93 (Silverman & Ollendick, 2005). In addition, factorial studies of the CRPBI have yielded the same three factors over samples varying in age and cultural background, providing additional evidence for the inventory's construct validity (Schludermann & Schludermann, 1970). In examining the criterion validity of the CRPBI, Litovsky and Dusek (1985) also reported that parents of adolescents with high self-esteem were rated as more accepting, provide more autonomy-promoting support, and are not as firm in making and enforcing rules as adolescents with low self-esteem.

Parental Bonding Instrument

The Parental Bonding Instrument (PBI; Parker, Tupling, & Brown, 1979) is a 25-item scale designed to measure adolescents' perceptions of the parent–child relationship. The measure identifies two subscales and their complementary opposites: caring (and indifference or rejection) and overprotection (and encouragement of autonomy or promotion of independence). Twelve items assess adolescents' perceptions of their parents as caring/indifferent or rejecting and 13 items assess overprotectiveness/promotion of autonomy (i.e., "my parents like me to make my own decisions"). Scores on the PBI range from 12 to 36 for caring, and from 13 to 39 for overprotectiveness with scores placing parents into one of four quadrants: optimal parenting (characterized by high caring and autonomy-promoting), affectionate constraint (characterized by high caring and high overprotection), affectionless control (characterized by low caring and high overprotection), and neglectful parenting (characterized by low caring and low overprotection). Studies examining the PBI have found high internal consistency for subscales with split-half coefficients of 0.88 for caring and 0.74 for overprotection (Mullis, Graf, & Mullis, 2009).

Rosenberg Self-Esteem Scale

The Rosenberg Self-Esteem Scale (SES; Rosenberg, 1965) is a 10-item self-report measure of global self-esteem (five with a positive orientation and five with a negative orientation) that assesses on a 5-point Likert scale (0 = strongly disagree to 4 = strongly agree), with higher scores indicative of higher self-esteem. The SES was originally developed to be used as a global measure of self-esteem in a sample of adolescents ($N = 5{,}024$) (Rosenberg, 1965) and has frequently since been considered the "gold standard" of measurement of self-esteem, often used as a model to test other measures of self-esteem. Psychometric studies have found evidence for the one-factor structure of the SES (Corwyn, 2000) although others have found evidence for a two-factor structure (delineating the positively worded and negatively worded items) (Farruggia, Chen, Greenberger, Dmitrieva, & Macek, 2004; Serretti, Olgiati, & Colombo, 2005). Internal consistency has been reported to range from 0.70 to 0.93 (Rosenberg, 1979; Wesley, 2003) and test–retest reliability over a

2-week interval has been reported to be 0.88 (Silber & Tippet, 1965). The validity for the SES has been reported in a number of studies. Specifically, Hatcher and Hall found support for the construct validity of the SES among African-American single mother (2009). The construct and convergent validity of the SES was supported with a sample of eating disordered individuals ($N=117$), as SES scores were significantly predictive of dieting disorder pathology (Griffiths et al., 1997) and the SES also showed convergent validity with the Ineffectiveness subscale of the Eating Disorder Inventory (EDI-2; Garner, 1991).

Coopersmith Self-Esteem Inventories

The Coopersmith Self-Esteem Inventories (SEIs; Coopersmith, 1981) are three self-report questionnaires intended to measure the evaluation a person makes with regard to him or herself. Each questionnaire involves items that contain generally favorable or unfavorable statements regarding the self and respondents are asked to indicate whether these are "like me" or "unlike me." The School Form is a 50-item inventory for 8–15-year-olds and contains four subscales pertaining to different self-esteem domains: peers, parents, school, and personal interests. The School Form also has an 8-item Lie Scale to assess defensiveness. The School Short Form contains the 25 items in the original form with the highest item-total correlations. The Adult Form is intended for individuals aged 15 and over and is adapted from the School Form. The Coopersmith Inventories are the most widely used self-esteem measures (Johnson, Redfield, Miller, & Simpson, 1983). In addition, there is much evidence supporting the SEIs reliability and validity. Specifically, internal consistency estimates ranging from 0.80 to 0.92 have been reported (Donaldson, 1974; Kimball, 1973; Spatz & Johnston, 1973) for the SEI. Split-half reliability has been reported with reliability coefficient of 0.87 for a sample of fifth and sixth graders ($N=104$) (Fullerton, 1972). Lane, White, and Henson (2002) conducted a reliability generalization (RG) study for the Coopersmith SEI compiling studies ($N=107$) that reported reliability data for the SEI. Ultimately, it was reported that internal consistency ranged from 0.50 to 0.95, and test–retest reliability ranged from 0.20 to 0.85. The SEI has been used across a wide variety of populations including individuals with tattoos or piercings (Carroll & Anderson, 2002), coping with stress (Marriage & Cummins, 2004), separation from parents (McCormick & Kennedy, 2000) and nicotine dependence (Guillon, Crocq, & Bailey, 2003).

Adolescent Autonomy Questionnaire

The Adolescent Autonomy Scale (Noom, Dekovic, & Meeus, 1999, 2001) is a 15-statement self-report measure meant to assess three aspects of autonomy: Attitudinal Autonomy, or the perception of goals by means of opportunities and desires (i.e., "I know what I want"); Emotional Autonomy, or the perception of independence through self-confidence and individuality (i.e., "I have the tendency to give in to others easily" reverse coded); and Functional Autonomy, or the perception of strategies by means of self-regulation and control (i.e., "I always go straight for my goal"). Respondents are asked to report the degree to which the statement is indicative of them on a 5-point scale ranging from "a very bad description of me" to "a very good description of me." Noom et al. (1999) studied 400 nonclinical adolescents aged 12–18 years along dimensions of social competence, academic competence, self-esteem, problem behavior and internalized distress. Cronbach alpha coefficients were 0.71 for the Attitudinal autonomy subscale, 0.60 for the Emotional autonomy subscale and 0.64 for the Functional autonomy subscale. Correlations between the subscales were found to range from 0.38 to 0.49, indicating that they referred to not only a general concept of autonomy but also different elements of autonomy. All aspects of autonomy were found to correlate positively with social competence, academic competence, and self-esteem, and correlate negatively with depressive thoughts. Attachment was also positively related to adjustment outcomes. There was a small positive relationship between autonomy and attachment, indicating that these are not opposite constructs from one another, but that they are also relatively independent measures. Convergent and divergent validity were established in a later study using the original sample (Noom et al., 2001) by reporting autonomy measures that correlated with perceptions of institutional goals, locus of control, and active coping. Additional research is warranted to continue to establish the psychometric properties for the Adolescent Autonomy Scale, however, given the gap regarding a child-report of autonomy, it has promising merit as a tool to measure autonomy in adolescents.

Promotion of Community Involvement

Involvement in activities outside of school is associated with positive outcomes in children (Denault & Poulin, 2009; Zarrett et al., 2008). Results from numerous studies reflect that the involvement in activities outside of school is associated with higher academic achievement (Darling et al., 2005; Eccles & Barber, 1999; Jordan & Nettles, 1999; Mahoney & Cairns, 1997; Mahoney, Cairns, & Farmer, 2003), a lower risk of engaging in risky behavior (i.e., risky sexual behavior, substance use, antisocial behavior) (Darling et al., 2005; Linville & Huebner, 2005), lower levels of internalizing problems (i.e., depression) (Bohnert, Kane, & Garber, 2008; Fredricks & Eccles, 2005; Mahoney et al. 2003), higher self-esteem (Barber, Eccles, & Stone, 2001), and more investment in the community (Denault & Poulin, 2009).

Children's Assessment of Participation and Enjoyment

The Children's Assessment of Participation and Enjoyment (CAPE; King et al., 2004, 2006) is a reliable and valid measure of children's participation appropriate for children and youth with and without disabilities for aged 6–21 years. The CAPE provides information about participation in formal and informal domains as well as in five activity types (i.e., recreational, active–physical, social, skill-based, and self-improvement activities). The items of the CAPE were generated from empirical literature, expert review, and pilot testing with children. CAPE test–retest reliability was evaluated with values for the CAPE activity type ranging from 0.72 to 0.81 (King et al., 2006). In addition, CAPE scores correlate with environmental, family and child variables, providing evidence for the CAPE's construct validity. Children are asked to indicate the activities they had participated in for the past 4 months, and how often on a 7-point scale (1 = "one time in the past 4 months" to 7 = "one time a day or more"). Parent or caregiver assistance in completing the CAPE is suggested as needed. Participation diversity (the sum of the number of different activities participated in), Participation intensity (calculated by dividing the sum of item frequency by the number of possible activities for a given level of scoring) and Enjoyment (measured by ratings provided on a 5-point scale of liking it from 1 = not at all to 5 = love it) scores are obtained for both formal and informal activities. The interview-assisted version of the CAPE involves a self-report component in which respondents report the number of activities they have participated in and with what frequency, and then the interview component, which assesses with whom, where and the degree of enjoyment for these activities. The self-administered CAPE is a single questionnaire that assesses all of this information through a self-report format. Psychometric properties for both versions have been reported to yield comparable results (King et al., 2004). The CAPE has been used in studies examining the enjoyment differences in children with and without disabilities toward formal vs. informal activities (King, Petrenchik, Law, & Hurley, 2009).

Effective Coparenting

Effective coparenting has been found to be an important factor in promoting positive child outcomes (Camera & Resnick, 1988; Feinberg, 2003). Coparenting counseling has been found to be efficacious in improving interparental communication and collaboration and decreasing parental conflict. Forgiveness has also been an important aspect of effective coparenting (Bonach, 2005; Gasper et al., 2009). A few recently developed measures assess domains that are specific to the degree to which parents are successful at coparenting. In addition, direct observation of the parents' behavior during the evaluation as well as collateral contacts will also provide useful information on this domain.

Parenting Alliance Measure

The Parenting Alliance Measure (PAM; Abidin & Konold, 1999) is a 20-item self-report measure designed to reflect the strength of the perceived alliance between parents of children aged 1–19 years. The measure takes approximately 10 min to complete and requires a third grade reading level. As mothers and fathers were found to differ significantly in the normative sample, raw scores, percentiles, and T-scores conversions are available for both groups. The Total Score for the PAM is an indication of the degree to which parents perceive themselves to be in a cooperative, communicative and mutually respectful alliance for the care of their children (Abidin & Konold, 1999). Higher scores are indicative of more strongly perceived alliance, whereas scores below the 20th percentile are indicative of marginal, problematic or dysfunctional (lowest). The PAM's development was guided by empirical research on family relations and was created based off of Abidin's 80-item Parenting Alliance Inventory (PAI; Abidin, 1992). The items were tested with parents and then reviewed by experts, after which it was reduced to 30 items. Finally, the PAI was tested with a sample of 512 parents and findings from factor loadings reduced it to the current 20-item version. Norms were based off of 1,214 parents from various backgrounds around the country and are reported to represent the nation's population characteristics.

The test authors have reported strong internal consistency on the PAM with alpha coefficients of 0.95 and higher. Test–retest reliability over a 4–6-week period has been reported at 0.88 for mothers and 0.64 for fathers (Abidin & Konold, 1999). Criterion-related validity was established by examining the PAM in relation to parenting stress, parent relationship quality, family functioning, child self-esteem, and social competence. The PAM was found to be negatively correlated with parenting stress, and positively correlated to family cohesion, family adaptability, and relationship quality. As further evidence of criterion-related validity, the authors compared parents from known groups. They found that married parents reported significantly more positive parenting alliances than separated or divorced parents. In addition, parents of children who had no history of receiving mental health services reported significantly stronger alliances than parents of children who had such histories, and parents of children who had engaged in delinquent behaviors had weaker PAM scores than parents of children who had not participated in delinquency. Finally, the authors considered parents of children with and without clinical diagnoses. Parents of children without diagnoses and parents of children with ADHD diagnoses reported stronger alliances than parents of children with oppositional defiant disorder (ODD) or conduct disorder (CD) (Abidin & Konold, 1999).

Enright Forgiveness Inventory

The Enright Forgiveness Inventory (EFI; Subkoviak et al., 1995) is a 60-item selfreport measure with a 6-point Likert scale (1 = strongly disagree to 6 = strongly agree) that assesses the level of forgiveness toward another who has wronged them. The EFI contains six subscales: positive affect, negative affect, positive behavior, negative behavior, positive cognition and negative cognition. Higher scores are indicative of higher levels of forgiveness. The EFI also contains 5 additional items of pseudo-forgiveness, which are not included in the overall score of the EFI. These items are intended to determine if the measure is capturing something other than genuine forgiveness. A score of 20 or higher on the pseudo-forgiveness items indicates that the rest of the profile may not be assessing genuine forgiveness. Additionally, a 1-item forgiveness scale (i.e., "To what degree have you forgiven the person whom you named in the inventory?") is included to capture the validity of the EFI's items and to ensure that forgiveness is being measured. The internal consistency of the EFI is 0.98 and the test–retest reliability is 0.86 (Enright & Rique, 2004). The construct validity of the EFI has been reported to be strong. The EFI has not been found to be correlated to measures of religiosity or social desirability (Enright & Rique, 2004). The EFI has been cross-culturally validated in over 5 countries (Enright & Fitzgibbons, 2000). Studies have frequently used the EFI as a measure of forgiveness with parents and couples (Lee & Enright, 2009; Orathinkal, Vansteenwegen, Enright, & Stroobants, 2007).

Taken together, it is apparent that measures do exist that assess constructs of the Promotive Factors Model. Although they may not have been intended for use in a child custody evaluation as a part of their development, and have not been normed for this population, they measure constructs that are very relevant and have been purported in the literature as being predictive of better outcomes in children. The measures described in this section are some of the measures that are available. Certainly, measuring children's adjustment at the time of the custody evaluation would be warranted, though measures for this were not included as a part of this discussion. It is important to be able to validly measure constructs to begin to add the potential for reliable and valid child custody evaluations. Now that methods for doing this have been reviewed, the next step is determining how these factors fit together and are weighed to yield consistent recommendations regarding custody arrangement. While every family is unique with different sets of strengths and risk factors, it is important to have a clear rationale guiding this attempt to predict the best interests of the child.

Actuarial Methodologies vs. Clinical Judgment

When looking at existing models for predicting future events, actuarial methodologies have gained significant support in the areas of predicting risk for violence or safety in children involved with child protection services (Baird, Wagner, Healy, & Johnson, 1999; Borum, 2000). Actuarial approaches to violence risk assessment employ formulas as the preferred model for predicting future violence that rely little on the clinical decision making of the evaluator (Grove & Meehl, 1996). Actuarial-based approaches rely on empirically derived risk factors that have been statistically and significantly related to violent behavior. Specifically, Child Protection Services (CPS) actuarial systems for risk assessment are based on empirical studies of CPS cases and future abuse/neglect outcomes. Factors are identified that have strong associations to future abuse/neglect. An actuarial instrument is used to assist in the identification of risk level of families involved (i.e., low, medium or high) (Baird et al., 1999). Actuarial-based systems are in contrast to clinical judgment, or consensus-based systems, in which evaluators rely on expert experience, intuition and interviewing skills to assess future risk of abuse or neglect. Clinical judgment has consistently been demonstrated as being relatively poor in accurately predicting future behavior (Grove & Meehl, 1996). Furthermore, a large body of research has reported that actuarial instruments can estimate future behavior more accurately than an individual not using actuarial information (Dawes et al., 1989; Meehl, 1954). While actuarial prediction might be helpful for some prediction assessments, others that involve a complex set of idiographic variables that are difficult to capture through empirical assessment alone. The Structured Professional Judgment (SPJ) model is a system that involves both clinical and actuarial strategies that was originally constructed for use with assessment of violence risk (Borum, 2000). The SPJ model is flexible in that allows for idiographic differences. In addition, it utilizes both actuarial methods, through the use of empirically supported risk factors, as well as clinical methods, through the use of judgments based on idiographic considerations, mitigating or exacerbating variables that affect factors' effects, and the situational or contextual variables of these factors (Borum, 2000). The Structured Professional Judgment model assists evaluators in focusing on "relevant data to gather during interviews and record reviews, so that the final judgment, though not statistical, is well informed by the best available research" (Borum, Bartel, & Forth, 2003, p. 4).

Research evaluating the utility of the Structured Professional Judgment model for assessing violence has been promising (Borum, 2003). Using the SPJ for the prediction of violence, an evaluator conducts a systematic assessment of predetermined risk factors (and, depending on the assessment, also a set of predetermined protective factors) that have significant empirical relationships with criterion violence in prior research. Each risk factor is considered and coded for severity; however, the ultimate determination regarding level of risk is made according to examiner's professional judgment.

Borum et al. (2003) developed the Structured Assessment of Violence Risk in Youth (SAVRY), which has been used with the SPJ in predicting violence. The SAVRY is designed to specifically focus on violence risk in adolescents. The SAVRY is composed of 24 risk items, divided into historical, individual, and social/contextual factors, along with six protective items. The risk items each have a three-level coding system (high, moderate, low) and the protective items have a two-level structure (absent, present). Specific risk and protective items for the SAVRY are:

Historical risk factors:

1. History of violence
2. History of nonviolent offending
3. Early initiation of violence
4. Past supervision/intervention failures
5. History of self-harm or suicide attempts
6. Exposure to violence in the home
7. Childhood history of maltreatment
8. Parental/caregiver criminality
9. Early caregiver disruption
10. Poor school achievement

Social/contextual risk factors:

11. Peer delinquency
12. Peer rejection
13. Stress and poor coping
14. Poor parental management
15. Lack of personal/social support
16. Community disorganization

Individual/clinical risk factors:

17. Negative attitudes
18. Risk taking/impulsivity
19. Substance-use difficulties
20. Anger management problems
21. Psychopathic traits
22. Attention deficit/hyperactivity difficulties
23. Poor compliance
24. Low interest/commitment to school

Protective factors:

25. Pro-social involvement
26. Strong social support
27. Strong attachments and bonds
28. Positive intervention toward intervention and authority
29. Strong commitment to school
30. Resilient personality traits

The SAVRY has shown significant correlations with existing measures of violence (Borum, Bartel, & Forth, 2003; Fitch, 2002), with predictive accuracy found to range from 0.74 to 0.80. The SAVRY appears to be a promising tool that uses empirically derived constructs to guide areas of assessment and have merit in terms of predictive validity. For this reason, The SAVRY was used as a guideline for developing a structured assessment measure for the EPFM. While similar to the SAVRY in its structure, the purpose of the EPFM Structured Assessment is to identify potential areas of risk as well as opportunities for promoting optimal child outcomes.

The Structured Assessment for the EPFM

Guided by literature on violence risk assessments and the Structured Professional Judgment model (Borum, 2000), guidelines are set forth for assessing factors in the EPFM. Consistent with ethical guidelines for child custody evaluators (APA, 1994), the structured assessment assesses data from multiple sources to assist in providing evidence to support or not support the presence of a specific factor. Risk prediction strategies that have been developed largely for assessing current and future risk in psycho-legal contexts have been tried in cases of child maltreatment, as well as relocation following divorce. Austin (2000) also used violence risk assessment methodologies and applied them to the child custody evaluation process. Austin describes this process as being different from prediction of harm caused by a specific perpetrator, to prediction of harm to a child caused by a specific environment (2000). The importance of predicting short-term child adjustment rather than long-term adjustment, in addition to measuring all relevant constructs is stressed in order to enhance the accuracy of predictions made for relocation cases (Austin, 2000). These are all important considerations for developing an assessment for evaluating whether egregious or promotive factors are present. Consistent with other risk assessments for violence, as well as the SAVRY, an evaluation of risk level is recommended for egregious factors from low, moderate to high and for promotive factors a dichotomous determination for present or absent is recommended. Distinct from the SAVRY, the EPFM Structured Assessment recommends the use of empirically supported measures, along with other sources of information to more accurately determine the presence of either risk or promotive factors. The EPFM Structured Assessment is only a guideline to assist in measuring empirically derived factors that have been found to predict child outcomes.

The EPFM Structured Assessment was developed for this model and has not been tested as to its reliability or validity. Longitudinal research to determine its ability to accurately evaluate for the presence of risk and promotive factors is warranted. These guidelines are provided below.

EPFM Structured Assessment

Egregious factors	Promotive factors
1. Poor parent–child relationship	1. Positive parenting
2. Poor parenting skills	2. Parental school involvement
3. Environmental instability	3. Promotion of interpersonal development
4. Parent mental health problems	4. Promotion of mental health
5. Excessive interparental conflict	5. Promotion of community involvement
	6. Effective coparenting

Structured Assessment for EPFM (for Parent X):

1) Does information gained from the clinical interview indicate the presence of egregious factor #X? _____Yes(1) _______No
   If Yes, What?
2) Does information gained from the empirically supported evaluation measures indicate the presence of egregious factor #X? ______Yes(1) _______No
   If Yes, What?

Chapter 5
A Preliminary Validation Study of the Model

Given the importance that child custody evaluations, and the reports created from these, have in the court's decision-making process, it is important to ensure that these evaluations and reports are conducted in a scientifically sound manner, validly assessing empirically relevant constructs and clearly explicating the rationale behind recommendations. The purpose of this study was to preliminarily examine judges' assessments of two different custody evaluations; one based on the Egregious/Promotive Factors Model and the other a more traditional, unspecified constructs model. In addition, this study intended to determine what factors influenced judge's decision making most, and their general feedback regarding the report they received. Family court judges were mailed sample reports that were created based on either the EPFM or an unspecified constructs (UC) report, relying more on clinical judgment. This study will be used to evaluate the impact of the EPFM.

Thus far, literature regarding the past and current state of child custody evaluations, child custody evaluation practices, state statutes regarding factors to consider in determining child custody, and results from longitudinal research regarding risk and promotive factors that predict outcomes for children have been reviewed. In addition, the EPFM has been described. The EPFM attempts to assess for the presence of empirically supported factors that have been shown to be predictive of outcomes for children. In addition, assessment tools that can validly measure these constructs have been discussed, and a structured assessment for the EPFM, designed after the Structured Professional Judgment model, has been developed. The structured assessment of the EPFM is proposed as an alternative to the existing child custody evaluations that appear to often be conducted using unspecified constructs. It is important to keep in mind, however, that the decisions made regarding child custody arrangements ultimately still lie in the hands of family court judges who preside over child custody hearings. Given the assumed importance of the child custody report provided by mental health professionals, it is necessary to review literature examining how custody evaluations impact judges' rulings, and what emphasis they place on the role of the mental health professional in guiding their rulings. Some literature has already been discussed as to why mental health professionals assumed the role of child custody evaluators. Reasons included: the emphasis on the psychological well being of the

L.W. Tolle and W.T. O'Donohue, *Improving the Quality of Child Custody Evaluations*,
DOI 10.1007/978-1-4614-3405-4_5, © Springer Science+Business Media, LLC 2012

child in custody arrangements (Bala & Saunders, 2003; Bolocofsky, 1989; Mason & Quirk, 1997), the ambiguity of the Best Interest of the Child doctrine (Melton, Petrila, Poythress, & Slobogin, 1997), and the ambiguous and often complex psychological factors (e.g., allegations of substance use, domestic violence, physical or sexual abuse, and mental illness) that frequently show up in custody evaluations (Bolocofsky, 1989; Mason & Quirk, 1997). Finally, it has been proposed that judges often find custody cases stressful and outside the realm of their profession, and therefore responsibilities are delegated to professionals who appear to have at least some training in psychology, family issues, and measurement (Kushner, 2006).

In an attempt to determine whether judges make use of information that the psychological literature has suggested to be predictive of children's psychological adjustment following divorce, Sorenson et al. (1997) examined case-specific data derived from reports provided to the court by Guardians ad Litem (GALs). GALs are trained professionals or volunteers who provide the court with information regarding the family and make recommendations regarding custody arrangements. The degree to which judges attended to this information versus statutory guidelines in making their decisions was examined, and results indicated that the statutory guidelines were most influential in decision making (Sorenson et al., 1997). Specifically, judges followed state statutes, attended to the nature of family relationships, and did not rely on a preference for one parent. Decision making appeared to be less impacted by information regarding the degree of interparental conflict, parental substance abuse, or the history of child abduction by one parent. Because this was an archival study, however, it is difficult to determine, from the judges' perspectives, what ultimately influenced their decision making.

In a separate study examining judicial decision making, Kunin, Ebbesen, and Konecni (1992) analyzed information from divorce investigation files and court records ($N=282$). Two factors were found to predict judges' decision making: the GAL recommendations and the child's preference. A significant relationship was found between the judges' decisions and the reports provided by the GAL with 60% of reports including specific recommendations. For 75% of the cases in which GALs made specific recommendations, judges were found to agree with these recommendations. In cases where GALs were not appointed, judges' decisions were predicted by the wishes of the child regarding custody placement.

In addition to studies examining archival records regarding judicial decision making, others have polled family court judges to compile a listing of the most important factors to consider for child custody evaluations. Some studies provided lists of factors and had judges rank-order how important they believed these to be in the child custody decision-making process (Lowery, 1981; Reidy, Silver, & Carlson, 1989). The most influential factors in guiding these judges' decisions were the children's age or developmental stage (Lowery, 1981), the wishes of adolescent children, custody investigation reports provided by court personnel, and testimony of parents and a court-appointed psychologist (Reidy et al., 1989). Wallace and Koerner (2003) interviewed family court judges ($N=18$) to determine what factors influenced the judges' decisions in child custody cases. Judges listed factors pertaining to the adjustment of the child, stability of the environment, and risk factors in the parents as being the most influential. The authors report that judges found recommendations by GALs and mental health professionals valuable, "but do not blindly accept their recommendations" (p. 186).

Waller and Daniel (2004) surveyed 97 judges regarding legal standards and personal biases that influence judicial custody decision making, issues that cause judges to order child custody evaluations, expectations regarding evaluation report components and evaluation procedures, parts of the report judges find useful for decision making, and finally the effect of the evaluation on litigation and judicial decision making. Findings indicated that judges were more likely to order custody evaluations when allegations of child physical or sexual abuse or parental unfitness were present. In addition, judges reported expectations of thorough evaluations and reports reflecting interviews with parents, children, significant others, psychological testing of all of these individuals, assessment of parenting skills, substance abuse, domestic violence, physical or sexual abuse, assessment of the parent–child relationship, and review of pertinent documents. Overall, judges indicated that findings from the evaluation, conclusions made from the psychiatric testing, and specific recommendations made by the evaluator were helpful and had a significant impact on their decision-making process (Waller & Daniel, 2004).

Hypotheses

Hypothesis 1

Judges provided with the EPFM-guided report will find it more empirically driven, will better understand the rationale behind its recommendations, and will be more satisfied with this report than judges who were provided with the unspecified constructs report.

Hypothesis 2

Judges provided with the EPFM-guided report will find the empirically based factors most important in determining their custody decisions, ultimately making these decisions in line with empirical literature.

Hypothesis 3

By better informing judges as to the empirical support for predicting child outcomes, custody decisions made by judges who have reviewed the EPFM-guided report will be more apt to follow recommendations provided by the evaluator, which are guided by empirical literature predicting poorer or positive outcomes in children.

Chapter 6
Methodology

The purpose of this study was twofold. The first was to define what empirically supported constructs have been found to predict better or poorer outcomes in children and to use these to create an empirically guided model for conducting child custody evaluations. The second was to compare Family Court Judges' attitudes and ultimate child custody recommendations that were based on an EPFM-guided report with an unspecified construct model report. Judges were randomly sent, via mail, either an EPFM-guided report or an unspecified constructs report concerning the same fictitious family and were asked to evaluate the report and provide recommendations for custody based on the report. In addition, judges were asked to rank-order the top five most important factors that influenced their decision.

Participants

In line with Phase I research guidelines (Rounsaville, Carroll, & Onken, 2001), an *N* of at least 30 (15 per condition) Family Court Judges were needed to be included in the study. Inclusion criteria were that participants be Family Court Judges currently residing in the USA. In order to maximize participant involvement, recruitment was done using two different methods. In the first method, packets containing an information sheet, which was used in lieu of the need for a signed Informed Consent form; a custody evaluation report—either the report guided by the Egregious/Promotive Factors Model, or an unspecified constructs report; a feedback form; and a stamped, addressed envelope to mail the feedback form back in, were sent to 422 Family Court Judges (211 of each condition) around the country (27 states). Professional addresses for judges were publically listed and found via Internet search engines (i.e., Google). In the second method, The National Council for Juvenile and Family Court Judges (NCJFCJ), based in Reno, NV, agreed to assist in the recruitment of Family Court Judges. The NCJFCJ was founded in 1937 and is dedicated to improving the effectiveness of courts and systems practice. More than 2,000 judges, referees,

L.W. Tolle and W.T. O'Donohue, *Improving the Quality of Child Custody Evaluations*, DOI 10.1007/978-1-4614-3405-4_6, © Springer Science+Business Media, LLC 2012

commissioners, masters, and other juvenile and family law professionals make up the members of the NCJFCJ. To assist in recruitment, the NCJFCJ sent out announcements via emails to its members with information about the study and included the student investigator's contact information for interest in participating. Eight emails were sent to the student investigator from members of the NCJFCJ indicating their interest in participating. Thirty-four questionnaires were returned following the mass mailing of packets, and another four were returned following the NCJFCJ announcements. Ultimately, 38 feedback forms were returned and 32 were completed (6 were returned blank). These resulting 32 completed questionnaires were included for the study. The participation of Judges was voluntary and anonymous.

Instruments

Judges were sent packets containing: an information sheet, either the EPFM-guided report or the unspecified constructs report, a feedback form, and a stamped, addressed envelope with which to return the completed feedback form. All of these forms were reviewed by the Institutional Review Board (IRB) for human subjects research and approved for use in this study.

Feedback Form

The feedback form sent to participants to complete was designed specifically for this study. The feedback form consists of 20 questions, 5 of which are demographic questions (i.e., sex, age, number of years as a Family Court Judge, number of child custody cases judge has presided over, and US State in which judge practices). The remaining items are a combination of open-ended, true–false, and 5-point Likert-scale questions. Judges were asked to give an open-ended response regarding what custody arrangement they would recommend given the report they reviewed. Judges were also asked to rank-order five factors that influenced this decision most. Additionally, Judges were asked to rate on a 5-point Likert scale the degree to which they felt the report was scientifically driven (from 1 being not scientific at all to 5 being very scientific), how clearly written they felt the report was (from 1 = not clear at all to 5 = very clear), and how acceptable they found the report (from 1 = not acceptable at all to 5 = very acceptable). In addition, four True/False questions were included regarding the completeness of the report, the rationale behind the recommendations made, if they felt the report covered important areas and if they would recommend custody evaluators to write reports this way. Finally, opportunities were given to provide open-ended feedback regarding what was liked or not liked about the report, what was unnecessary, what would improve the report, and any final comments about the report.

Custody Reports

Fictitious custody reports were created to test how Judges' reacted to and how recommendations differed between the unspecified constructs and EPFM-guided custody evaluation reports. Both reports presented the same family (divorcing parents John and Jane Doe, aged 38 and 35, respectively, and their children Judy, 6 and Jimmy, 3). The ages of the children were decided upon because they are old enough not to be physically dependent on their mother (i.e., no longer of breastfeeding age), but yet not of age to give preference relative to the custody arrangement. These ages provide the least amount of confounds as determined by child custody literature (Guttman, Ben-Archer, & Lazar, 1999).

Typical custody reports can range from 10 to 200 pages. In order to ensure judge participation and to distil the reports to a reasonable length, the reports sent to judges included a brief statement of the makeup of the family, conclusions regarding both parents and children, and recommendations to the court regarding custody arrangement and psychological treatment. Because of this, lengthy histories regarding each parent, lengthy discussions of testing, detailed summaries of collateral reports, background information and summaries of materials brought by each parent, discussion regarding observations of home environments, and observed child–parent interactions were not included in either report. A disclaimer at the top of each report reads: "NOTE: For the purposes of ease and efficiency in reading these recommendations, no summary of background materials, collateral reports, parents interviews, child interviews, or testing is included, however, please assume that these were conducted and included previously in the report." Included in the reports is information alluding to these being done (i.e., discussion of results of testing, discussion of review of materials, collateral references, observations with parents and children, and interviewing of children).

Both reports provided five recommendations each, and both recommended therapy for the 6-year-old child, as well as co-parenting classes for the parents. Both reports discuss a past history of domestic violence (before the children were born) and some strain in the relationship between Judy and John, with Judy saying negative things about John, which may have come from Jane (both of which are meant to relate to poor co-parenting). Both parents also discuss Jane being the primary parent before separation. In addition, both reports involved the same allegations by each parent to keep the content consistent. These allegations were:

- Jane felt John was not invested in the children and wanted to "win" the custody case rather than have the children. Jane also felt that John's supervision of the children was inadequate.
- John alleged that Jane has problems with alcohol abuse and that Judy is frequently tardy to school when Jane takes her.

The reports are differentiated in regard to the style in which they were written. The unspecified constructs report was based on common child custody evaluation practices that have been reported in previous studies (Bow & Quinnell, 2002; Gourley & Stolberg, 2000). This report used subjective language like "it is my opinion to a reasonable degree of psychological certainty," and makes statements regarding allegations that appear to be conclusory without providing a rationale other than expert opinion. In addition, the unspecified constructs report uses projective testing including the Child Apperception Test and the Rorschach, as well as testing results for both parents using the MMPI-2. These tests were selected again, based on previous studies citing commonly used tests in child custody evaluator practices (Ackerman & Ackerman, 1997; Keilin & Bloom, 1986). Ultimately, the evaluator makes custody recommendations to give Jane sole physical and legal custody (because she has been the primary parent), and provides one evening and every other Saturday to John with no overnights, citing that the children are not attached to him.

The EPFM-guided report examines each parent for risk and promotive factors and provides evidence for or against each egregious factor (all egregious factors were ruled out for both parents). In addition, two promotive factors were found to be present for each parent, indicating that they both have positive attributes that could enhance their children's outcomes. The allegations cited by each parent are addressed by discussing objective evidence (i.e., absence of police reports, CPS involvement, report from professionals involved with the family such as the pediatrician) and using this information to rule out factors. The ultimate recommendations outlined in the EPFM-guided report are to give parents joint physical and legal custody, but to place the children with Jane 66% of the time, and John 33% of the time, so that the children have a primary home, which is consistent with empirical research on child outcomes in custody arrangements (Emery, 1999). The EPFM-guided report also provided literature and references related to research on children's adjustment to divorce and explicated the rationale for the provided recommendations.

Chapter 7
Results

One important aspect for this study was to examine and compare patterns in how judges make their custody recommendations based on either an empirically guided custody reports or an unspecified constructs report. Demographic data for the participant judges were also collected, and of the final sample ($N = 32$), 19 were identified as male and 13 as female. Participants practiced in 14 US States representing several different geographical regions (i.e., the Pacific Northwest, New England, South, South East, Mid West, West, etc.) of the country. The mean age of participants was 55.3 (range = 44–70, median = 58, modal age = 60); the mean length of time in years that participants worked as judges was 10.12 (range = 1–25 years, median = 9.5, mode = 3); and the mean number of custody cases judges had been involved in, during their careers, was 495.5 (range = 1–4,000, median = 200, mode = 100). Analyses were conducted to determine whether significant differences between groups existed with regard to age, gender, experience in years, or number of custody cases involved in, and none were found to be significant. Table 7.1 illustrates the demographic data of the participants involved. Table 7.2 displays the relationship of these data and reflects that age and number of years as a judge were statistically and significantly positively correlated. Number of cases involved in were not significantly associated with either age or years as a judge.

Quality of the Report

Judges were asked to respond to three questions regarding their perceived quality of the report. These questions are on a 5-point Likert scale and address three domains of the report: how scientifically driven they found the report to be (1 = Not Scientific at All, to 5 = Very Scientific), how clearly written they found the report to be (1 = Not Clear at All, to 5 = Very Clear), and how acceptable the reported was found to be (1 = Not Acceptable at All, to 5 = Very Acceptable). The mean rating for the entire

L.W. Tolle and W.T. O'Donohue, *Improving the Quality of Child Custody Evaluations*, DOI 10.1007/978-1-4614-3405-4_7, © Springer Science+Business Media, LLC 2012

Table 7.1 Demographic information of participants

	Frequency	*M*	SD	Range
Gender				
Female	13			
Male	19			
Age (in years)		55.3	6.5	44–70
Experience as family judge (in years)		10.1	6.9	1–25
Custody cases involved in (#)		495.5	836.5.5	1–4,000

Table 7.2 Correlation matrix of demographic information

	No. of cases involved in	No. of years as a judge	Age
No. of cases involved in			
Pearson correlation	1.000	−0.06	0.004
Sig. (two-tailed)		0.76	0.98
No. of years as a judge			
Pearson correlation	−0.06	1.000	0.43[a]
Sig. (two-tailed)	0.76		0.02
Age			
Pearson correlation	0.004	0.43[a]	1.000
Sig. (two-tailed)	0.98	0.02	

[a]Correlation is significant at the 0.05 level (two-tailed)

sample regarding how scientifically driven the report was found to be was 2.9 (SD = 1.0). The mean rating for how clearly written the report was found to be was 3.6 (SD = 0.98), and finally the mean rating for how acceptable the report was found to be was 2.9 (SD = 1.24).

Means for these ratings were also examined by version of the report. For completed feedback questionnaires regarding the EPFM-guided report, the mean rating for how scientifically driven it was perceived to be was 3.12 (SD = 0.96); the mean for how clearly written it was perceived to be was 3.81 (SD = 0.98); and the mean for how acceptable it was found to be was 3.38 (SD = 1.14). Feedback questionnaires regarding the unspecified constructs report yielded means of 2.62 (SD = 1.10) for how scientifically driven it was, 3.38 (SD = 0.96) for how clearly written it was, and 2.40 (SD = 1.18) for how acceptable it was. One-way analyses of variance were conducted to determine whether significant differences existed in these ratings between groups. ANOVAs for how scientifically driven the report was, in addition to how clearly the report was written, were not significant based on the version of the report, with $F(1, 30) = 1.91$, $p = 0.18$ and $F(1, 30) = 1.63$, $p = 0.21$, respectively. The one-way ANOVA for acceptability of the report and version of the report was found to be significant, however, with $F(1, 29) = 5.42$, $p < 0.027$. Subsequent analyses were conducted to control for potential covariates. When controlling for age, similar findings were observed [scientifically driven: $F(1, 30) = 1.06$, $p = 0.36$; clearly written: $F(1, 30) = 1.26$, $p = 0.30$; acceptability: $F(1, 30) = 3.82$, $p < 0.04$].

However, when controlling for number of years as a judge or number of cases involved in, the rating for acceptability between groups is no longer statistically significant [$F(1, 30)=2.68$, $p=0.09$; $F(1, 30)=2.36$, $p=0.12$]. This indicates that judges who received the EPFM-guided report found the report to be significantly more acceptable than judges who received the unspecified constructs report; however, when correcting for potential covariates with the exception of age, the differences no longer reach a statistically significant level.

In addition to these three questions regarding each report's quality, four True/False questions were included that were also meant to assess the report's quality. These items included: "Overall I felt the report was complete," "Overall I felt the report covered important factors," "Overall I clearly understood the reasoning behind the report," and "I would recommend custody evaluators write reports this way." Options to provide open-ended reasoning for respondents' answers to these questions were also provided and will be described further. For the first item, completeness of the report, 9 respondents (28%) from the total sample answered "true," while 22 (69%) answered "false." Twenty-two respondents provided reasoning behind their answer and responses included: "Too much information left out," "Not enough detail to justify the conclusions," and "Need more information from collateral sources." For the second True/False item regarding the report covering important areas, 23, or (72%) of the total sample answered "true" while 7 (22%) answered "false." Eleven (34.4%) respondents provided reasoning for their answers. Responses from participants who answered "true" include: "It was complete yet succinct, and got to the point while also attempting to be objective," and "I liked the Egregious/Promotive Factors Model." Responses from participants who answered "false" include: "Too much left out," and "Too much rumor with too little evidence." The third True/False item regarding the reasoning behind the report yielded 21 "true" responses (65.6% of the sample), and 9 "false" responses (28.1% of the sample). Seven participants provided an explanation for their responses and of these, all responded "false" to the item. These included: "Because it wasn't revealed," and "It seemed very biased." Finally, for the fourth True/False item regarding recommended custody evaluators write the way the report they received was written, 16 (50%) responded "true" and 13 (40.6%) responded "false." Seventeen participants (53.1%) provided explanation for their answers. Respondents' explanations for "true" answers included: "I liked the factors model" and "gives basic information in clear, comprehensive manner." Respondents' who answered "false" and provided explanations for their answer reported: "Needs to contain more information," "Not objective," and "Incomplete, pseudoscientific approach."

Fisher's exact chi-square analyses were conducted to determine whether significant differences between groups existed for the perceived quality of the reports received. Regarding the completeness of the report, 6 participants receiving the EPFM-guided report responded "true" and 10 reported "false," while 3 participants answered "true" and 12 participants answered "false" from the unspecified constructs report group. Two-sided, Fisher's exact chi-square analysis of completeness and version yielded nonsignificant results $\chi^2(1, N=31)=1.15$,

Table 7.3 Quality of the report by version

	EPFM UC report						
	M	SD	*M*	SD	*F*		*p*
Degree of scientifically driven	3.12	96	2.62	1.09	1.91		0.18
Degree of clarity	3.81	98	3.38	96	1.63		0.21
Degree of acceptability	3.38	1.15	2.40	1.18	5.42		0.03[a]
	EPFM		UC report		Total		Fisher's exact *p* (two-sided)
	T	*F*	*T*	*F*	*T*	*F*	
The report was complete	6	10	3	12	9	22	0.43
The report covered important areas	14	2	9	5	23	7	0.20
The report had clear rationale	14	2	7	7	21	9	0.046[a]
I would recommend evaluators write reports this way	12	4	4	9	16	13	0.03[a]

[a] Significance at the 0.05 level

$p=0.43$. Regarding whether or not the report covered important factors, 14 respondents answered "true" from the EPFM-guided report group and 9 participants answered "true" from the UC report group. The remaining respondents answered "false" (2 for the EPFM-guided report group and 5 for the UC report group). Analysis of this second item also yielded nonsignificant results $\chi^2(1, N=30)=2.25$, $p=0.20$. Regarding the third item, concerning clarity of the reasoning behind the report, 14 respondents from the EPFM-guided report group reported "true" responses while only 2 reported "false." Concerning the UC report group, seven participants responded with "true" and seven answered "false." Two-sided chi-square analysis of reasoning behind the report yielded significant findings with $\chi^2(1, N=30)=5.00$, $p=0.046$. Finally, regarding whether participants would recommend reports be written similar to the one they reviewed, 12 participants answered "true" and 4 answered "false" from the EPFM-guided report group. Of the UC report group, four participants answered "true" and nine answered "false." Two-sided chi-square analysis of writing of the report yielded significant findings with $\chi^2(1, N=29)=5.67$, $p=0.027$. Table 7.3 provides descriptive information for significant findings.

To examine whether the quality of the report was associated with judges' age, number of years as a judge, or number of cases involved in, Pearson correlations were conducted. Table 7.4 reflects that no statistically significant associations between demographic factors and rated quality of the report were observed. Statistically significant positive correlations were noted among the factors for rated quality of the report. Significant correlations are noted in Table 7.4.

Table 7.4 Correlation matrix of demographic data and quality of the report

	No. of cases involved	No. of years as judge	Age	Scientific	Clear	Acceptable
No. of cases involved						
Pearson *r*	1.00	–0.06	0.01	–0.15	–0.05	0.02
p		0.76	0.98	0.42	0.81	0.92
No. of years as a judge						
Pearson *r*	–0.06	1.00	0.43[a]	–0.10	–0.18	0.02
p	0.76		0.02	0.59	0.32	0.92
Age						
Pearson *r*	0.01	0.43[a]	1.00	0.21	0.28	0.26
p	0.98	0.02		0.25	0.13	0.17
Scientific						
Pearson *r*	–0.15	–0.10	0.21	1.00	0.58[b]	0.48[b]
p	0.42	0.59	0.25		0.00	0.01
Clear						
Pearson *r*	–0.05	–0.18	0.28	0.58[b]	1.00	0.62[b]
p	0.81	0.32	0.13	0.00		0.00
Acceptable						
Pearson *r*	0.02	0.02	0.26	0.48[b]	0.62[b]	1.00
p	0.92	0.92	0.17	0.006	0.00	

[a]Correlation is significant at the 0.05 level (two-tailed)
[b]Correlation is significant at the 0.01 level (two-tailed)

Factors Ranked as Important in Guiding Recommendations

As a part of the feedback questionnaire, judges were asked to list the five factors that most influenced their custody recommendations. Of the judges ($N=32$) who completed the questionnaire, 2 (6%) did not report any reasons that guided their decision making, 2 listed only one factor that guided their decision, 1 respondent listed two factors, 5 (15%) listed three factors, 9 (28%) listed four, and 13 (40%) listed five factors that guided their decision making. No significant differences were found regarding the number of reasons listed given the version of the report (i.e., EPFM-guided or UC report) judges received ($F=0.49$, $p=0.489$). The mean number of reasons given for judges receiving the EPFM-guided report was 3.94 (SD=1.34). The mean number of reasons given for judges receiving the unspecified constructs report was 3.56 (SD=1.67).

Responses related to reasons for recommendations were coded, and some overlap was noted between what judges receiving the EPFM-guided report listed and what was listed by judges receiving the unspecified constructs report. Responses were grouped based on similar themes yielding a total of 18 different reasons that were provided by judges. These reasons were: (1) Jane's role as the historical parent, (2) Lack of egregious or limiting factors, (3) Parenting skills, (4) Promotive factors, (5) Emotional stability of the parents, (6) Environmental stability, (7) Interparental conflict, (8) Developmental stages of the children, (9) The children's adjustment, (10) Psychological testing, (11) Parent–child relationships, (12) Father's lack of concern or poor judgment, (13) The mother is bonded more closely to children, (14) Collateral sources, (15) Recommendations of the evaluator, (16) Poor quality of the report, (17) Wishes of the children, and (18) Both parents are flawed.

Eight factors were reported as overlapping and five factors were unique to each group. Factors were determined to be overlapping by at least one respondent from both groups citing it as important. Specifically, when looking at the total sample, reasons listed as being the most important in guiding decisions of custody arrangement that were most frequently cited and were overlapping between groups included: mom as historical primary parent [frequency count = 14 (44%); EPFM-guided $N = 5$, UC report $N = 9$], lack of egregious or limiting factors [frequency count = 14 (44%); EPFM-guided $N = 7$, UC report $N = 7$], interparental conflict [frequency count = 10 (31%); EPFM-guided $N = 7$, UC report $N = 3$], children's adjustment [frequency count = 8 (25%); EPFM-guided $N = 2$, UC report $N = 6$], the parent–child relationship [frequency count = 8 (25%); EPFM-guided $N = 4$, UC report $N = 4$], environmental stability [frequency count = 6 (19%); EPFM-guided $N = 5$, UC report $N = 1$], developmental level of the children [frequency count = 5 (16%); EPFM-guided $N = 1$, UC report $N = 4$], and psychological testing [frequency count = 5 (16%); EPFM-guided $N = 1$, UC report $N = 4$].

Some differences were also noted between groups. Specifically, five reasons were uniquely cited by the judges receiving the EPFM-guided report. These included: promotive factors (frequency count = 9; 56%), parenting skills (frequency count = 6; 37%), emotional stability (frequency count = 5; 31%), collateral sources (frequency count = 1; 0.6%), and recommendations of the evaluator (frequency count = 1; 0.6%). An additional five reasons were uniquely cited by judges receiving the UC report, these included: father's poor judgment/lack of concern (frequency count = 10; 63%), mother more closely bonded to children (frequency count = 4; 25%), evaluator inconsistencies (frequency count = 1; 0.6%), wishes of the children (frequency count = 1; 0.6%), and parents are both flawed (frequency count = 1; 0.6%). Upon examining differences between groups, variation in the factors guiding decision making emerged. The eight most frequently cited factors for each group is reported in Table 7.5.

While there appeared to be overlap between groups, the rank of important factors between groups was quite different. The most frequently cited reason guiding decision making for judges who received the EPFM-guided report was the promotive factors that were discussed. This was followed by a lack of egregious factors and interpersonal conflict as the next two most frequently cited reasons. Followed by these reasons, emotional stability of the parents, environmental stability, and Jane's historical role as primary parent were all reported at the same frequency. Finally, the parent–child relationship was cited as the eighth most frequently cited decision-making factor for judges receiving the EPFM-guided report. In looking at judges' responses, based on the unspecified constructs report, the father's perceived poor judgment and lack of concern for the children was the most frequently cited factor that was reported as important in custody arrangement decision making. This was followed by Jane's historical role as the primary parent, little evidence of limiting

Table 7.5 Factors listed as most important

Version			
EPFM		UC report	
Factor	Frequency count	Factor	Frequency count
Promotive factors	9	Father's poor judgment/lack of concern	10
Lack of egregious factors	7	Jane as primary parent	9
Interparental conflict	7	No evidence of limiting factors	7
Parenting skills	6	Children's adjustment	6
Emotional stability	5	Ages/developmental stages of the children	4
Environmental stability	5	Psychological testing	4
Jane as primary parent	5	Parent–child relationship	4
Parent–child relationship	4	Interparental conflict	3

factors, the children's adjustment, the ages and stages of the children, psychological testing, the parent–child relationship, and finally interparental conflict.

Analyses were conducted to examine any potential significant relationship between the custody decisions judges made and reasons reported by judges that influenced these decisions. These cross-tabulated frequency tests were found to be nonsignificant [recommendation × first reason = $\chi^2(10, N=32)=13.23$, $p=0.21$; recommendation × second reason = $\chi^2(10, N=32)=13.03$, $p=0.22$; recommendation × third reason = $\chi^2(11, N=32)=18.12$, $p=0.11$; recommendation × fourth reason = $\chi^2(9, N=32)=11.82$, $p=0.22$; recommendation × fifth reason = $\chi^2(9, N=32)=14.0$, $p=0.12$]. This indicates that judges who ordered joint custody, judges who ordered custody to the mother with every other weekend with the father, judges who ordered sole custody to the mother, and judges who did not make recommendations did not differ significantly in the reasons reported that influenced these decisions.

Custody Recommendations

Analyses were conducted to determine whether the version of the report received by judges was associated with significant differences in the resulting recommendations for custody arrangements. Open-ended responses for custody arrangements were coded and resulted in four different responses: (1) joint custody with equal/close to equal (i.e., 30–40%) time with the father, but primary home with the mother; (2) sole custody to the mother, with some visitation with the father (every other weekend, with overnights); (3) sole custody to the mother with no overnights to the father, visitation with the children one evening during the week and weekend day; and (4) I would not make recommendations based on this evaluation. It should be noted that the EPFM-guided report recommended that the primary home be with the mother and a 66%/33% split, with the father having visitation with the children Thursdays–Tuesdays every other week. The unspecified constructs model report recommended that sole custody be awarded to the mother with dinner one weekday per week and every other Saturday with the father and no overnights.

Cross-tabulated frequencies were conducted to statistically examine whether a difference in custody recommendations existed between judges who reviewed either the EPFM-guided report or the unspecified constructs report and statistically significant differences were found, $\chi^2(3,\ N=32)=15.851,\ p=0.001$. Table 7.6 reports the frequencies of recommendations made by version of the report that was reviewed, and Fig. 7.1 reports these data in bar chart form.

Of the judges who received the EPFM-guided report that recommended joint or a shared parenting custody arrangement, 87.5% ($N=14$) ultimately made this decision as well. Of the remaining two judges who received the EPFM-guided report, one reported that the father should receive less time than recommended (every other

Table 7.6 Recommendation vs. version crosstabulation

	Version		
	EPFM	UC	Total
Recommendation			
Shared/joint	14	3	17
Primary w/mother, e.o. weekend w/father	1	9	10
Sole w/mother	0	2	2
Wouldn't make recs.	1	2	3
Total	16	16	32

$\chi^2(3, N=32)=15.851, p=0.001$

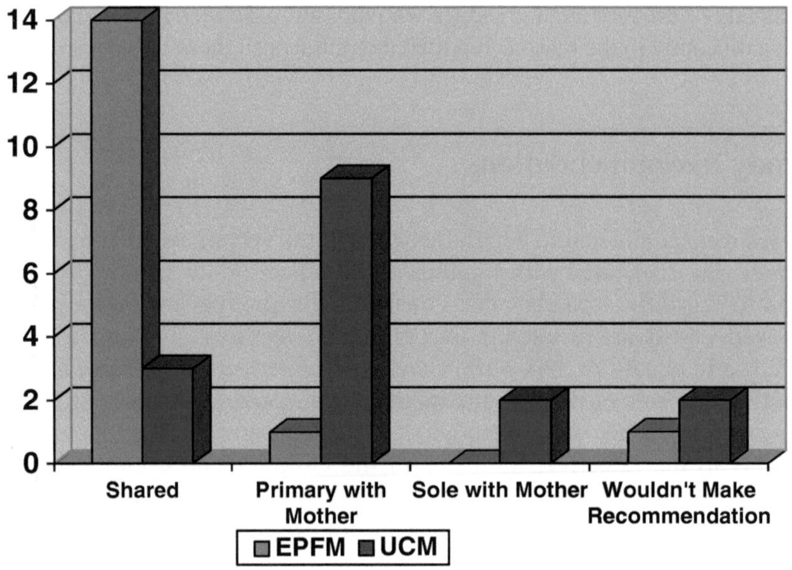

Fig. 7.1 Custody outcomes from judges, by version of report

weekend) and the other reported that they would not be able to make a custody decision based on the information provided. Of the judges who received the unspecified constructs report that recommended sole custody to the mother, 56.2% ($N=9$) recommended that the mother be given primary custody, with the father receiving overnight visitation every other weekend. Of this sample, only two judges recommended sole custody to the mother, which was in line with what the report recommended. In addition, only three judges decided that the father should receive dramatically more time with his children (including more of a joint/shared parenting or 60/40 type of custody arrangement) than the unspecified constructs report recommended. The final two judges who received the unspecified constructs report declared that they would not make recommendations based on the evaluation report they received. Overall, judges who reviewed the EPFM-guided report were more likely to adopt the recommendations of the evaluator than judges who reviewed the unspecified constructs report. In addition, judges who reviewed the unspecified constructs report were more likely to recommend more time with the father than the evaluator, however, not as much so as to recommend joint custody and shared parenting.

To determine whether custody recommendations differed by judges' gender, cross-tabulated frequencies were conducted. Results of Fisher's exact chi-square analyses yielded nonsignificant findings [$\chi^2(3, N=32)=1.12, p=0.77$]. Specifically, of the male judge respondents ($N=19$), 11 (58%) recommended shared/joint custody, 6 (32%) recommended primary custody with the mother with overnights and alternating weekends with the father, 1 recommended sole custody with the mother, and 1 reported that he would not be able to make a recommendation based on the report he received. Of the female judge respondents ($N=11$), six (55%) recommended shared/joint custody, four (36%) recommended primary custody with the mother with overnights and alternating weekends with the father, one recommended sole custody with the mother, and two reported that she would not be able to make recommendations based on the report received.

Finally, analyses were conducted to determine whether custody recommendations differed by judges' reported age, number of years as a judge, and number of cases. These findings were nonsignificant as well. Table 7.7 provides information regarding these data.

Table 7.7 Recommendations by age, number of years as a judge, and number of cases presided over

	Joint/ shared	Primary w/mom	Sole w/mom	Wouldn't make recommendation	*F*	*p*
Judge age						
M	54.56	56.10	59.00	54.00	0.35	0.79
SD	7.65	5.61	1.41	6.23		
No. of years as a Judge						
M	10.65	10.30	2.00	12.00	1.02	0.40
SD	7.43	5.79	1.41	9.17		
No. of cases presided over						
M	528.50	256.67	1,150.00	600.00	0.65	0.59
SD	1,048.10	313.16	1,202.08	360.55		

M mean, *SD* standard deviation

Additional Feedback Regarding the Report

Judges had the opportunity to respond to open-ended questions regarding what they liked, did not like, what they believed would improve the report, what they thought was unnecessarily included in the report, and final comments about the report. Responses to open-ended questions were coded and examined by version of the report received.

What Was Liked About the Report

Among judges who received the EPFM-guided report, 13 (81%) responded to the open-ended question regarding things that they liked. Ten judges (63%) reported that they liked the Egregious/Promotive Factors Model, one judge reported that he liked the clarity of the model, one judge reported that he liked the references listed at the end, and one judge reported that he felt the report was thorough from a psychological point of view. Ten judges (63%) who received the unspecified constructs report responded to the open-ended question regarding what they liked about the report they received. Of these, four judges (25%) reported that they liked the clarity of the model, two judges reported that they felt the description of testing outcomes was reported fairly completely, one judge reported that he liked the brevity of the report, one reported that he liked that the report came to a conclusion, and two judges reported that they liked nothing about the report.

What Was Not Liked About the Report

Eleven of the 16 judges (69%) who received the EPFM report provided information regarding what they did not like about the report. Of these 11, ten (63%) reported that they thought not enough background information was provided in the report. The remaining judge reported that he felt the report did not focus enough on the children. Of the 16 judges who received the unspecified constructs report, 14 (88%) provided responses regarding things that they did not like. Eight judges (50%) reported that they felt the report was not helpful, included conclusory statements or seemed biased. The other six judges provided different responses for things they did not like, including: counseling for the younger child was not recommended, it was not clear regarding "he said/she said" statements, it did not acknowledge limitations of the psychological tests used, not enough background information was provided, and two judges felt that the report was dismissive of Jane's reported alcohol use.

What Could Improve the Report

Nine judges (56%) who received the EPFM report provided responses to an open-ended question regarding what would improve the report. Six (37%) of these respondents reported that they would have liked to have read more background information. Of the three remaining judges, one reported that he would have wanted to have seen identification of the collateral sources, one would have wanted the term "unsubstantiated" to "not applicable," and one reported that they would have wanted the same factors examined for each parent. Eleven judges (69%) who received the unspecified constructs report provided responses on how to improve the report. Of these 11 judges, 6 reported that they would have liked more background information, 3 would have liked to have seen how the conclusions were arrived at, 1 would have liked to have seen fewer legal conclusions and more information about the parents' personalities, and finally one judge reported that he felt the report should have "stuck to the facts more and drawn conclusions from there."

What Was Unnecessary About the Report

Of the 16 judges who received the EPFM report, only 3 provided responses to the open-ended question about what was unnecessary about the report. Of these 3, two judges reported that the reference cited in the text was unnecessary and should just be included at the end. The remaining judge reported that "obvious research statements" were unnecessary. Of the 16 judges who received the unspecified constructs report, 7 (44%) provided responses to the open-ended question about what was unnecessary about the report. Five of these judges reported that they felt the evaluator's statement that the case was one of his worst was unnecessary and the remaining two judges reported that the personal conclusions of the writer were unnecessary.

Final Comments About the Report

Finally, judges were given the opportunity to provide final comments about the report. Of the 16 judges who received the EPFM, 9 (56%) provided responses to the final comments section. Four judges reported that they liked the Egregious/Promotive Factors Model, one reported that it was very "fact-based and would be very capable of defending in court," another reported it was "much better than a lot of the stuff I usually get," and another judge reported that they liked the recommendation of coparenting counseling. Finally, one judge reported that the report focused too much on "buzzwords" and did not look at the practicalities, and another judge reported that he would have liked to have seen more about the collaterals. Six judges (37%)

who received the unspecified constructs report provided final comments regarding the report they received. Of these six judges, two reported that the report had little "true value." One judge reported that the report would not be helpful and would "probably be disregarded in my analysis." Another judge stated, "I thought it was well-written and gave me adequate information to assist in my recommendation." An additional judge stated that it is "good to have a clear report but it should provide factual information." Finally, a judge reported, "my reaction to this report is much like ones I see: too much 'soft science' and unsubstantiated opinion."

Chapter 8
Discussion of the Preliminary Validation Study's Results

This study's first aim was to conduct a thorough literature review to determine what empirically supported constructs or factors have been shown to predict better or poorer outcomes in children for the purpose of guiding child custody evaluations. Review of the literature yielded consistent findings across five domains that predicted poorer outcomes in children: a poor parent–child relationship, poor parenting skills, environmental instability, parent mental health problems, and excessive interparental conflict (O'Donohue, Beitz, & Cummings, 2007). Several of these factors overlap with state statutes that provide important areas to assess in child custody cases. In addition, these factors are consistent with poorer adjustment in children post-divorce. In addition to egregious factors, a number of promotive factors have been consistently reported in the literature as predictive of positive outcomes in children. Six factors that were repeatedly reported in research include: positive parenting, parental school involvement, promotion of interpersonal development, promotion of mental health, promotion of community involvement, and effective coparenting. The 11 factors that were identified were not intended to be an exhaustive list of areas that might be important to assess; there are potentially others that are specific to cases that should also be included. The field is unclear about what areas are important to assess, and state statutes are inconsistent regarding what important areas should be covered in custody cases. This study looked at several decades of longitudinal research, in addition to research specific to the context of divorce, to obtain factors that are consistently demonstrated as being important to the positive development of children. In looking at the existing, ambiguous guidelines currently available to child custody evaluators (e.g., APA, 1994; American Psychiatric Association Task Force on Clinical Assessment in Child Custody, 1988), it is anticipated that knowledge about the importance of these factors will provide an important contribution to the body of research related to child custody evaluations.

Previous studies have demonstrated that child custody evaluators have little guidance in how to conduct a valid child custody evaluation. This study's second aim was to propose a preliminary model for conducting child custody evaluations that is based on empirical evidence. Based on the literature predicting poorer and

L.W. Tolle and W.T. O'Donohue, *Improving the Quality of Child Custody Evaluations*, DOI 10.1007/978-1-4614-3405-4_8, © Springer Science+Business Media, LLC 2012

positive outcomes in children, the Egregious/Promotive Factors Model (EPFM) was created. In order to ensure that these factors can be reliably and validly assessed, a thorough review of existing psychological assessments was conducted and measures with good psychometric properties that assess the factors of the EPFM were provided. Several of these, in particular those that are suggested for assessment of egregious factors, are widely used measures and considered the "gold standard" for assessing their respective domains. While these measures were not created to be used in the child custody context, they do assess domains that are important in this context. Some measures for the promotive factors are relatively new measures and need further research to provide additional evidence supporting their psychometric properties. In addition to suggesting evaluation measures that assess these constructs, a structured assessment guide was developed that was adapted from existing predictive risk assessments for violence. The structured assessment of the EPFM will help child custody evaluators to rule in or out both egregious and promotive factors, and determine the level of risk for any egregious factor as well as the presence or absence of promotive factors. It is anticipated that the EPFM, with its empirically supported factors and suggested evaluation measures, will provide greatly needed guidelines for child custody evaluators and move the science of child custody evaluations forward. Additional research is needed to show reliability of this model and eventually, and potentially most importantly, to show its predictive validity.

The third aim of this study was to preliminarily assess what family court judges base their decision making on in terms of child custody placements. Specifically, this study had three hypotheses. The first hypothesis was that judges provided with the EPFM-guided report will find it more empirically driven, will understand the rationale behind its recommendations more, and will overall be more satisfied with this report than judges who were provided with the unspecified constructs report. In some ways, this hypothesis was supported. Judges who reviewed the EPFM-guided report found it to be: (1) significantly more acceptable; (2) significantly more clear in its rationale; (3) and they were significantly more likely to recommend evaluators write their reports they way the EPFM-guided report was written than judges who reviewed the unspecified constructs report. Other measures regarding the EPFM report in contrast to the unspecified constructs report were found to be statistically nonsignificant. Judges who reviewed the EPFM reported positive things that they liked about the report and final comments that reflected its positive receipt. Discussion regarding these findings is provided in addition to a discussion of the study's limitations, implications, and areas for future research.

The second hypothesis questioned whether judges provided with the EPFM-guided report will find these factors most important in determining their ultimate decision regarding custody. This hypothesis was also supported. Judges provided with the EPFM-guided report ranked promotive factors, the lack of egregious factors, interparental conflict, parenting skills, emotional stability, environmental stability, the mother's role as the primary parent, and the parent–child relationship as being the most frequently cited reasons guiding their decision making. With the exception of the mother's role as primary parent, the rest of these factors are part of the EPFM, reflecting that judges were influenced by this model, which is guided by empirical evidence that predicts poorer or positive outcomes in children. A difference was noted regarding the factors that judges receiving the unspecified constructs report cited as reasons guiding their decision making. Specifically, these judges cited problems the father was having, the mother's role as primary parent, no evidence of limiting factors, the children's adjustment, the ages and developmental stages of the children, psychological testing, the parent–child relationship, and parental conflict most frequently in guiding decisions regarding custody.

Finally, the third hypothesis questioned whether judges provided with an EPFM-guided report will follow the recommendations provided by the report to make their custody decisions, thereby making decisions that are supported by research predicting child outcomes. This hypothesis was supported and judges provided with the EPFM-guided report made statistically significant (at the 0.05 level) different custody decisions than judges provided with the unspecified constructs report. Eighty-seven percent of the judges provided with the EPFM-guided report adopted the recommendations of the report, whereas judges provided with the unspecified constructs report had much more variability in their custody decisions. The possible reasons behind these results are examined later in this dissertation.

Differences in Custody Recommendations Relative to the Report Version

The EPFM-guided report and the unspecified constructs report differed in the recommendations they provided. The EPFM-guided report recommended joint custody, with the mother having the primary home for the children, but the father having Thursdays to Tuesday evenings every other week. The unspecified constructs report recommended sole custody to Jane and one evening during the week and every other Saturday with the father with no overnights. The EPFM-guided report provided rationale for these recommendations based on empirical literature. The unspecified constructs report used some projective testing and other psychological testing in addition to clinical judgment to base recommendations on. The custody decisions made by judges who reviewed the EPFM-guided report and custody decisions made by judges who reviewed the unspecified constructs report were different at a statistically significant level. When asked to provide a decision regarding custody arrangements for the family based on the report judges had reviewed, 14 of the 16 judges, or 87.5%, who reviewed the EPFM-guided report adopted the recommendations of the evaluator. This is higher than the 75% of judges who were found to agree with recommendations provided by court personnel in previous studies (Kunin, Ebbesen, & Konecni, 1992). Of the remaining two judges, one recommended sole custody to the mother, and the other reported that he would not make a decision based on the report. Judges who received the EPFM-guided report in general more clearly understood the rationale behind the report, found the report to be highly acceptable, liked the format of the report, and found the promotive factors, in addition to the egregious factors, to be highly influential in their decision making. Though not found to be significant at the statistical level, ratings for the EPFM-guided report were higher than ratings for the unspecified constructs report across all items. This provides a good base of support for the utility of the EPFM as an empirically driven model to guide custody evaluations that is liked by judges and has been found to influence their decision making regarding child custody.

Additional findings from judges who completed feedback questionnaires regarding the unspecified constructs report are discussed as well. Regarding the custody decisions reported by judges who reviewed the unspecified constructs report, only two judges adopted completely the recommendations set forth by the unspecified constructs report. Fifty-six percent of the judges who reviewed the unspecified constructs report modified the time to include one overnight with the father every other weekend. This is not a dramatic change from the recommendations provided, in that the father would have received 1 day every other weekend, the overnight would have added some additional time to this. Three judges decided to provide substantially more time with the father than the report recommended (more of a split or joint custody arrangement) and two judges reported that they would not make a decision based on the report received. Regarding their ratings of factors that influenced decision making, judges who reviewed the unspecified constructs report appeared to have been swayed by the biasing language used in the report. Examples of this were seen by the top two most frequently cited reasons provided by judges who received the unspecified constructs report—negative things about the father and the mother being the historical primary parent. In the report regarding this factor, the evaluator reports that both parents assert to being the primary parent, but the evaluator reports that it is "clearly" the mother who has been the primary parent, without providing evidence to support this. These findings are interesting given that judges who reviewed the unspecified constructs report reported lower ratings for how scientifically driven they found the report to be, as well as lower ratings for how acceptable they found the report to be. Additionally, judges who reviewed this report were more likely to find it incomplete, have an unclear rationale, and would not recommend evaluators write reports this way.

Despite these negative findings, judges still made custody decisions based on the report received and ranked things that guided this decision from the report. Overall, it appears that judges receiving the EPFM-guided report were more likely to adopt the recommendations of the evaluator than judges receiving the unspecified constructs report. Additionally, judges who reviewed the unspecified constructs report and did not agree with the recommendations completely, largely modified them only slightly and did not deviate too far from them.

Limitations

There were several limitations to this study, one of which was the low response rate from the family court judges. Previous research using survey methodology with family court judges have also yielded low response rates (Reidy, Silver, & Carlson,

1989; Stamps, Kunen, & Rock-Faucheux, 1997). To account for this, attempts were made to distribute a greater number of questionnaire packets to potential participants. In addition, study materials were consciously shortened to attempt to decrease the burden on requiring the participants to invest a lot of time in completing the measures. A total of 422 questionnaire packets were distributed, and 38 were returned, which is a 9% response rate. Of these 38, 32 were completed and 6 were returned blank. It is unknown how many potential participants were sent email announcements from the National Council for Juvenile and Family Court Judges. Over 2,000 individuals make up its membership, which would be the maximum number reached; however, it is unknown how closely these emails are read. Ultimately, it is unknown what accounted for this especially low response rate.

One very fortunate finding from the returned and completed questionnaires was the equal distribution of responses from each version of the report (16 in both groups). While the return of one report's questionnaire over another might provide some insight as to the low response rate, the fact that both were returned at an equal rate makes the version received a less likely reason. The main limitation of having a low sample size is the difficulty with which generalizations can be made from this analysis to a larger population. It is possible that the study did not have enough statistical power to detect other meaningful differences. Despite the low statistical power, positive trends were nonetheless noted. Specifically, report measures of degree of clarity and degree of scientifically driven were rated higher for the EPFM-guided report than for the unspecified constructs report. In addition, many more judges who received the EPFM-guided report thought that it covered important areas than judges who received the unspecified constructs report; however, this did not reach statistical significance. It is possible that these did not reach statistical significance because of the low statistical power, though it is important to note these trends. However, due to the low number of participants, it is not possible to make strong conclusions from these data.

An additional limitation of this study was initially an attempt to decrease the time burden on judges reviewing the custody evaluation report and completing the subsequent feedback questionnaire. Frequently, extensive background information is provided in child custody reports regarding interviews with the parents, interviews with the child, interviews with collateral sources, observations from the home environment, a time log of how much time was spent doing what and number of times spent with each parent for what given amount of time, and results from psychological testing. To increase participation through shortening the reports, and because information regarding these areas in addition to the rationale behind the provided recommendations was what was important to stress and distinguish between reports, much of the background information was cut out. A disclaimer was provided at the top of each report in bold that these sections were taken out specifically to cut down on reading time; however, it should be assumed that all of these were conducted. In addition, these are alluded to in both reports as being conducted. Given the number of judges who reported that they felt too much information was left out, it is possible that these reports were shortened too much. One judge, however, noted the time it took her to complete the review of the report and the questionnaire and made a note in the margin of her feedback questionnaire that it took longer than was estimated in the information sheet. Condensing pertinent information into succinct, yet still thorough reports proved to be a challenge, and it is unknown how this affected responses to additional questions on the feedback questionnaire. Future studies testing this model may need to extend the length of reports and provide some sort of compensation for judges reviewing it.

Finally, because this study used a between-subjects design, it did not provide an opportunity for judges to review both reports and with the knowledge of the content provided in each version, to decide which one was superior. Future research should include within-subjects designs to further assess this. In addition, because the reports differed not only in their writing styles and rationales but also in the recommendations that were ultimately made, this presents a confound in that it is not known for certain why judges adopted the recommendations of the evaluator (i.e., because the evaluator made a recommendation for joint custody, or because of the EPFM). Future research should keep recommendations across versions the same to further explore what influences judges who receive the EPFM-guided report or an unspecified constructs report.

Implications

The finding that judges who received the unspecified constructs report were not found to deviate far from the recommendations of the evaluator may be consistent with extant literature that suggests that custody cases are stressful for judges and outside the realm of their profession. Judges may feel hesitant to completely go against the recommendations of mental health professionals who are thought of as being natural professionals in conducting custody evaluations with the Best Interest of the Child criteria in mind (Kushner, 2006). This may also be consistent with the notion that psychologists act as "consultants" to the court and educate judges about the complexities involved in the child custody evaluation (Stahl, 1994). Additionally, it has been reported that "judges are more likely to base decisions on sound behavioral science disciplines, especially developmental psychology. The findings of these disciplines go beyond common sense and are useful antidotes to personal prejudices that easily cloud decisions in this area" (Galatzer-Levy & Kraus, 1999, p. 442). These notions perpetuate the idea that all mental health professionals practicing in this area, conducting child custody evaluations, are using sound behavioral science practices to guide their decision making. While many perhaps do, it is clear that there has not been a consistent way in which this is done, and more importantly, judges and the court are not aware of and may not be exposed to these professionals to be able to tell them apart from those who rely on clinical judgment.

In addition, reports that rely on clinical judgment are still used to guide decision making and even if judges do not find those reports helpful, may still be biased by them, or be cautious to deviate far from them. It is positive that several of the judges who received the unspecified constructs report ordered more time with the father than the evaluator had recommended, which is more in line with what would be associated with better outcomes for the children and therefore consistent with the Best Interest of the Child. It is impossible to know what difference giving the father one overnight every other weekend as opposed to 1 day every other weekend would have on child outcomes. Given the methodological problems in researching outcomes for children of divorced homes, there are numerous barriers to conducting this type of research. For example, children cannot ethically be randomly selected to different custody arrangements and other methods of information gathering such as longitudinal research, archival research, or retrospective research cannot easily control for variables. An additional aspect of child custody decisions that might mitigate poor recommendations would be to make predictions for short-term adjustment and continually monitor outcomes and adjust accordingly. For example, if a factor is identified that may negatively impact a child (i.e., unemployment or little parenting experience), custody arrangement could be established and once this factor is remediated by securing a job or by passing a parenting skills class, this arrangement could be revisited and altered.

The finding that judges who reviewed the unspecified constructs report had more variability in their custody decisions than judges who reviewed the EPFM-guided report has important implications. Judges who reviewed the EPFM-guided report were more likely to adopt the recommendations of the evaluator, and felt more positively about this report than judges who received the unspecified constructs report. The EPFM reduces variability by focusing on 11 specific factors that have been shown to predict child outcomes. The structured assessment for the EPFM provides a framework for determining the presence of the salient egregious and promotive factors as well as assigning level of risk to the egregious factors.

Results from the judges' feedback forms indicate that the quality of the report and the clear rationale supporting the recommendations allowed judges who received the EPFM-guided report to adopt the recommendations of the evaluator. The much higher rate of agreement among judges who received the EPFM-guided report would indicate that this sort of model would go a long way toward establishing uniform guidelines for child custody evaluators. It should be pointed out that the decision of judges responding did not appear to significantly differ by state, suggesting that differing state statutes did not appear to impact decisions. As previously discussed, the heterogeneity inherent in the differing state guidelines related to child custody evaluations could be problematic in ensuring uniformity of evaluations across states. For the sample included in this study, the EPFM appears to have potential utility for evaluators across the country.

An additional interesting finding from this study was the vast degree of variability among the judges' responses. This variability was observed both between and within the two groups and across all items included in the feedback form. Judges varied in the custody decisions that they made as well as the variables that were ranked which were reported to influence these decisions. In addition, a wide variety of responses were noted in the open-ended questions on the feedback form. Broadest variability from the final comments about the report are characterized by responses such as, "The report was very fact-based and would be very capable of defending in court" and "My reaction to this report is much like the ones I see: too much 'soft science' and unsubstantiated opinion." Judges in both groups varied in their responses related to what was liked, not liked, what was unnecessary, and what could improve the report. In examining the results of this small study, inter-rater reliability of judges was not strong and judges' responses were highly individualized. Based on these findings, it is easy to see why custody decisions can be so variable.

In keeping with the current recognition of the importance of openness and transparency, the EPFM provides a template that allows for a clear basis upon which parents involved in a child custody evaluation will be assessed. All parties involved in a child custody evaluation process (from parents, attorneys, mental health professionals, professional collateral sources, to family court judges) benefit from this transparency. By clearly explicating the important factors that parents are being assessed on and making these factors known at the outset of the evaluation, parents have the opportunity to be involved in the process and respond to information related to risk or egregious factors. The accountability of evaluation outcomes and the mental health professionals conducting these evaluations is greatly enhanced by basing the outcomes on measurable variables as opposed to the evaluator's clinical judgment. One important consideration of utilizing the EPFM in future custody practices is the cost of custody evaluations. This model attempts to cut down on time spent assessing factors unnecessarily by utilizing simple screening tools. Much of the cost of evaluations can be the time spent testing. One would not advocate for the use of extensive testing unless it is warranted. By focusing on areas of concern, the potential for time spent on less important areas is minimized. It is important to examine other potential ways to make quality, evidence-based custody evaluations more efficient and thus less costly for the parents involved.

Future Directions

Findings from this study which indicate preliminary support for the utility of the EPFM are encouraging. Additional research should continue to develop this model and apply it to broader applications. It is possible that factors should be added or subtracted to improve the EPFM's breadth. For example, including a history of domestic violence or criminal history in general as a separate and distinct factor from interparental conflict may add to its completeness. A number of state statutes regarding the best interest of the child include these as separate factors to consider and it may be an improvement to the EPFM to follow this.

As previously mentioned, within-subject studies that would allow for the direct comparison of the EPFM with an unspecified constructs model would be an important next step in evaluating the EPFM's utility. Future research should more tightly control variables including keeping recommendations the same, as well as extending the length of the report and providing incentive for judges to participate (including monetary compensation for participation). In addition to testing the EPFM further with family court judges, it may be useful to test it with divorce attorneys to gain their perspective. In addition, research examining the psychometric properties including the reliability and validity of the EPFM and its structured assessment should be conducted. Specifically important to the EPFM would be further research demonstrating that it has high inter-rater reliability as well as establishing its construct and predictive validity. In order to further assess the validity of the EPFM, longitudinal and cross-sectional studies using the EPFM, assessing children's outcomes along the egregious and promotive factors will provide additional evidence supporting the construct and predictive validity of the model. If this model is determined through future research to be of clinical utility, dissemination and training of evaluators in this model would finally be an important contribution to science behind child custody evaluation practices.

Conclusions

In conclusion, this study provided preliminary support for the EPFM as a guideline for conducting child custody evaluations. The EPFM was developed based on empirical evidence that has been shown to predict outcomes in children. It suggests assessments that may assist in measuring evidence of egregious and promotive factors in families to assist in making custody recommendations that are consistent with the Best Interests of the Child. Overall, judges who received the EPFM-guided report found it to have a clear rationale, to be acceptable, and reported that they would want custody evaluators to write reports in the same way. Furthermore, judges who received the EPFM-guided report reviewed it more positively than judges who received the unspecified constructs report across all areas of the report, even though not all of these domains reached statistical significance. Judges who received the EPFM-guided report cited the egregious and promotive factors as being influential in their custody decision, and a high percentage of judges adopted the recommendations of the evaluator. In total, support was found for the three hypotheses of this study. Based on these favorable outcomes, additional research to further refine and develop the EPFM is warranted.

Appendix A
Best Interest of the Child by State Laws

Alabama

The court shall in every case consider joint custody but may award any form of custody which is determined to be in the best interest of the child. In determining whether joint custody is in the best interest of the child, the court shall consider the same factors considered in awarding sole legal and physical custody and all of the following factors: (1) the agreement or lack of agreement of the parents on joint custody. (2) The past and present ability of the parents to cooperate with each other and make decisions jointly. (3) The ability of the parents to encourage the sharing of love, affection, and contact between the child and the other parent. (4) Any history of or potential for child abuse, spouse abuse, or kidnapping. (5) The geographic proximity of the parents to each other as this relates to the practical considerations of joint physical custody. (Based on Alabama State Divorce Code – Chapter 3, Sections 30-3-150 and 30-3-152.)

Alaska

In Alaska, the court shall consider the following when making a custody decision:

(a) The physical, emotional, mental, religious, and social needs of the child.
(b) The capability and desire of each parent to meet these needs.
(c) The child's wishes if the child is of sufficient age and capacity to form a preference.
(d) The relationship each child has with each parent.
(e) The length of time the child has lived in a stable, satisfactory environment and the desirability of maintaining continuity.
(f) The willingness and ability of each parent to facilitate and encourage a close and continuing relationship between the other parent and the child, except that

L.W. Tolle and W.T. O'Donohue, *Improving the Quality of Child Custody Evaluations*, DOI 10.1007/978-1-4614-3405-4, © Springer Science+Business Media, LLC 2012 the court may not consider this willingness and ability if one parent shows that the other parent has sexually assaulted or engaged in domestic violence against the parent or a child, and that a continuing relationship with the other parent will endanger the health or safety of either the parent or the child.

(g) Any evidence of domestic violence or abuse.

(h) Evidence that substance abuse by either parent or other members of the household directly affects the emotional or physical well-being of the child.

(i) Other factors that the court considers pertinent. (Alaska Dissolution Statutes – Sections: 25-24-150 and 25.24.090.)

In Alaska, as with all other states, the court will always be looking out for the best interests of the children. What you want or your spouse wants is not really relevant until the court says it is. Many parents go to custody hearings not realizing that they must portray themselves as the best custodial parent rather pleading to the court that they simply deserve the children. The court would much prefer the parents to decide who should have custody, but if they can't, the court will do it for them.

Arizona

25-403. Custody; best interests of child

A. The court shall determine custody, either originally or on petition for modification, in accordance with the best interests of the child. The court shall consider all relevant factors, including:

1. The wishes of the child's parent or parents as to custody.
2. The wishes of the child as to the custodian.
3. The interaction and interrelationship of the child with the child's parent or parents, the child's siblings and any other person who may significantly affect the child's best interest.
4. The child's adjustment to home, school, and community.
5. The mental and physical health of all individuals involved.
6. Which parent is more likely to allow the child frequent and meaningful continuing contact with the other parent.
7. Whether one parent, both parents, or neither parent has provided primary care of the child.
8. The nature and extent of coercion or duress used by a parent in obtaining an agreement regarding custody.
9. Whether a parent has complied with chapter 3, article 5 of this title.
10. Whether either parent was convicted of an act of false reporting of child abuse or neglect under section 13-2907.02.

B. In a contested custody case, the court shall make specific findings on the record about all relevant factors and the reasons for which the decision is in the best interests of the child.

25-403.01. Sole and joint custody

A. In awarding child custody, the court may order sole custody or joint custody. This section does not create a presumption in favor of one custody arrangement over another. The court in determining custody shall not prefer a parent as custodian because of that parent's sex.
B. The court may issue an order for joint custody over the objection of one of the parents if the court makes specific written findings of why the order is in the child's best interests. In determining whether joint custody is in the child's best interests, the court shall consider the factors prescribed in section 25-403, subsection A and all of the following:

   1. The agreement or lack of an agreement by the parents regarding joint custody.
   2. Whether a parent's lack of agreement is unreasonable or is influenced by an issue not related to the best interests of the child.
   3. The past, present, and future abilities of the parents to cooperate in decision-making about the child to the extent required by the order of joint custody.
   4. Whether the joint custody arrangement is logistically possible.

C. The court may issue an order for joint custody of a child if both parents agree and submit a written parenting plan and the court finds such an order is in the best interests of the child. The court may order joint legal custody without ordering joint physical custody.

25-403.02. Parenting plans

A. Before an award is made granting joint custody, the parents shall submit a proposed parenting plan that includes at least the following:

   1. Each parent's rights and responsibilities for the personal care of the child and for decisions in areas such as education, health care, and religious training.
   2. A schedule of the physical residence of the child, including holidays and school vacations.
   3. A procedure by which proposed changes, disputes, and alleged breaches may be mediated or resolved, which may include the use of conciliation services or private counseling.
   4. A procedure for periodic review of the plan's terms by the parents.
   5. A statement that the parties understand that joint custody does not necessarily mean equal parenting time.

B. If the parents are unable to agree on any element to be included in a parenting plan, the court shall determine that element. The court may determine other factors that are necessary to promote and protect the emotional and physical health of the child.

Arkansas

In Arkansas, the court will act in the best interest of the children and will give equal consideration to both the mother and the father when making a custody decision.

The court may consider the preferences of the child if the child is of a sufficient age and capacity to reason, regardless of chronological age; the past and future roles of the parents; and past domestic violence.(Arkansas Code – Title 9 – Chapters: 13–101.)

In Arkansas, as with all other states, the court will always be looking out for the best interests of the children. What you want or your spouse wants is not really relevant until the court says it is. Many parents go to custody hearings not realizing that they must portray themselves as the best custodial parent rather pleading to the court that they simply deserve the children. The court would much prefer the parents to decide who should have custody, but if they can't, the court will do it for them.

California

In California, the court shall consider the following when making a custody decision:

1. The health, safety, and welfare of the child.
2. Any history of abuse by one parent or any other person seeking custody against any of the following: (a) any child to whom he or she is related by blood or affinity or with whom he or she has had a caretaking relationship, no matter how temporary. (b) The other parent. (c) A parent, current spouse, or cohabitant, of the parent or person seeking custody, or a person with whom the parent or person seeking custody has a dating or engagement relationship.
3. The nature and amount of contact with both parents.
4. The habitual or continual illegal use of controlled substances or habitual or continual abuse of alcohol by either parent. (California Code – Sections: 3011, 3020, 3024, 3040, and 3042.)

In California, as with all other states, the court will always be looking out for the best interests of the children. What you want or your spouse wants is not really relevant until the court says it is. Many parents go to custody hearings not realizing that they must portray themselves as the best custodial parent rather pleading to the court that they simply deserve the children. The court would much prefer the parents to decide who should have custody, but if they can't, the court will do it for them.

Colorado

The court, upon the motion of either party or upon its own motion, may make provisions for custody and parenting time that the court finds are in the child's best interests In determining the best interests of the child for purposes of custody and parenting time, the court shall consider all relevant factors, including: (a) the wishes of the child's parents as to parenting time; (b) the wishes of the child if he or she is sufficiently mature to express reasoned and independent preferences as to the parenting time schedule; (c) the interaction and interrelationship of the child with his or her parents, his or her siblings, and any other person who may significantly affect the child's best interests; (d) the child's adjustment to his or her home, school, and community; (c) the mental and physical health of all individuals involved, except that a disability alone shall not be a basis to deny or restrict parenting time; (f) the ability of the parties to encourage the sharing of love, affection, and contact between the child and the other party; (g) whether the past pattern of involvement of the parties with the child reflects a system of values, time commitment, and mutual support; (h) the physical proximity of the parties to each other as this relates to the practical considerations of parenting time; (i) whether one of the parties has been a perpetrator of child abuse or neglect under section 18-6-401, C.R.S., or under the law of any state, which factor shall be supported by credible evidence; (j) whether one of the parties has been a perpetrator of spouse abuse as defined in subsection (4) of this section, which factor shall be supported by credible evidence; (k) the ability of each party to place the needs of the child ahead of his or her own needs. (Colorado Statutes – Article 10 – Sections: 14-20-123, 14-20-124, and 14-20-129.)

Connecticut

In making or modifying any order with respect to custody or visitation, the court shall (1) be guided by the best interests of the child, giving consideration to the wishes of the child if the child is of sufficient age and capable of forming an intelligent preference, provided in making the initial order the court may take into consideration the causes for dissolution of the marriage or legal separation if such causes are relevant in a determination of the best interests of the child, and (2) consider whether the party satisfactorily completed participation in a parenting education program established pursuant to section 46b-69b.There shall be a presumption, affecting the burden of proof, that joint custody is in the best interests of a minor child where the parents have agreed to an award of joint custody or so agree in open court at a hearing for the purpose of determining the custody of the minor child or children of the marriage. If the court declines to enter an order awarding joint custody, the court shall state in its decision the reasons for denial of an award of joint custody. (Connecticut General Statutes – Title 46b – Chapter 56 and 84.)

Delaware

In Delaware, the Court shall consider all relevant factors in making a child custody decision including:

(a) The wishes of the child's parent or parents as to his or her custody and residential arrangements.
(b) The wishes of the child as to his or her custodian(s) and residential arrangements.

(c) The interaction and interrelationship of the child with his or her parents, grandparents, siblings, persons cohabiting in the relationship of husband and wife with a parent of the child, any other residents of the household or persons who may significantly affect the child's best interests.
(d) The child's adjustment to his or her home, school and community.
(e) The mental and physical health of all individuals involved.
(f) Past and present compliance by both parents with their rights and responsibilities to their child.
(g) Evidence of domestic violence.
(h) The criminal history of any party or any other resident of the household including whether the criminal history contains pleas of guilty or no contest or a conviction of a criminal offense. (Delaware Code – Title 13 – Chapters: 722.)

In Delaware, as with all other states, the court will always be looking out for the best interests of the children. What you want or your spouse wants is not really relevant until the court says it is. Many parents go to custody hearings not realizing that they must portray themselves as the best custodial parent rather pleading to the court that they simply deserve the children. The court would much prefer the parents to decide who should have custody, but if they can't, the court will do it for them.

District of Columbia

In determining the care and custody of a child, the best interest of the child shall be the primary consideration. To determine the best interest of the child, the court shall consider all relevant factors, including, but not limited to:

(a) The wishes of the child as to his or her custodian, where practicable.
(b) The wishes of the child's parent or parents as to the child's custody.
(c) The interaction and interrelationship of the child with his or her parent or parents, his or her siblings, and any other person who may emotionally or psychologically affect the child's best interest.
(d) The child's adjustment to his or her home, school, and community.
(e) The mental and physical health of all individuals involved.
(f) Evidence of an intrafamily offense as defined in section 16-1001(5).
(g) The capacity of the parents to communicate and reach shared decisions affecting the child's welfare.
(h) The willingness of the parents to share custody.
(i) The prior involvement of each parent in the child's life.
(j) The potential disruption of the child's social and school life.
(k) The geographic proximity of the parental homes as this relates to the practical considerations of the child's residential schedule.
(l) The demands of parental employment.
(m) The age and number of children.
(n) The sincerity of each parent's request.
(o) The parent's ability to financially support a joint custody arrangement.

(p) The impact on Temporary Assistance for Needy Families, or Program on Work, Employment, and Responsibilities, and medical assistance.
(q) The benefit to the parents.

Florida

In Florida, the court will determine custody, notwithstanding that the child is not physically present in this state at the time of filing any proceeding under this chapter, if it appears to the court that the child was removed from this state for the primary purpose of removing the child from the jurisdiction of the court in an attempt to avoid a determination or modification of custody. The court shall determine custody with the best interests of the child and in accordance with the Uniform Child Custody Jurisdiction and Enforcement Act.

The court will ensure that each minor child has frequent and continuing contact with both parents after the parents separate or the marriage of the parties is dissolved and to encourage parents to share the rights and responsibilities, and joys of childrearing. After considering all relevant facts, the father of the child shall be given the same consideration as the mother in determining the primary residence of a child irrespective of the age or sex of the child. (Florida Statutes – Chapters: 61.13.)

Georgia

In Georgia, the court may look into all the circumstances of the parties, including but not limited to the parental suitability of each parent, the needs of the child, the prior role of each parent, the wishes of the child, the location of the residences of each parent, and any agreement between the parents.

The court may consider in a proceeding in which the custody of a child or visitation by a parent is at issue and in which the court has made a finding of family violence.

If the child has reached the age of 14 years, the child shall have the right to select the parent with whom he or she desires to live. The child's selection shall be controlling, unless the parent so selected is determined not to be a fit and proper person to have the custody of the child.

If the child has reached the age of at least 11 but not 14 years, the court shall consider the desires, if any, and educational needs of the child in determining which parent shall have custody. (Georgia Code – Sections: 19-9-1 and 19-9-51.)

Hawaii

The court will award custody to either parent or both parents according to the best interests of the child. The court may also consider frequent, continuing, and meaningful contact of each parent with the child unless the court finds that a parent is unable to act in the best interest of the child.

In Hawaii, with any custody arrangement, the court shall award reasonable visitation to parents, grandparents, siblings, and any person interested in the welfare of the child in the discretion of the court, unless it is shown that rights of visitation are detrimental to the best interests of the child.

The court will consider the following when domestic violence is an issue:

1. The primary factor the safety and well-being of the child and of the parent who is the victim of family violence.
2. The perpetrator's history of causing physical harm, bodily injury, or assault or causing reasonable fear of physical harm, bodily injury, or assault to another person.
3. If a parent is absent or relocates because of an act of family violence by the other parent, the absence or relocation shall not be a factor that weighs against the parent in determining custody or visitation. (Hawaii Statutes – Title 580 – Chapters: 46.)

Idaho

1. In an action for divorce the court may, before and after judgment, give such direction for the custody, care, and education of the children of the marriage as may seem necessary or proper in the best interests of the children. The court shall consider all relevant factors which may include:

   (a) The wishes of the child's parent or parents as to his or her custody.
   (b) The wishes of the child as to his or her custodian.
   (c) The interaction and interrelationship of the child with his or her parent or parents, and his or her siblings.
   (d) The child's adjustment to his or her home, school, and community.
   (e) The character and circumstances of all individuals involved.
   (f) The need to promote continuity and stability in the life of the child.
   (g) Domestic violence as defined in section 39-6303, Idaho Code, whether or not in the presence of the child.

Illinois

The court shall determine custody in accordance with the best interest of the child and shall not consider marital conduct. The court shall consider all relevant factors including: (1) the wishes of the child's parent or parents as to his custody; (2) the wishes of the child as to his custodian; (3) the interaction and interrelationship of the child with his parent or parents, his siblings, and any other person who may significantly affect the child's best interest; (4) the child's adjustment to his home, school, and community; (5) the mental and physical health of all individuals involved; (6) the physical violence or threat of physical violence by the child's potential custodian, whether directed against the child or directed against another person; (7) the occurrence of ongoing or repeated abuse, whether directed against the child or directed against another person; and (8) the willingness and ability of each parent to facilitate and encourage a close and continuing relationship between the other parent and the child.

When the court is to determine whether or not a joint custody arrangement is in the best interests of the children, it shall consider the following factors: (1) the wishes of the child's parent or parents as to his custody; (2) the wishes of the child as to his custodian; (3) the interaction and interrelationship of the child with his parent or parents, his siblings, and any other person who may significantly affect the child's best interest; (4) the child's adjustment to his home, school, and community; (5) the mental and physical health of all individuals involved; (6) the physical violence or threat of physical violence by the child's potential custodian, whether directed against the child or directed against another person; (7) the occurrence of ongoing abuse, whether directed against the child or directed against another person; (8) the willingness and ability of each parent to facilitate and encourage a close and continuing relationship between the other parent and the child; and (9) whether one of the parents is a sex offender. (750 Illinois Compiled Statutes – Chapter 5 – Sections: 602, 603, and 610.)

Indiana

In Indiana, the court shall consider all relevant factors when making a custody award, including the following:

1. The age and sex of the child.
2. The wishes of the child's parents.
3. The wishes of the child, with more consideration given to the child's wishes if the child is at least fourteen (14) years of age.
4. The interaction and interrelationship of the child with: (a) the child's parents; (b) the child's siblings; and (c) any other person who may significantly affect the child's best interest.
5. The child's adjustment to home, school, and community.
6. The mental and physical health of all individuals involved.
7. Evidence of a pattern of domestic or family violence by either parent.
8. Evidence that the child has been cared for by a de facto custodian. (Indiana Code – Title 31 – Article 15 – Chapters: 17-2-8, 17-2-8.5, and 17-2-15.)

Iowa

In considering what custody arrangement is in the best interest of the minor child, the court shall consider the following factors: (a) whether each parent would be a suitable custodian for the child. (b) Whether the psychological and emotional needs and development of the child will suffer due to lack of active contact with and attention from both parents. (c) Whether the parents can communicate with each other regarding the child's needs. (d) Whether both parents have actively cared for the child before and since the separation. (e) Whether each parent can support the other parent's relationship with the child. (f) Whether the custody arrangement is in accord with the child's wishes or whether the child has strong opposition, taking into consideration the child's age and maturity. (g) Whether one or both the parents agree or are opposed to joint custody. (h) The geographic proximity of the parents. (i) Whether the safety of the child, other children, or the other parent will be jeopardized by the awarding of joint custody or by unsupervised or unrestricted visitation. (j) Whether a history of domestic abuse exists. (Iowa Code – Section 598.41.)

Kansas

In Kansas, when determining custody of the children, the court shall consider all relevant factors, including but not limited to:

1. The length of time that the child has been under the actual care and control of any person other than a parent and the circumstances relating thereto.
2. The desires of the child's parents as to custody or residency.
3. The desires of the child as to the child's custody or residency.
4. The interaction and interrelationship of the child with parents, siblings, and any other person who may significantly affect the child's best interests.
5. The child's adjustment to the child's home, school, and community.
6. The willingness and ability of each parent to respect and appreciate the bond between the child and the other parent and to allow for a continuing relationship between the child and the other parent.
7. Evidence of spousal abuse. (Kansas Statutes – Chapter 60 – Article 16 – Subject: 1610.)

Kentucky

In Kentucky, the court shall determine custody in accordance with the best interests of the child and equal consideration shall be given to each parent and to any de facto custodian.

Both parents will be given equal consideration and the court shall consider all relevant factors including:

1. The wishes of the child's parent or parents, and any de facto custodian, as to his custody.
2. The wishes of the child as to his custodian.

3. The interaction and interrelationship of the child with his parent or parents, his siblings, and any other person who may significantly affect the child's best interests.
4. The child's adjustment to his home, school, and community.
5. The mental and physical health of all individuals involved.
6. Information, records, and evidence of domestic violence.
7. The extent to which the child has been cared for, nurtured, and supported by any de facto custodian.
8. The intent of the parent or parents in placing the child with a de facto custodian.
9. The circumstances under which the child was placed or allowed to remain in the custody of a de facto custodian, including whether the parent now seeking custody was previously prevented from doing so as a result of domestic violence and whether the child was placed with a de facto custodian to allow the parent now seeking custody to seek employment, work, or attend school. (Kentucky Statutes – Title 35 – Chapters: 403.270.)

Louisiana

In Louisiana, the court will keep the best interests of the children at the forefront of all custody decisions by considering:

(a) The love, affection, and other emotional ties between each party and the child.
(b) The capacity and disposition of each party to give the child love, affection, and spiritual guidance and to continue the education and rearing of the child.
(c) The capacity and disposition of each party to provide the child with food, clothing, medical care, and other material needs.
(d) The length of time the child has lived in a stable, adequate environment, and the desirability of maintaining continuity of that environment.
(e) The permanence, as a family unit, of the existing or proposed custodial home or homes.
(f) The moral fitness of each party, insofar as it affects the welfare of the child.
(g) The mental and physical health of each party.
(h) The home, school, and community history of the child.
(i) The reasonable preference of the child, if the court deems the child to be of sufficient age to express a preference.
(j) The willingness and ability of each party to facilitate and encourage a close and continuing relationship between the child and the other party.
(k) The distance between the respective residences of the parties.
(l) The responsibility for the care and rearing of the child previously exercised by each party. (Louisiana Code of Civil Procedure – Article: 131, 132, 133, and 134.)

Maine

In Maine, when deciding a child custody arrangement, the court shall consider the following factors:

1. The age of the child.
2. The relationship of the child with the child's parents and any other persons who may significantly affect the child's welfare.
3. The preference of the child, if old enough to express a meaningful preference.
4. The duration and adequacy of the child's current living arrangements and the desirability of maintaining continuity.
5. The stability of any proposed living arrangements for the child.
6. The motivation of the parties involved and their capacities to give the child love, affection, and guidance.
7. The child's adjustment to the child's present home, school, and community.
8. The capacity of each parent to allow and encourage frequent and continuing contact between the child and the other parent, including physical access.
9. The capacity of each parent to cooperate or to learn to cooperate in child care.
10. Methods for assisting parental cooperation and resolving disputes and each parent's willingness to use those methods.
11. The effect on the child if one parent has sole authority over the child's upbringing.
12. The existence of domestic abuse between the parents, in the past or currently, and how that abuse affects.
13. The existence of any history of child abuse by a parent.
14. All other factors having a reasonable bearing on the physical and psychological well-being of the child.
15. A parent's prior willful misuse of the protection from abuse process.
16. If the child is under 1 year of age, whether the child is being breast-fed.
17. The existence of a parent's conviction for a sex offense or a sexually violent offense. (Maine Revised Statutes – Title 19A – Sections: 1501, 1653.)

Maryland

In Maryland, joint or sole custody arrangements will be awarded to either parent or both with the best interest of the children in mind. There are no standard factors that would be automatically considered by the court, but the normal factors are, but not limited to, age, health, parent's contributing roles, child's wishes, etc.

The court will examine the following facts when deciding which parent would be entitled to keep the marital home in the property award:

1. The best interests of any child.
2. The interest of each party in continuing: (a) to use the family use personal property or any part of it, or to occupy or use the family home or any part of it

as a dwelling place; or (b) to use the family use personal property or any part of it, or to occupy or use the family home or any part of it for the production of income.

3. Any hardship imposed on the party whose interest in the family home or family use personal property is infringed on by an order issued under §§8-207 through 8-213 of this subtitle. (Maryland Code – Family Law Chapter – Sections: 5-203, 8-207, 8-208, and 9-101.)

Massachusetts

In determining what custody arrangement would be in the best interest of the child, the court shall consider all relevant facts including, but not limited to, whether any member of the family abuses alcohol or other drugs or has deserted the child and whether the parties have a history of being able and willing to cooperate in matters concerning the child.

If the issue of custody is contested and either party seeks shared legal or physical custody, the parties, jointly or individually, shall submit to the court at the trial a shared custody implementation plan setting forth the details of shared custody including, but not limited to, the child's education; the child's health care; procedures for resolving disputes between the parties with respect to child-raising decisions and duties; and the periods of time during which each party will have the child reside or visit with him, including holidays and vacations, or the procedure by which such periods of time shall be determined.

The court shall consider the shared custody implementation plans submitted by the parties. The court may issue a shared legal and physical custody order and, in conjunction therewith, may accept the shared custody implementation plan submitted either by the party or by the parties jointly or may issue a plan modifying the plan or plans submitted by the parties. The court may also reject the plan and issue a sole legal and physical custody award to either parent. A shared custody implementation plan issued or accepted by the court shall become part of the judgment in the action, together with any other appropriate custody orders and orders regarding the responsibility of the parties for the support of the child. (Massachusetts General Laws – Chapter 208 – Sections: 28 and 31.)

Michigan

In Michigan, when establishing a child custody order, the court will act in the best interests of the children and consider the following factors:

1. The love, affection, and other emotional ties existing between the parties involved and the child.
2. The capacity and disposition of the parties involved to give the child love, affection, and guidance and to continue the education and raising of the child in his

or her religion or creed, if any.

3. The capacity and disposition of the parties involved to provide the child with food, clothing, medical care, or other remedial care recognized and permitted under the laws of this state in place of medical care and other material needs.
4. The length of time the child has lived in a stable, satisfactory environment, and the desirability of maintaining continuity.
5. The permanence, as a family unit, of the existing or proposed custodial home or homes.
6. The moral fitness of the parties involved.
7. The mental and physical health of the parties involved.
8. The home, school, and community record of the child.
9. The reasonable preference of the child, if the court considers the child to be of sufficient age to express preference.
10. The willingness and ability of each of the parties to facilitate and encourage a close and continuing parent–child relationship between the child and the other parent or the child and the parents.
11. Domestic violence, regardless of whether the violence was directed against or witnessed by the child.
12. Any other factor considered by the court to be relevant to a particular child custody dispute. (Michigan Compiled Laws – Sections: 552.16 and 722.23.)

Minnesota

(a) "The best interests of the child" means all relevant factors to be considered and evaluated by the court including:

   1. The wishes of the child's parent or parents as to custody.
   2. The reasonable preference of the child, if the court deems the child to be of sufficient age to express preference.
   3. The child's primary caretaker.
   4. The intimacy of the relationship between each parent and the child.
   5. The interaction and interrelationship of the child with a parent or parents, siblings, and any other person who may significantly affect the child's best interests.
   6. The child's adjustment to home, school, and community.
   7. The length of time the child has lived in a stable, satisfactory environment and the desirability of maintaining continuity.
   8. The permanence, as a family unit, of the existing or proposed custodial home.
   9. The mental and physical health of all individuals involved; except that a disability, as defined in section 363A.03, of a proposed custodian or the child shall not be determinative of the custody of the child, unless the proposed custodial arrangement is not in the best interest of the child.
   10. The capacity and disposition of the parties to give the child love, affection, and guidance, and to continue educating and raising the child in the child's culture and religion or creed, if any.

11. The child's cultural background.
12. The effect on the child of the actions of an abuser, if related to domestic abuse, as defined in section 518B.01, that has occurred between the parents or between a parent and another individual, whether or not the individual alleged to have committed domestic abuse is or ever was a family or household member of the parent.
13. Except in cases in which a finding of domestic abuse as defined in section 518B.01 has been made, the disposition of each parent to encourage and permit frequent and continuing contact by the other parent with the child. The court may not use one factor to the exclusion of all others. The primary caretaker factor may not be used as a presumption in determining the best interests of the child. The court must make detailed findings on each of the factors and explain how the factors led to its conclusions and to the determination of the best interests of the child.

(b) The court shall not consider conduct of a proposed custodian that does not affect the custodian's relationship to the child.

Subd. 1a. Evidence of false allegations of child abuse.

The court shall consider evidence of a violation of section 609.507 in determining the best interests of the child.

Subd. 2. Factors when joint custody is sought.

In addition to the factors listed in subdivision 1, where either joint legal or joint physical custody is contemplated or sought, the court shall consider the following relevant factors:

(a) The ability of parents to cooperate in the rearing of their children.
(b) Methods for resolving disputes regarding any major decision concerning the life of the child, and the parents' willingness to use those methods.
(c) Whether it would be detrimental to the child if one parent were to have sole authority over the child's upbringing.
(d) Whether domestic abuse, as defined in section 518B.01, has occurred between the parents.

The court shall use a rebuttable presumption that upon request of either or both parties, joint legal custody is in the best interests of the child. However, the court shall use a rebuttable presumption that joint legal or physical custody is not in the best interests of the child if domestic abuse, as defined in section 518B.01, has occurred between the parents.

If the court awards joint legal or physical custody over the objection of a party, the court shall make detailed findings on each of the factors in this subdivision and explain how the factors led to its determination that joint custody would be in the best interests of the child.

Subd. 3. Custody order.

(a) Upon adjudging the nullity of a marriage, or in a dissolution or separation proceeding, or in a child custody proceeding, the court shall make such further order as it deems just and proper concerning:

1. The legal custody of the minor children of the parties which shall be sole or joint.
2. Their physical custody and residence.
3. Their support. In determining custody, the court shall consider the best interests of each child and shall not prefer one parent over the other solely on the basis of the sex of the parent.

(b) The court shall grant the following rights to each of the parties, unless specific findings are made under section 518.68, subdivision 1. Each party has the right of access to, and to receive copies of, school, medical, dental, religious training, and other important records and information about the minor children. Each party has the right of access to information regarding health or dental insurance available to the minor children. Each party shall keep the other party informed as to the name and address of the school of attendance of the minor children. Each party has the right to be informed by school officials about the children's welfare, educational progress and status, and to attend school and parent–teacher conferences. The school is not required to hold a separate conference for each party. In case of an accident or serious illness of a minor child, each party shall notify the other party of the accident or illness, and the name of the health care provider and the place of treatment. Each party has the right to reasonable access and telephone contact with the minor children. The court may waive any of the rights under this section if it finds it is necessary to protect the welfare of a party or child.

Subd. 4. Repealed, 1986 c 406 s 9

Subd. 5. Repealed, 1986 c 406 s 9

Subd. 6. Departure from guidelines based on joint custody. An award of joint legal custody is not a reason for departure from the guidelines in section 518.551, subdivision 5.

Mississippi

Child custody: If the parents can't come to a mutual agreement concerning custody, the court shall base its decision on the best interests of the child. There is no presumption that either parent is better suited for custody based on gender. In making an order for custody to either parent or both parents jointly, the court may require the parents to submit a plan for the implementation of the custody order. If custody is disputed, there shall be a rebuttable presumption that it is detrimental to the child, and not in the best interest of the child, to be placed in sole custody, joint legal custody or joint physical custody of a parent who has a history of perpetrating family violence. (Based on MS Code, Title 93, Section 93-5-24.)

Missouri

In Missouri, the court will act in the best interest of the children and shall consider all relevant factors including:

1. The wishes of the child's parents as to custody and the proposed parenting plan submitted by both parties.
2. The needs of the child for a frequent, continuing, and meaningful relationship with both parents and the ability and willingness of parents to actively perform their functions as mother and father for the needs of the child.
3. The interaction and interrelationship of the child with parents, siblings, and any other person who may significantly affect the child's best interests.
4. Which parent is more likely to allow the child frequent, continuing, and meaningful contact with the other parent.
5. The child's adjustment to the child's home, school, and community.
6. The mental and physical health of all individuals involved.
7. The intention of either parent to relocate the principal residence of the child.
8. The wishes of a child as to the child's custodian. (Missouri Statutes – Title 30 – Chapter 452 – Sections: 375 and 400.)

Montana

In Montana, the court will make a custody award that is best for the children involved by considering these factors:

(a) The wishes of the child's parent or parents.
(b) The wishes of the child.
(c) The interaction and interrelationship of the child with the child's parent or parents and siblings and with any other person who significantly affects the child's best interest.
(d) The child's adjustment to home, school, and community.
(e) The mental and physical health of all individuals involved.
(f) Physical abuse or threat of physical abuse by one parent against the other parent or the child.
(g) Chemical dependency, or chemical abuse on the part of either parent.
(h) Continuity and stability of care.
(i) Developmental needs of the child.

(j) Whether a parent has knowingly failed to pay birth-related costs that the parent is able to pay, which is considered to be not in the child's best interests.
(k) Whether a parent has knowingly failed to financially support a child that the parent is able to support, which is considered to be not in the child's best interests.
(l) Whether the child has frequent and continuing contact with both parents, which is considered to be in the child's best interests unless the court determines, after a hearing, that contact with a parent would be detrimental to the child's best interests.
(m) Adverse effects on the child resulting from continuous and vexatious parenting plan amendment actions. (Montana Code – Section 40 – Titles: 4-104, 4-108 and 4-212.)

Nebraska

In Nebraska, the court will consider the following factors to determine what is in the best interest of the children:

1. The relationship of the minor child to each parent prior to the commencement of the action or any subsequent hearing.
2. The desires and wishes of the minor child if of an age of comprehension regardless of chronological age, when such desires and wishes are based on sound reasoning.
3. The general health, welfare, and social behavior of the minor child.
4. Credible evidence of abuse inflicted on any family or household member. The court will not make a decision based on gender, so each parent is given an equal opportunity in all custody decisions. (Nebraska Statutes – Chapter 42 – Section: 364.)

Nevada

In Nevada, the sole consideration of the court is the best interest of the child. When determining the best custody award to order, the court shall consider, but not limited to:

1. The wishes of the child if the child is of sufficient age and capacity to form an intelligent preference as to his custody.
2. Any nomination by a parent or a guardian for the child.
3. Whether either parent or any other person seeking custody has engaged in an act of domestic violence. (Nevada Statutes – Chapter 125 – Sections: 480 and 490.)

New Hampshire

In determining parental rights and responsibilities, the court shall be guided by the best interests of the child, and shall consider the following factors: (a) the relationship of the child with each parent and the ability of each parent to provide the child with nurture, love, affection, and guidance. (b) The ability of each parent to assure that the child receives adequate food, clothing, shelter, medical care, and a safe environment. (c) The child's developmental needs and the ability of each parent to meet them, both in the present and in the future. (d) The quality of the child's adjustment to the child's school and community and the potential effect of any change. (e) The ability and disposition of each parent to foster a positive relationship and frequent and continuing physical, written, and telephonic contact with the other parent, except where contact will result in harm to the child or to a parent. (f) The support of each parent for the child's contact with the other parent as shown by allowing and promoting such contact. (g) The support of each parent for the child's relationship with the other parent. (h) The relationship of the child with any other person who may significantly affect the child. (i) The ability of the parents to communicate, cooperate with each other, and make joint decisions concerning the children. (j) Any evidence of abuse, and the impact of the abuse on the child and on the relationship between the child and the abusing parent. (k) If a parent is incarcerated, the reason for and the length of the incarceration, and any unique issues that arise as a result of incarceration. (l) Any other additional factors the court deems relevant. (New Hampshire Statutes – Chapters: 458:17.)

New Jersey

In New Jersey, the court will award a custody arrangement by considering the following:

1. The physical, emotional, religious and everyday needs of the children.
2. The wishes of the child is deemed to be of sufficient age and maturity. (New Jersey Statutes – Title 2 A – Chapters: 34-23.)

New Mexico

In New Mexico, the court make a custody award with the best interests of the children in mind. The factors the court will consider are as follows:

1. The wishes of the child's parent or parents as to his custody.
2. The wishes of the child as to his custodian.

3. The interaction and interrelationship of the child with his parents, his siblings, and any other person who may significantly affect the child's best interest.
4. The child's adjustment to his home, school, and community.
5. The mental and physical health of all individuals involved. Also, if the child is 14 years or older, the court will consider his or her wishes. (New Mexico Statutes – Article 4 – Sections: 40-4-9 and 40-4-9.1.)

New York

In New York, the court shall require verification of the status of any child of the marriage with respect to such child's custody and support, including any prior orders, and shall enter orders for custody and support as, in the court's discretion, justice requires, having regard to the circumstances of the case and of the respective parties and to the best interests of the child. (Consolidated Laws of New York – Domestic Relations Laws – Article 13 – Sections: 240.)

North Carolina

In North Carolina, the court shall consider all relevant factors including acts of domestic violence between the parties, the safety of the child, and the safety of either party from domestic violence by the other party and shall make findings accordingly. The goal of the court is to always protect the children an act in their best interests. The courts shall not favor one parent over the other on the basis of gender. (North Carolina Statutes – Chapter 50 – Sections: 50-13.2.)

North Dakota

For the purpose of custody, the best interests and welfare of the child are determined by the court's consideration and evaluation of all factors affecting the best interests and welfare of the child. These factors include all of the following when applicable: (a) the love, affection, and other emotional ties existing between the parents and child. (b) The capacity and disposition of the parents to give the child love, affection, and guidance and to continue the education of the child. (c) The disposition of the parents to provide the child with food, clothing, medical care, or other remedial care recognized and permitted under the laws of this state in lieu of medical care, and other material needs. (d) The length of time the child has lived in a stable satisfactory environment and the desirability of maintaining continuity. (e) The permanence, as a family unit, of the existing or proposed custodial home.

(f) The moral fitness of the parents. (g) The mental and physical health of the parents. (h) The home, school, and community record of the child. (i) The reasonable preference of the child, if the court deems the child to be of sufficient intelligence, understanding, and experience to express a preference. (j) Evidence of domestic violence. (k) The interaction and interrelationship, or the potential for interaction and interrelationship, of the child with any person who resides in, is present, or frequents the household of a parent and who may significantly affect the child's best interests. The court shall consider that person's history of inflicting, or tendency to inflict, physical harm, bodily injury, assault, or the fear of physical harm, bodily injury, or assault, on other persons. (l) The making of false allegations not made in good faith, by one parent against the other, of harm to a child. (m) Any other factors considered by the court to be relevant to a particular child custody dispute. (North Dakota Century Code – Volume 3A – Chapters: 14-05-22, 14-09-06, 14-09-06.1, and 14-09-06.2.)

Ohio

When husband and wife are living separate and apart from each other, or are divorced, and the question as to the parental rights and responsibilities for the care of their children and the place of residence and legal custodian of their children is brought before a court of competent jurisdiction, they shall stand upon an equality as to the parental rights and responsibilities for the care of their children and the place of residence and legal custodian of their children, so far as parenthood is involved.

In determining the best interest of a child, whether on an original decree allocating parental rights and responsibilities for the care of children or a modification of a decree allocating those rights and responsibilities, the court shall consider all relevant factors, including, but not limited to: (a) the wishes of the child's parents regarding the child's care; (b) the child's wishes and concerns as to the allocation of parental rights and responsibilities concerning the child, the wishes and concerns of the child, as expressed to the court; (c) the child's interaction and interrelationship with the child's parents, siblings, and any other person who may significantly affect the child's best interest; (d) the child's adjustment to the child's home, school, and community; (e) the mental and physical health of all persons involved in the situation; (f) the parent more likely to honor and facilitate court-approved parenting time rights or visitation and companionship rights; (g) whether either parent has failed to make all child support payments, including all arrearages, that are required of that parent pursuant to a child support order under which that parent is an obligor; (h) whether either parent previously has been convicted of or pleaded guilty to any criminal offense involving any act that resulted in a child being an abused child or a neglected child; (i) whether the residential parent or one of the parents subject to a shared parenting decree has continuously and willfully denied the other parent's right to parenting time in accordance with an order of the court; (j) whether either parent has established a residence, or is planning to establish a residence, outside this state.

In determining whether shared parenting is in the best interest of the children, the court shall consider all of these additional relevant factors, including, but not limited to, (a) the ability of the parents to cooperate and make decisions jointly, with respect to the children; (b) the ability of each parent to encourage the sharing of love, affection, and contact between the child and the other parent; (c) any history of, or potential for, child abuse, spouse abuse, other domestic violence, or parental kidnapping by either parent; (d) the geographic proximity of the parents to each other, as the proximity relates to the practical considerations of shared parenting; (e) the recommendation of the guardian ad litem of the child, if the child has a guardian ad litem. (Ohio Code – Sections: 3105.21, 3109.03, 1309.04, and 1309.051.)

Oklahoma

In Oklahoma, the court will explore all possibilities for a custody arrangement that is best for the children. Custody shall be awarded in a way which assures the frequent and continuing contact of the child with both parents. When awarding custody to either parent, the court:

(a) Shall consider, among other facts, which parent is more likely to allow the child or children frequent and continuing contact with the noncustodial parent.
(b) Shall not prefer a parent as a custodian of the child because of the gender of that parent. (Oklahoma Statutes – Title 43 – Sections: 109 and 112 and Title 10 – Sections: 21.1.)

Oregon

A general parenting plan may include a general outline of how parental responsibilities and parenting time will be shared and may allow the parents to develop a more detailed agreement on an informal basis. However, a general parenting plan must set forth the minimum amount of parenting time and access a noncustodial parent is entitled to have.

A detailed parenting plan may include, but need not be limited to, provisions relating to: (a) residential schedule; (b) holiday, birthday, and vacation planning; (c) weekends, including holidays, and school in-service days preceding or following weekends; (d) decision making and responsibility; (e) information sharing and access; (f) relocation of parents; (g) telephone access; (h) transportation; and (i) methods for resolving disputes.

In determining custody of a minor child under ORS 107.105 or 107.135, the court shall give primary consideration to the best interests and welfare of the child. In determining the best interests and welfare of the child, the court shall consider the following relevant factors: (a) the emotionalities between the child and other family members; (b) the interest of the parties in and attitude toward the child; (c) the desirability of continuing an existing relationship; (d) the abuse of one parent by the other; (e) the preference for the primary caregiver of the child, if the caregiver is deemed fit by the court; and (f) the willingness and ability of each parent to facilitate and encourage a close and continuing relationship between the other parent and the child. However, the court may not consider such willingness and ability if one parent shows that the other parent has sexually assaulted or engaged in a pattern of behavior of abuse against the parent or a child, and that a continuing relationship with the other parent will endanger the health or safety of either the parent or the child. (Oregon Statutes – Volume 2 – Sections: 107.105, 107.137, 107.169.)

Pennsylvania

In Pennsylvania, the court will order partial custody or visitation to either parent with the best interests of the children as a standard for all decisions. The court shall consider, among other factors, which parent is more likely to encourage, permit, and allow frequent and continuing contact and physical access between the noncustodial parent and the child. In addition, the court shall consider each parent and adult household member's present and past violent or abusive conduct which may include, but is not limited to, abusive conduct as defined under the act of October 7, 1976 (P.L.1090, No.218), known as the Protection From Abuse Act.

Rhode Island

In Rhode Island, after making a custody decision that is in the best interest of the children, the court shall provide for the reasonable right of visitation by the natural parent not having custody of the children, except upon the showing of cause why the right should not be granted. The court shall mandate compliance with its order by both the custodial parent and the children. In the event of noncompliance, the noncustodial parent may file a motion for contempt in family court. Upon a finding by the court that its order for visitation has not been complied with, the court shall exercise its discretion in providing a remedy, and define the noncustodial parent's visitation in detail. However, if a second finding of noncompliance by the court is made, the court shall consider this to be grounds for a change of custody to the noncustodial parent.

South Carolina

In South Carolina, when making a custody award the court will consider the child's preference if it is deemed to be appropriate. The court shall place weight upon the preference based on the child's age, experience, maturity, judgment, and ability to express a preference. The court will also consider evidence of domestic violence, the current situation and nature of the divorce, and the religious faith of the parents. The court will not award custody based on the gender of the parent. (Code of Laws for South Carolina – Chapter 3; Sections 20-3-160, 20-7-100, and 20-7-1520.)

South Dakota

When minor children are involved in a divorce, the South Dakota courts will do everything possible to help lessen the emotional trauma the children may be experiencing. If the parents cannot come to an agreement regarding the issues involving the children, the court will establish the custody order at its discretion.

The court will award sole or joint custody based on the standards of what is in the best interests of the children. The court will consider the following: marital misconduct only if it is relevant to the further well-being of the child; the child wishes depending on age and maturity; and the expressed desires of the parents. The court will not discriminate based on the parents gender.

Tennessee

In Tennessee, the court will take into consideration the following primary factors when determining what custody arrangement is best for a child:

(a) The love, affection, and emotional ties between the parents and child.
(b) The importance of continuity and the length of time the child has lived in a stable and satisfactory environment.
(c) Whether there has been any domestic violence or physical or mental abuse to the child, spouse, or any other person and whether a parent has had to relocate to avoid such violence.
(d) The stability of the family unit.
(e) The mental and physical health of the parents.
(f) The home, school, and community record of the child.
(g) The reasonable preference of a child over 12 years of age.
(h) The character and behavior of any person who lives in or visits the parent's home and such person's interactions with the child.
(i) Each parent's past and potential performance of parenting duties, including a willingness and ability to facilitate and encourage a close and continuing parent–child relationship with the other parent. (Tennessee Code – Volume 6A, Title 36, Sections 36-4-106.)

Texas

(a) The court will strive to promote the amicable settlement of disputes between the parties to a suit, the parties may enter into a written agreement containing provisions for conservatorship and possession of the child and for modification of the agreement, including variations from the standard possession order.
(b) If the court finds that the agreement is in the child's best interest, the court shall render an order in accordance with the agreement.
(c) Terms of the agreement contained in the order or incorporated by reference regarding conservatorship or support of or access to a child in an order may be enforced by all remedies available for enforcement of a judgment, including contempt, but are not enforceable as a contract.
(d) If the court finds that the agreement is not in the child's best interest, the court may request the parties to submit a revised agreement or the court may render an order for the conservatorship and possession of the child.

If a written agreement of the parents is filed with the court, the court shall render an order appointing the parents as joint managing conservators only if the agreement:

1. Designates the conservator who has the exclusive right to designate the primary residence of the child and: (A) establishes, until modified by further order, the geographic area within which the conservator shall maintain the child's primary residence; or (B) specifies that the conservator may designate the child's primary residence without regard to geographic location.
2. Specifies the rights and duties of each parent regarding the child's physical care, support, and education.
3. Includes provisions to minimize disruption of the child's education, daily routine, and association with friends.
4. Allocates between the parents, independently, jointly, or exclusively, all of the remaining rights and duties of a parent provided by Chapter 151.
5. Is voluntarily and knowingly made by each parent and has not been repudiated by either parent at the time the order is rendered.
6. Is in the best interest of the child.

A child aged 12 years or older may file with the court in writing the name of the person who is the child's preference to have the exclusive right to designate the primary residence of the child, subject to the approval of the court. (Texas Code – Family Code – Chapters: 5-153.004–153.434.)

Utah

In determining whether the best interest of a child will be served by ordering physical custody, the court shall consider the following factors: (a) whether the physical, psychological, and emotional needs and development of the child will benefit from joint legal or physical custody; (b) the ability of the parents to give first priority to the welfare of the child and reach shared decisions in the child's best interest; (c) whether each parent is capable of encouraging and accepting a positive relationship between the child and the other parent, including the sharing of love, affection, and contact between the child and the other parent; (d) whether both parents participated in raising the child before the divorce; (e) the geographical proximity of the homes of the parents; (f) the preference of the child if the child is of sufficient age and capacity to reason so as to form an intelligent preference as to joint legal or physical custody; (g) the maturity of the parents and their willingness and ability to protect the child from conflict that may arise between the parents; (h) the past and present ability of the parents to cooperate with each other and make decisions jointly; (i) any history of, or potential for, child abuse, spouse abuse, or kidnapping; and (j) any other factors the court finds relevant.

The court shall, in every case, consider joint custody but may award any form of custody which is determined to be in the best interest of the child.

The children may not be required by either party to testify unless the trier of fact determines that extenuating circumstances exist that would necessitate the testimony of the children be heard, and there is no other reasonable method to present their testimony.

The court may inquire of the children and take into consideration the children's desires regarding future custody or parent-time schedules, but the expressed desires are not controlling and the court may determine the children's custody or parent-time otherwise. The desires of a child aged 16 years or older shall be given added weight, but is not the single controlling factor.

In awarding custody, the court shall consider, among other factors the court finds relevant, which parent is most likely to act in the best interests of the child, including allowing the child frequent and continuing contact with the noncustodial parent as the court finds appropriate.

If the court finds that one parent does not desire custody of the child, or has attempted to permanently relinquish custody to a third party, it shall take that evidence into consideration in determining whether to award custody to the other parent.

Neither the husband nor wife can remove the other or their children from the homestead without the consent of the other, unless the owner of the property shall in good faith provide another homestead suitable to the condition in life of the family; and if a husband or wife abandons his or her spouse, that spouse is entitled to the custody of the minor children, unless a court of competent jurisdiction shall otherwise direct. (Utah Code – Sections: 30-2-10, 30-3-5, and 30-3-10.)

Vermont

In Vermont, the court will order custody to either parent or both by considering the following factors:

(a) The relationship of the child with each parent and the ability and disposition of each parent to provide the child with love, affection, and guidance.

(b) The ability and disposition of each parent to assure that the child receives adequate food, clothing, medical care, other material needs, and a safe environment.
(c) The ability and disposition of each parent to meet the child's present and future developmental needs.
(d) The quality of the child's adjustment to the child's present housing, school and community and the potential effect of any change.
(e) The ability and disposition of each parent to foster a positive relationship and frequent and continuing contact with the other parent.
(f) The quality of the child's relationship with the primary care provider, if appropriate given the child's age and development.
(g) The relationship of the child with any other person who may significantly affect the child.
(h) The ability and disposition of the parents to communicate, cooperate with each other and make joint decisions concerning the children where parental rights and responsibilities are to be shared or divided.
(i) Evidence of abuse. (Vermont Statutes – Title 15 – Section 664.)

Virginia

In Virginia, joint or sole custody will be awarded by the court to the father or the mother or both based on the best interests of the children standard. The court will consider all relevant factors on a case-by-case basis, but the following is a list of typical factors taken into consideration when determining a custody arrangement that is best for the children. These factors are, but are not limited to, the age of the children, the health of the children, the wishes of the children, the parental roles of each parent, and the needs of the children. (Virginia Code – Title 20 – Sections: 20-107.2.)

Washington

In Washington, the court will award sole or joint child custody to either the mother, father or both with the best interests of the children as the standard for any decision. All custody cases must have a proposed parenting plan or agreement to be presented to the court for approval before the final order is put in place.

The primary goals of the parenting plan are to:

1. Provide for the child's physical care.
2. Maintain the child's emotional stability.
3. Provide for the child's changing needs as the child grows and matures, in a way that minimizes the need for future modifications to the permanent parenting plan.
4. Set forth the authority and responsibilities of each parent with respect to the child.
5. Minimize the child's exposure to harmful parental conflict.

6. Encourage the parents to meet their responsibilities to their minor children through agreements in the permanent parenting plan, rather than by relying on judicial intervention.
7. To otherwise protect the best interests of the child. (Revised Code of Washington – Title 26 – Chapters: 26.09.181 and 26.09.220.)

Custody, whether joint or sole, will be awarded to the father or the mother or both based on the best interests of the children. With each petition filed with minor children, the parties must also have a proposed parenting plan to be approved by the court.

The objectives of the permanent parenting plan are to: (a) provide for the child's physical care; (b) maintain the child's emotional stability; (c) provide for the child's changing needs as the child grows and matures, in a way that minimizes the need for future modifications to the permanent parenting plan; (d) set forth the authority and responsibilities of each parent with respect to the child (e) minimize the child's exposure to harmful parental conflict; (f) encourage the parents to meet their responsibilities to their minor children through agreements in the permanent parenting plan, rather than by relying on judicial intervention; and (g) to otherwise protect the best interests of the child.

The permanent parenting plan shall contain provisions for resolution of future disputes between the parents, allocation of decision-making authority, and residential provisions for the child.

The plan shall allocate decision-making authority to one or both parties regarding the children's education, health care, and religious upbringing. The parties may incorporate an agreement related to the care and growth of the child in these specified areas, or in other areas, into their plan. Regardless of the allocation of decision making in the parenting plan, either parent may make emergency decisions affecting the health or safety of the child. (a) Each parent may make decisions regarding the day-to-day care and control of the child while the child is residing with that parent. (b) When mutual decision making is designated but cannot be achieved, the parties shall make a good-faith effort to resolve the issue through the dispute resolution process.

The plan shall include a residential schedule which designates in which parent's home each minor child shall reside on given days of the year, including provision for holidays, birthdays of family members, vacations, and other special occasions.

If a parent fails to comply with a provision of a parenting plan or a child support order, the other parent's obligations under the parenting plan or the child support order are not affected. Failure to comply with a provision in a parenting plan or a child support order may result in a finding of contempt of court.

The court shall approve agreements of the parties allocating decision-making authority, or specifying rules in the areas listed in RCW 26.09.184(4)(a), when it finds that: (1) the agreement is consistent with any limitations on a parent's decision-making authority mandated by RCW 26.09.191; and (2) the agreement is knowing and voluntary.

The court shall make residential provisions for each child which encourage each parent to maintain a loving, stable, and nurturing relationship with the child, consistent with the child's developmental level and the family's social and economic circumstances. The court shall consider the following factors: (1) the relative strength, nature, and stability of the child's relationship with each parent, including whether a parent has taken greater responsibility for performing parenting functions relating to the daily needs of the child; (2) the agreements of the parties, provided they were entered into knowingly and voluntarily; (3) each parent's past and potential for future performance of parenting functions; (4) the emotional needs and developmental level of the child; (5) the child's relationship with siblings and with other significant adults, as well as the child's involvement with his or her physical surroundings, school, or other significant activities; (6) the wishes of the parents and the wishes of a child who is sufficiently mature to express reasoned and independent preferences as to his or her residential schedule; and (7) each parent's employment schedule, and shall make accommodations consistent with those schedules. Factor (1) shall be given the greatest weight.

The court may order that a child frequently alternate his or her residence between the households of the parents for brief and substantially equal intervals of time only if the court finds the following: (1) no limitation exists under RCW 26.09.191; (2) (A) the parties have agreed to such provisions and the agreement was knowingly and voluntarily entered into; or (B) the parties have a satisfactory history of cooperation and shared performance of parenting functions; the parties are available to each other, especially in geographic proximity, to the extent necessary to ensure their ability to share performance of the parenting functions; and (3) the provisions are in the best interests of the child. (Revised Code of Washington – Title 26 – Chapters: 26.09.181, 26.09.220.)

West Virginia

In West Virginia, the court will always make a decision in the child's best interests, by facilitating:

A. Stability of the child.
B. Parental planning and agreement about the child's custodial arrangements and upbringing.
C. Continuity of existing parent–child attachments.
D. Meaningful contact between a child and each parent.
E. Caretaking relationships by adults who love the child, who know how to provide for the child's needs, and who place a high priority on doing so.
F. Security from exposure to physical or emotional harm.
G. Expeditious, predictable decision making and avoidance of prolonged uncertainty respecting arrangements for the child's care and control. (West Virginia Code – Sections: 48-9-102, 48-9-201, and 48-11-201.)

If the parents agree to one or more provisions of a parenting plan, the court shall so order, unless it makes specific findings that: (1) the agreement is not knowing or voluntary; or (2) the plan would be harmful to the child.

The primary objective of the court is to serve the child's best interests, by facilitating: (1) stability of the child; (2) parental planning and agreement about the child's custodial arrangements and upbringing; (3) continuity of existing parent–child attachments; (4) meaningful contact between a child and each parent; (5) caretaking relationships by adults who love the child, know how to provide for the child's needs, and who place a high priority on doing so; (6) security from exposure to physical or emotional harm; and (7) expeditious, predictable decision making and avoidance of prolonged uncertainty respecting arrangements for the child's care and control. (West Virginia Code – Sections: 48-9-102, 48-9-201, and 48-11-201.)

Wisconsin

In determining legal custody and periods of physical placement, the court shall consider all facts relevant to the best interest of the child. The court may not prefer one potential custodian over the other on the basis of the sex or race of the custodian. The court shall consider reports of appropriate professionals if admitted into evidence when legal custody or physical placement is contested. The court shall consider the following factors in making its determination: (a) the wishes of the child's parent or parents. (b) The wishes of the child, which may be communicated by the child or through the child's guardian ad litem or other appropriate professional. (c) The interaction and interrelationship of the child with his or her parent or parents, siblings, and any other person who may significantly affect the child's best interest. (d) The child's adjustment to the home, school, religion, and community. (e) The mental and physical health of the parties, the minor children, and other persons living in a proposed custodial household. (f) The availability of public or private child care services. (g) Whether one party is likely to unreasonably interfere with the child's continuing relationship with the other party. (h) Whether there is evidence that a party engaged in abuse, as defined in s. 813.122 (1) (a), of the child, as defined in s. 48.02 (2). (i) Whether there is evidence of interspousal battery as described under s. 940.19 or 940.20 (1m) or domestic abuse as defined in s. 813.12 (1) (a). (j) Whether either party has or had a significant problem with alcohol or drug abuse. (k) Such other factors as the court may in each individual case determine to be relevant.

Wyoming

In Wyoming, the court will always attempt to make a child custody and visitation decision that is best for the children by addressing the following factors:

1. The quality of the relationship each child has with each parent.
2. The ability of each parent to provide adequate care for each child throughout each period of responsibility, including arranging for each child's care by others as needed.

3. The relative competency and fitness of each parent.
4. Each parent's willingness to accept all responsibilities of parenting, including a willingness to accept care for each child at specified times and to relinquish care to the other parent at specified times.
5. How the parents and each child can best maintain and strengthen a relationship with each other.
6. How the parents and each child interact and communicate with each other and how such interaction and communication may be improved.
7. The ability and willingness of each parent to allow the other to provide care without intrusion, respect the other parent's rights and responsibilities, including the right to privacy.
8. Geographic distance between the parents' residences.
9. The current physical and mental ability of each parent to care for each child.
10. Any other factors the court deems necessary and relevant. (Wyoming Statutes – Title 20 – Chapters: 20-2-104, 20-2-107, and 20-2-201.)

Appendix B
Brief Screen

Brief Screen for Egregious Factors:

What concerns do you have regarding your ex-spouse that might negatively impact your child(ren)?

____
____
____

Do you have concerns about your ex-spouses' relationship with your child(ren)? If so, what?

____
____
____

Do you have concerns about your ex-spouses' parenting skills? If so, what?

____
____
____

Do you have concerns about the environmental stability (i.e., including the safety of the home environment, substance abuse problems, potential for abuse or neglect) as related to your ex-spouse? If so, what?

____
____
____

Do you have concerns about the emotional stability of your ex-spouse? If so, what?

____
____
____

Do you have concerns about the level of conflict between yourself and your ex-spouse? If so, what?

____
____
____

L.W. Tolle and W.T. O'Donohue, *Improving the Quality of Child Custody Evaluations*,
DOI 10.1007/978-1-4614-3405-4, © Springer Science+Business Media, LLC 2012

Appendix C
Structured Assessment Form for the EPFM

Structured Assessment for EPFM (For Parent X):

Egregious Factors

Poor Parent–Child Relationship

1. Does information gained from the clinical interview indicate the presence of a poor parent–child relationship? _____Yes(1) _______No
   If Yes, What?
2. Does information gained from the empirically supported evaluation measures indicate presence of a poor parent–child relationship? ______Yes(1) _______No
   If Yes, What?
3. Does information gained from existing legal or professional documents indicate the presence of a poor parent–child relationship? _______Yes(1) _______No
   If Yes, What?
4. Does information gained from an interview or assessments of the child indicate presence of a poor parent–child relationship? _______Yes(1) _______No
   If Yes, What?
5. Does information gained from professional collateral sources indicate the presence of a poor parent–child relationship?_______Yes(1)_______No
   If Yes, What?
6. Is there information gained from the home visit or child-parent observation that indicates the presence of a poor parent–child relationship? ______Yes(1) ________No
   If Yes, What?

L.W. Tolle and W.T. O'Donohue, *Improving the Quality of Child Custody Evaluations*,
DOI 10.1007/978-1-4614-3405-4, © Springer Science+Business Media, LLC 2012

7. Is there other information that indicates the presence of a poor parent–child relationship (i.e., spouse-report)? _____Yes(1)______No
   If Yes, What?
8. Is there information that mitigates this poor parent–child relationship (i.e., treatment is being sought/currently undergoing treatment, child is adjusting well, etc.)?_____Yes(−1)______No
   If Yes, What?
9. Is there information that indicates that a poor parent–child relationship is not present? _____Yes(−1) _____No
   If Yes, What?
   Total Risk Score:__________ Risk Level:___________

Poor Parenting Skills

1. Does information gained from the clinical interview indicate the presence of poor parenting skills? _____Yes(1) _______No
   If Yes, What?
2. Does information gained from the empirically supported evaluation measures indicate the presence of poor parenting skills? ______Yes(1) _______No
   If Yes, What?
3. Does information gained from existing legal or professional documents indicate the presence of poor parenting skills? _______Yes(1) _______No
   If Yes, What?
4. Does information gained from an interview or assessments of the child indicate the presence of poor parenting skills? _______Yes(1) _______No
   If Yes, What?
5. Does information gained from professional collateral sources indicate the presence of poor parenting skills?_______Yes(1)_______No
   If Yes, What?
6. Is there information gained from the home visit or child-parent observation that indicates the presence of poor parenting skills? ______Yes(1) ________No
   If Yes, What?
7. Is there other information that indicates the presence of poor parenting skills (i.e., spouse-report)? _____Yes(1)______No
   If Yes, What?
8. Is there information that mitigates poor parenting skills (i.e., treatment is being sought/currently undergoing treatment, child is adjusting well, heavy involvement of grandparents or other positive adults, etc.)?_____Yes(−1)______No
   If Yes, What?
9. Is there information that indicates that poor parenting skills are not present? _____Yes(−1) _____No
   If Yes, What?
   Total Risk Score: ________ Risk Level:__________

Environmental Instability

1. Does information gained from the clinical interview indicate the presence of environmental instability? _____Yes(1) _______No
   If Yes, What?
2. Does information gained from the empirically-supported evaluation measures indicate the presence of environmental instability? ______Yes(1) _______No
   If Yes, What?
3. Does information gained from existing legal or professional documents indicate the presence of environmental instability? _______Yes(1) _______No
   If Yes, What?
4. Does information gained from an interview or assessments of the child indicate the presence of environmental instability? _______Yes(1) _______No
   If Yes, What?
5. Does information gained from professional collateral sources indicate the presence of environmental instability?_______Yes(1)_______No
   If Yes, What?
6. Is there information gained from the home visit or child-parent observation that indicates the presence of environmental instability? ______Yes(1) ________No
   If Yes, What?
7. Is there other information that indicates the presence of environmental instability (i.e., spouse-report)? _____Yes(1)______No
   If Yes, What?
8. Is there information that mitigates environmental instability (i.e., treatment is being sought/currently undergoing treatment, child is adjusting well, etc.)?_____Yes(−1)______No
   If Yes, What?
9. Is there information that indicates that environmental instability is not present?
   _____Yes(−1) _____No
   If Yes, What?
   Total Risk score: __________ Risk Level:__________

Parent Mental Health Problems

Structured Assessment for EPFM (For Parent X):

1. Does information gained from the clinical interview indicate the presence of mental health problems? _____Yes(1) _______No
   If Yes, What?
2. Does information gained from the empirically-supported evaluation measures indicate the presence of mental health problems? ______Yes(1) _______No
   If Yes, What?

3. Does information gained from existing legal or professional documents indicate the presence of mental health problems? _______Yes(1) _______No
   If Yes, What?
4. Does information gained from an interview or assessments of the child indicate the presence of mental health problems? _______Yes(1) _______No
   If Yes, What?
5. Does information gained from professional collateral sources indicate the presence of mental health problems?_______Yes(1)_______No
   If Yes, What?
6. Is there information gained from the home visit or child-parent observation that indicates the presence of mental health problems? ______Yes(1) ________No
   If Yes, What?
7. Is there other information that contributes to indicate presence of mental health problems (i.e., spouse-report)? _____Yes(1)______No
   If Yes, What?
8. Is there information that mitigates mental health problems (i.e., treatment is being sought/currently undergoing treatment, child is adjusting well, etc.)?_____Yes(−1)______No
   If Yes, What?
9. Is there information that indicates that mental health problems are not present? _____Yes(−1) _____No
   If Yes, What?
   Total Risk Score: _________ Risk Level: ___________

Excessive Interparental Conflict

1. Does information gained from the clinical interview indicate the presence of excessive interparental conflict? _____Yes(1) _______No
   If Yes, What?
2. Does information gained from the empirically-supported evaluation measures indicate the presence of excessive interparental conflict? ______Yes(1) _______No
   If Yes, What?
3. Does information gained from existing legal or professional documents indicate the presence of excessive interparental conflict? _______Yes(1) _______No
   If Yes, What?
4. Does information gained from an interview or assessments of the child indicate the presence of excessive interparental conflict? _______Yes(1) _______No
   If Yes, What?
5. Does information gained from professional collateral sources indicate the presence of excessive interparental conflict?_______Yes(1)_______No
   If Yes, What?

6. Is there information gained from the home visit or child-parent observation that indicates the presence of excessive interparental conflict? ______Yes(1) ________No
   If Yes, What?
7. Is there other information that contributes to indicate the presence of excessive interparental conflict (i.e., spouse-report)? _____Yes(1)______No
   If Yes, What?
8. Is there information that mitigates excessive interparental conflict (i.e., treatment is being sought/currently undergoing treatment, child is adjusting well, etc.)?_____Yes(−1)______No
   If Yes, What?
9. Is there information that indicates that excessive interparental conflict is not present? _____Yes(−1) _____No
   If Yes, What?
   Total Risk Score: _________ Risk Level:_________

Promotive Factors

Positive Parenting

What evidence (based on parent interviews, information from assessments provided, information from child interviews or assessments, information from the child observations or home visit, information from collateral sources, information from professional or legal documents or other sources) makes it apparent that this parent exhibits characteristics of positive parenting?
_____Absent ______Present

Parental School Involvement

What evidence (based on parent interviews, information from assessments provided, information from child interviews or assessments, information from the child observation or home visit, information from collateral sources, information from professional or legal documents or other sources) makes it apparent that this parent is invested in parental school involvement?
_____Absent ______Present

Promotion of Interpersonal Development

What evidence (based on parent interviews, information from assessments provided, information from child interviews or assessments, information from the child

observation or home visit, information from collateral sources, information from professional or legal documents or other sources) makes it apparent that this parent promotes their child(ren)'s interpersonal development?
______Absent______Present

Promotion of Mental Health

What evidence (based on parent interviews, information from assessments provided, information from child interviews or assessments, information from the child observation or home visit, information from collateral sources, information from professional or legal documents or other sources) makes it apparent that this parent promotes their child(ren)'s mental health?
______Absent______Present

Promotion of Community Involvement

What evidence (based on parent interviews, information from assessments provided, information from child interviews or assessments, information from the child observation or home visit, information from collateral sources, information from professional or legal documents or other sources) makes it apparent that this parent promotes their child(ren)'s community involvement?
______Absent_______Present

Effective Coparenting

What evidence (based on parent interviews, information from assessments provided, information from child interviews or assessments, information from the child observation or home visit, information from collateral sources, information from professional or legal documents or other sources) makes it apparent that this parent exhibits characteristics of effective coparenting?
______Absent_______Present

References

Abidin, R. R. (1990). *Parenting Stress Index.* Charlottesville: Pediatric Psychology Press.

Abidin, R. R. (1992). The determinants of parenting behavior. *Journal of Clinical Child Psychology, 21*, 407–412.

Abidin, R. R., & Konold, T. R. (1999). *Parenting alliance measure.* Odessa: Psychological Assessment Resources.

Achenbach, T. M. (1991a). *Manual for the child behavior checklist 4-18 and 1991 profile.* Burlington: University of Vermont, Department of Psychiatry.

Achenbach, T. M. (1991b). *Manual for the teacher's report form and 1991 profile.* Burlington: University of Vermont, Department of Psychiatry.

Achenbach, T. M., & Edelbrock, C. (1983). *Manual for the child behavior checklist and revised child behavior profile.* Burlington: University Associates in Psychiatry.

Ackerman, M. J. (1995). *Clinician's guide to custody evaluations.* New York: Wiley.

Ackerman, M. J., & Ackerman, M. (1997). Custody evaluation practices: A survey of experienced professionals (revisited). *Professional Psychology: Research and Practice, 28*, 137–145.

Adamsons, K., & Pasley, K. (2006). Coparenting following divorce and relationship dissolution. In M. Fine & J. Harvey (Eds.), *Handbook of divorce and relationship dissolution.* New York: Erlbaum.

Ahrons, C. R., & Tanner, J. L. (2003). Adult children and their fathers: Relationship changes 20 years after parental divorce. *Family Relations, 52*, 340–351.

Ainsworth, M. D., & Witting, B. A. (1969). Attachment and exploratory behavior of one-year olds in a strange situation. In B. M. Foss (Ed.), *Determinants of infant behavior IV.* London: Methuen.

Albrecht, S. L. (1980). Reactions and adjustments to divorce: Differences in the experiences of males and females. *Family Relations, 29*, 59–68.

Albrecht, S. L., Bahr, H. M., & Goodman, K. L. (1983). *Divorce and remarriage: Problems, adaptation and adjustments.* Westport: Greenwood Press.

Amato, P. R. (2000). The consequences of divorce for adults and children. *Journal of Marriage and the Family, 62*, 1269–1287.

Amato, P. R. (2001). Children of divorce in the 1990s: An update of the Amato and Keith (1991) meta-analysis. *Journal of Family Psychology, 15*(3), 355–370.

Amato, P. R. (2006). Marital discord, divorce, and children's well-being: Results from a 20-year longitudinal study of two generations. In A. Clarke-Stewart & J. Dunn (Eds.), *Families count: Effects on child and adolescent development* (pp. 179–202). New York: Cambridge University Press.

Amato, P. R., & Gilbreth, J. G. (1999). Nonresident fathers and children's well-being: A meta-analysis. *Journal of Marriage and the Family, 61*(3), 557–573.

Amato, P. R., & Keith, B. (1991). Parental divorce and well being of children: A meta-analysis. *Psychological Bulletin, 110*, 26–46.

L.W. Tolle and W.T. O'Donohue, *Improving the Quality of Child Custody Evaluations*,
DOI 10.1007/978-1-4614-3405-4, © Springer Science+Business Media, LLC 2012

Amato, P. R., & Rezac, S. J. (1994). Contact with nonresident parents, interparental conflict, and children's behavior. *Journal of Family Issues, 15*, 191–207.

American Academy for Child and Adolescent Psychiatry. (1997). *Practice parameters for child custody evaluation.* Washington: AACAP.

American Academy of Pediatrics, Council on Children With Disabilities. (2006). Identifying infants and young children with developmental disorders in the medical home: An algorithm for developmental surveillance and screening. *Pediatrics, 118*(2006), 405–420.

American Law Institute. (1996). *Principles of the law of family dissolution: Analysis and recommendations: Tentative draft no. 2.* Philadelphia: American Law Institute Executive Office.

American Psychiatric Association. (1994). *DSM IV Diagnostic and Statistical – Manual* (4th ed.). Washington: American Psychiatric Association.

American Psychiatric Association. (2000). *Diagnostic and statistical manual of mental disorders* (4-TRth ed.). Washington: Task Force.

American Psychiatric Association Task Force on Clinical Assessment in Child Custody. (1988). *Child custody consultation: Report of the Task Force on Clinical Assessment in Child Custody.* Washington: American Psychiatric Association.

American Psychological Association. (1994). Guidelines for child custody evaluations in divorce proceedings. *American Psychologist, 49*(7), 677–680.

Archer, R. P., Aiduk, R., Griffin, R., & Elkins, D. E. (1996). Incremental validity of the MMPI-2 content scales in a psychiatric sample. *Assessment, 3*, 79–90.

Armsden, G. C., & Greenberg, M. T. (1987). The Inventory of Parent and Peer Attachment: Individual differences and their relationship to psychological well-being in adolescence. *Journal of Youth and Adolescence, 16*, 427–454.

Arnold, D. S., O'Leary, S. G., Wolff, L. S., & Acker, M. M. (1993). The parenting scale: A measure of dysfunctional parenting in discipline situations. *Psychological Assessment, 5*, 137–144.

Association of Family and Conciliation Courts. (1994). *Model standards for child custody evaluation.* Madison: Author.

Austin, W. G. (2000). A forensic psychology model of risk assessment for child custody relocation law. *Family & Conciliation Courts Review, 38*(2), 192–207.

Baird, C., Wagner, D., Healy, T., & Johnson, K. (1999). Risk assessment in child protective services: Consensus and actuarial model reliability. *Child Welfare, 99*, 723–748.

Baker, J. (2003). *Divorce in America.* Downloaded 23 August 2008 at: http://divorcesource.wordpress.com/2008/01/01/divorce-in-america/.

Baker, L. A. (2007). The biology of family relationships: What behavior genetic studies tell us about interactions within families. *DePaul Law Review/Darby, 56*, 857–66.

Bala, N., & Saunders, A. (2003). Understanding the family context: Why the law of expert evidence is different in family law cases. *Canadian Family Law Quarterly, 20*, 277–238.

Baldwin, A. L., Baldwin, C., & Cole, R. E. (1990). Stress resistant families and stress resistant children. In J. Rolf, A. S. Masten, K. Cicchetti, K. H. Nuechterlein, & S. Weinstraub (Eds.), *Risk and protective factors in the development of psychopathology* (pp. 384–404). Cambridge: Cambridge University Press.

Ball, S. A., Rounsaville, B. J., Tennen, H., & Kranzler, H. R. (2001). Reliability of personality disorder symptoms and personality traits in substance-dependent inpatients. *Journal of Abnormal Psychology, 110*(2), 341–352.

Ballou, M., Barry, J., Billinghan, K., Weinger Boorstein, B., Butler, C., Gershber, R., Heim, J., Lirianio, D., McGovern, S., Nicastro, S., Romaniello, J., Vasquez-Nuttall, K., & White, C. (2000). Psychological model for judicial decision making in emergency child placement. *American Journal of Orthopsychiatry, 71*(4), 416–425.

Barber, B. L., Eccles, J. S., & Stone, M. R. (2001). Whatever happened to the jock, the brain and the princess? Young adult pathways linked to adolescent activity involvement and social identity. *Journal of Adolescent Research, 16*(5), 429–455.

Basco, M. R., Bostic, J. Q., Davies, D., Rush, A. J., Witte, B., Hendrickse, W. et al. (2000). Methods to improve diagnostic accuracy in a community mental health setting. *American Journal of Psychiatry, 157*, 1599–1605.

Baum, N. (2003). Divorce process variables and the co-parental relationship and parental role fulfillment of divorced parents. *Family Process, 42*(1), 117–31.
Baum, N. (2004). Coping with "absence-presence:" non-custodial fathers parenting behavior. *American Journal of Orthopsychiatry, 74*, 316–324.
Baumrind, D. (1967). Child care practices anteceding three patterns of preschool behavior. *Genetic Psychology Monographs, 75*(1), 43–88.
Baumrind, D. (1971). Current patterns of parental authority. *Developmental Psychology Monograph, 41*(Pt 2).
Baumrind, D. (1991). The influence of parenting style on adolescent competence and substance use. *Journal of Early Adolescence, 11*(1), 56–95.
Bausermann, R. (2002). Child adjustment in joint-custody versus sole-custody arrangements: A meta-analytic review. *Journal of Family Psychology, 16*, 91–102.
Beardslee, W. R., Versage, E. M., & Gladstone, T. R. (1998). Children of affectively ill parents: A review of the past 10 years. *Journal of the American Academy of Child and Adolescent Psychiatry, 37*, 1134–1141.
Beck, A. T., Steer, R. A., & Brown, G. K. (1996). *Beck Depression Inventory – 2nd Edition Manual.* San Antonio: The Psychological Corporation.
Beck, A. T., Steer, R. A., & Garbin, M. G. (1988). Psychometric properties of the Beck Depression Inventory: Twenty-five years of evaluation. *Clinical Psychology Review, 8*, 77–100.
Beck, A. T., Ward, C. H., Mendelson, M., Mock, J., & Erbaugh, J. (1961). An inventory for measuring depression. *Archives of General Psychiatry, 4*, 561–571.
Ben-Porath, Y. S., Butcher, J. N., & Graham, J. R. (1991). Contribution of the MMPI-2 content scales to the differential diagnosis of schizophrenia and major depression. *Psychological Assessment, 3*, 634–640.
Bertoia, C., & Drakich, J. (1993). The fathers' rights movement, contradictions in rhetoric and practice. *Journal of Family Issues, 14*(4), 592–615.
Bessmer, J. L., Brestan, E. V., & Eyberg, S. M. (2005). The dyadic parent-child interaction coding system II (DPICS II): Reliability and validity with mother child dyads. Manuscript in preparation.
Bickham, N. L., & Fiese, B. H. (1997). Extension of the children's perceptions of interparental conflict scale for use with late adolescents. *Journal of Family Psychology, 11*(2), 246–250.
Bigras, M., LaFreniere, P. J., & Dumas, J. E. (1996). Discriminant validity of the parent and child scales of the parenting stress index. *Early Education and Development, 7*(2), 167–178.
Black, M. M., & Matula, K. (1999). *Essentials of Bayley Scales of Infant Development II Assessment.* New York: Wiley.
Bohnert, A. M., Kane, P., & Garber, J. (2008). Organized activity participation and internalizing and externalizing symptoms: Reciprocal relations during adolescence. *Journal of Youth and Adolescence, 37*(2), 239–250.
Bolocofsky, D. N. (1989). Use and abuse of mental health experts in child custody determinations. *Behavioral Sciences and the Law, 7*(2), 197–213.
Bonach, K. (2005). Factors contributing to quality coparenting: Implications for family policy. *Journal of Divorce and Remarriage, 43*(3/4), 79–103.
Bonach, K., & Sales, E. (2002). Forgiveness as a mediator between post divorce cognitive processes and coparenting quality. *Journal of Divorce and Remarriage, 38*(1/2), 17–38.
Booth, A., Brinkerhoff, D., & White, D. (1984). Impact of parental divorce on courtship. *Journal of Marriage and the Family, 46*, 85–94.
Borum, R. (2000). Assessing violence risk among youth. *Journal of Clinical Psychology, 56*, 1263–1287.
Borum, R. (2003). Managing at-risk juvenile offenders in the community. *Journal of Contemporary Criminal Justice, 19*, 114–137.
Borum, R., Bartel, P., & Forth, A. (2003). *Manual for the structured assessment of violence risk in youth (SAVRY): Version 1.1.* Tampa: University of South Florida.
Bow, J. (2006). Review of empirical research on child custody practice. *Journal of Child Custody, 3*(1), 23–50.

Bow, J. N., & Quinnell, F. A. (2002). A critical review of child custody evaluation reports. *Family Court Review, 40*(2), 164–176.

Bowlby, J. (1969). *Attachment and loss: Vol. 1. Attachment*. New York: Basic Books.

Braver, S. L., Wolchik, S. A., Sandler, I. N., Sheets, V. L., Fogas, B., & Bay, R. C. (1993). A longitudinal study of noncustodial parents: Parents without children. *Journal of Family Psychology, 7*(1), 9–23.

Bray, J. H. (1991). Psychosocial factors affecting custodial and visitation arrangements. *Behavioral Science and the Law, 9*, 419–437.

Brennan, P. A., Hammen, C., Anderson, M. J., Bor, W., Najman, J. M., & Williams, G. M. (2000). Chronicity, severity, and timing of maternal depressive symptoms: Relationships with child outcomes at age 5. *Developmental Psychology, 36*(6), 759–766.

Brestan, E. V., Foote, R. C., & Eyberg, S. M. (2005). The dyadic parent-child interaction coding system II (DPICS II): Reliability and validity with father child dyads. Manuscript in preparation.

Bricklin, B. (1990). *Bricklin Perceptual Scales*. Furlong: Village Publishing.

Bricklin, B. (1995). *The custody evaluation handbook: Research-based solutions and applications*. New York: Brunner/Mazel.

Bronstein, P., Stoll, M. F., Clauson, J., Abrams, C. L., & Briones, M. (1994). Fathering after separation or divorce: Factors predicting children's adjustment. *Family Relations, 43*, 469–479.

Brown, B. B., & Haung, B. H. (1995). Examining parenting practices in different peer contexts. In *Implications for adolescent trajectories, handbook of adolescent psychology* (2nd ed., pp. 363–394). New York: Wiley.

Brubaker, R., & Szakowski, A. (2000). Parenting practices and behavior problems among deaf children. *Child & Family Behavior Therapy, 22*, 13–28.

Buchanan, C., Maccoby, E., & Dornbusch, S. (1991). Caught between parents: Adolescents' experience in divorced homes. *Child Development, 62*, 1008–1029.

Buchanan, C. M., Maccoby, E. E., & Dornbusch, S. M. (1996). *Adolescents after divorce*. Cambridge, MA: Harvard University Press.

Budd, K. S., & Holdsworth, M. J. (1996). Issues in clinical assessment of minimal parenting competence. *Journal of Clinical Child Psychology, 25*(1), 2–14.

Buehler, C., & Gerard, J. M. (1995). Divorce law in the United States: A focus on child custody. *Family Relations, 44*, 439–458.

Buehler, C., Krishnakumar, A., Stone, G., Anthony, C., Pemberton, S., Gerard, J., & Barber, B. K. (1998). Interparental conflict styles and youth problem behaviors: A two-sample replication study. *Journal of Marriage and the Family, 60*, 119–132.

Buri, J. R. (1989). Self-esteem and appraisals of parental behavior. *Journal of Adolescent Research, 4*(1), 33–49.

Buri, J. R. (1991). Parental Authority Questionnaire. *Journal of Personality Assessment, 57*, 110–119.

Butcher, J. N., Dahlstrom, W. G., Graham, J. R., Tellegen, A., & Kaemmer, B. (1989). *Manual for the restandardized Minnesota Multiphasic Personality Inventory: MMPI-2*. Minneapolis: University of Minnesota Press.

Butler, N., & Bynner, J. M. (1997). *1970 British Cohort Study: Ten year follow-up*. Colchester: UK Data Archive.

Butler, N., & Bynner, J. M. (2003). *1970 British Cohort Study: Sixteen year follow-up*. Colchester: UK Data Archive.

Butler, N., Dowling, S., & Osborn, A. (1990). *1970 British Cohort Study: Five-year follow-up*. Colchester: UK Data Archive.

Caldwell, B. M., & Bradley, R. H. (1984). *Home observation for measurement of the environment*. Little Rock: University of Arkansas.

Camera, K., & Resnick, G. (1988). Interparental conflict and co-operation: Factors moderating children's post divorce adjustment. In E. M. Hetherington & J. D. Arasteh (Eds.), *Impact of divorce single parenting and stepparenting on children*. Hillsdale: Lawrence Erlbaum.

Canty-Mitchell, J., & Zimet, G. D. (2000). Psychometric properties of the Multidimensional Scale of Perceived Social Support in urban adolescents. *American Journal of Community Psychology, 28*(3), 391–400.

Carbonneau, R., Eaves, L. J., Silberg, J. L., Simonoff, E., & Rutter, M. (2002). Assessment of the within-family environment in twins: Absolute versus differential ratings, and relationship with conduct problems. *Journal of Child Psychology and Psychiatry, 43*, 1064–1074.

Carbonneau, R., Rutter, M., Simonoff, E., Silberg, J. L., Eaves, L. J., & Maes, H. H. (2001). The twin inventory of relationships and experiences (TIRE): Psychometric properties of a measure of the nonshared and shared environmental experiences of twins and singletons. *International Journal of Methods in Psychometric Research, 10*, 72–85.

Carlson, E. A. (1998). A prospective longitudinal study of attachment disorganization/disorientation. *Child Development, 69*, 1107–1128.

Carnegie Corporation of New York. (1992). *A matter of time: Risk and opportunities in the nonschool hours*. New York: Carnegie Corporation of New York.

Carr, G. D., Moretti, M. M., & Cue, B. J. H. (2005). Evaluating parenting capacity: Validity problems with the MMPI-2, PAI, CAPI, and ratings of child adjustment. *Professional Psychology: Research and Practice, 36*(2), 188–195.

Carroll, L., & Anderson, R. (2002). Body piercing, tattooing, self-esteem and body investment in adolescent girls. *Adolescence, 37*, 627–637.

Catalano, R. F., Gainey, R. R., Fleming, C. B., Haggerty, K. P., & Johnson, N. O. (1999). An experimental intervention with families of substance abusers: One-year follow-up of the focus on families project. *Addiction, 94*, 241–254.

Catalano, R. F., Haggerty, K. P., Fleming, C. B., Brewer, D. D., & Gainey, R. R. (2002). Children of substance abusing parents: Current findings from the focus on families project. In R. J. McMahon & R. D. V. Peters (Eds.), *The effects of parental dysfunction on children* (pp. 179–204). New York: Kluwer Academic/Plenum.

Chamberlain, R., & Chamberlain, G. (1989). *1970 British cohort study: Birth and 22-month subsample, 1970–1972*. Colchester: UK Data Archive.

Chambless, D. L., Baker, M. J., Baucom, D. H., Beutler, L. E., Calhoun, K. S., Crits- Christoph, P. (1998). Update on empirically validate therapies, II. *Clinical Psychologist, 66*, 7–18.

Chassin, L., Pillow, D. R., Curran, P. J., Molina, B. S., & Barrera, M. (1993). Relation of parental alcoholism to early adolescent substance use: A test of three mediating mechanisms. *Journal of Abnormal Psychology, 102*(1), 3–19.

Chassin, L., Pitts, S. C., DeLucia, C., & Todd, M. (1999). A longitudinal study of children of alcoholics: Predicting young adult substance use disorders, anxiety, and depression. *Journal of Abnormal Psychology, 108*(1), 106–119.

Child Welfare Information Gateway. (2005). *Determining the best interests of the child: Summary of state laws*. Downloaded May 2008 at: www.childwelfare.gov/systemwide/laws_policies/statutes/best_interest.cfm.

Cicchetti, D., & Toth, S. L. (1998). The development of depression in children and adolescents. *American Psychologist, 53*(2), 221–241.

Clark, R. M. (1983). *Family life and school achievement*. Chicago: University of Chicago Press.

Clark, R. (1985). *The Parent-Child Early Relational Assessment instrument and manual*. Madison: Author, Department of Psychiatry, University of Wisconsin Medical School.

Clark, B. K. (1995). Acting in the best interest of the child: Essential components of a child custody evaluation. *Family Law Quarterly, 29*, 20–38.

Clark, R., Tluczek, A., & Gallagher, K. C. (2004). Assessment of parent-child early relational disturbances. In R. Del Carmen & A. Carter (Eds.), *Assessment of mental health disorders in infants and toddlers* (pp. 25–60). Oxford: Oxford University Press.

Coffman, J. K., Guerin, D. W., & Gottfried, A. W. (2006). Reliability and validity of the Parent-Child Relationship Inventory (PCRI): Evidence from a longitudinal cross-informant investigation. *Psychological Assessment, 18*(2), 209–14.

Coie, J. D., Dodge, K. A., & Coppotelli, H. (1982). Dimensions and types of social status: A cross-age perspective. *Developmental Psychology, 18*, 557–570.

Cole, D. A., Warren, D. E., Dallaire, D. H., LaGrange, B., Travis, R., & Ciesla, J. A. (2007). Early predictors of helpless thoughts and behaviors in children: Developmental precursors to depressive cognitions. *Clinical Child Psychology & Psychiatry, 12*(2), 295–312.

Collins, W. A., Maccoby, E. E., Steinberg, E. M., Hetherington, E. M., & Bornstein, M. H. (2000). Contemporary research on parenting: The case for nature and nurture. *American Psychologist, 55*(2), 218.

Conger, R. D., Neppl, T., Kim, K. J., & Scaramella, L. V. (2003). Angry and aggressive behavior across three generations: A prospective, longitudinal study of parents and children. *Journal of Abnormal Child Psychology, 31*, 143–160.

Coopersmith, S. (1981). *Self-esteem inventories*. Palo Alto: Consulting Psychologists Press.

Corwyn, R. F. (2000). The factor structure of global self-esteem among adolescents and adults. *Journal of Research in Personality, 34*, 357–379.

Council on Children with Disabilities, Section on Developmental Behavioral Pediatrics, Bright Futures Steering Committee. (2006). Identifying infants and young children with developmental disorders in the medical home: An algorithm for developmental surveillance and screening. *Pediatrics, 118*(1), 405–426.

Couton, C., & Irwin, M. (2009). Parental and community level correlates of participation in out-of school activities among children living in low income neighborhoods. *Children and Youth Services Review, 31*(3), 300–308.

Crowley, J. E. (2003). *The politics of child support in America*. New York: Cambridge University Press.

Cummings, E. M., & Davies, P. T. (2002). The effects of marital conflict on children: Recent advances and emerging themes in process-oriented research. *Journal of Child Psychology & Psychiatry, 43*(1), 31–63.

Cummings, E. M., Davies, P. T., & Simpson, K. S. (1994). Marital conflict, gender, and children's appraisals and coping efficacy as mediators of child adjustment. *Journal of Family Psychology, 8*, 141–149.

Dadds, M. R., Maujean, A., & Fraser, J. A. (2003). Parenting and Conduct Problems in children: Australian data and psychometric properties of the Alabama Parenting Questionnaire. *Australian Psychologist, 38*(3), 238–241.

Dahlem, N. W., Zimet, G. D., & Walker, R. R. (1991). The Multidimensional Scale of Perceived Social Support: A confirmation study. *Journal of Clinical Psychology, 47*, 756–761.

Dallaire, D. H., Pineda, A. Q., Cole, D. A., Ciesla, J. A., Jacquez, F., LaGrange, B., & Bruce, A. E. (2006). Relation of positive and negative parenting to children's depressive symptoms. *Journal of Clinical Child and Adolescent Psychology, 35*(2), 313–322.

Damon, W. (Series Ed.) & Eisenberg, N. (Vol. Ed.). (1998). *Handbook of child psychology: Vol. 3. Social, emotional, and personality development* (5th ed.). New York: Wiley.

Darling, N., Caldwell, L. L., & Smith, R. (2005). Participation in school-based extracurricular activities and adolescent adjustment. *Journal of Leisure Research, 37*(1), 51–76.

Davis, K. (1977). The American family in relation to demographic change. In C. R. Westoff & R. Parke (Eds.), *Demographic and social aspects of population growth* (Vol. 1).: Commission on Population Growth and the American Future.

Dawe, S., Frye, S., Best, D., Moss, D., Atkinson, J., Evans, C., et al. (2007). *Drug use in the family: Impacts and implications for children*. Canberra: Australian National Council on Drugs.

Dawes, R. M., Faust, D. E., & Meehl, P. E. (1989). Clinical versus actuarial judgment. *Science, 243*, 1668–1674.

De Wit, D. J., Lipman, E., Manzano-Munguia, M., Bisanz, J., Graham, K., Offord, D. R., O'Neill, E., Pepler, D., & Shaver, K. (2007). Feasibility of a randomized controlled trial for evaluating the effectiveness of the Big Brothers Big Sisters community match program at the national level. *Children and Youth Services Review, 29*(3), 383–404.

Demo, D. H., & Acock, A. C. (1988). The impact of divorce on children. *Journal of Marriage and the Family, 50*(3), 619–648.

Denault, A. S., & Poulin, F. (2009). Intensity and breadth of participation in organized activities during the adolescent years: Multiple associations with youth outcomes. *Youth and Adolescence, 38*(9), 199–213.

Deskins, M. M. (2005). The Dyadic Parent-Child Interaction Coding System II: Reliability and validity with school-age dyads. *Dissertation Abstracts International, 66*, 2302B.

Diareme, S., Tsiantis, J., & Tsitoura, S. (1997). Cross-cultural validation of the child abuse potential inventory in Greece: A preliminary study. *Child Abuse and Neglect, 21*(11), 1067–1079.

Dodge, K. A., Malone, P. S., Lansford, J. E., Miller-Johnson, S., Pettit, G. S., & Bates, J. E. (2006). Toward a dynamic developmental model of the role of parents and peers in early onset substance use. In A. Clarke-Stewart & J. Dunn (Eds.), *Families count: Effects on child and adolescent development* (pp. 104–131). New York: Cambridge University Press.

Donaldson, T. S. (1974). *Affective testing in the Alum Rock voucher schools*. Santa Monica: RAND.

Dornbusch, S. M., Ritter, P. L., Leiderman, P. L., Roberts, D. F., & Fraleigh, M. J. (1987). The relation of parenting style to adolescent school performance. *Child Development, 58*(5), 143–160.

Downey, G., & Coyne, J. C. (1990). Children of depressed parents: An integrative review. *Psychological Bulletin, 108*, 50–76.

Drozd, L. M., Kuehnle, K., & Walker, L. E. A. (2004). Safety first: A model for understanding domestic violence in child custody and access disputes. *Journal of Child Custody, 1*(2), 75–103.

Dubow, E. F., & Ullman, D. G. (1987). *The measurement of children's social support: The development of a self-report scale*. Paper presented at the meeting of the Midwestern Psychological Association, Chicago.

Dubow, E. F., & Ullman, D. G. (1989). Assessing social support in elementary school children: The survey of children's social support. *Journal of Clinical Child Psychology, 18*(1), 52–64.

Dunn, J., Davies, L., O'Connor, T. G., & Sturgess, W. (2001). Family lives and friendships: The perspectives of children in step-, single-parent and nonstep families. *Journal of Family Psychology, 15*(2), 272–287.

Durbin, D. L., Darling, N., Steinberg, L., & Brown, B. B. (1993). Parenting style and peer group membership among European American adolescence. *Journal of Research on Adolescence, 3*, 87–100.

Dwyer, S. A., Graham, J. R., & Ott, E. K. (1992). *Psychiatric symptoms associated with the MMPI-2 content scales*. Unpublished manuscript, Kent State University, Kent.

Eccles, J., & Barber, B. L. (1999). Student council, volunteering, basketball, or marching band: What kind of extracurricular participation matters? *Journal of Adolescent Research, 14*(1), 10–43.

Elias, M. J., & Haynes, N. M. (2008). Social competence, social support and academic achievement in minority, low-income, urban elementary school children. *School Psychology Quarterly, 23*(4), 474–495.

Emery, R. (1982). Interparental conflict and the children of discord and divorce. *Psychological Bulletin, 9*, 310–330.

Emery, R. E. (1999). *Marriage, divorce, and children's adjustment*. California: Sage.

Emery, R. E., Otto, R. K., & O'Donohue, W. T. (2005). A critical assessment of child custody evaluations: Limited science and a flawed system. *Psychological Science in the Public Interest, 6*(1), 1–29.

Enright, R. D., & Fitzgibbons, R. P. (2000). *Helping clients forgive: An empirical guide for resolving anger and restoring hope*. Washington: American Psychological Association.

Enright, R. D., & Rique, J. (2004). *Manual for the Enright Forgiveness Inventory*. Redwood City: Mind Garden.

Epstein, J. (1995). School/family/community partnerships: Caring for the children we share. *Phi Delta Kappan, 76*(9), 701–12.

Essau, C. A., Sasagawa, S., & Frick, P. J. (2006). Psychometric properties of the Alabama Parenting Questionnaire. *Journal of Child and Family Studies, 15*(5), 597–616.

Estrada, P., Arsenio, W. F., Hess, R. D., & Holloway, S. D. (1987). Affective quality of the mother-child relationships: Longitudinal consequences for children's school relevant cognitive functioning. *Developmental Psychology, 23*, 210–215.

Ewing, J. A. (1984). Detecting alcoholism: The CAGE questionnaire. *Journal of the American Medical Association, 252*, 1905–1907.

Eyberg, S. M., Nelson, M. M., Duke, M., & Boggs, S. R. (2005). *Manual for the dyadic parent-child interaction coding system* (3rd ed.). Available on-line at www.PCIT.org.

Eyberg, S. M., & Robinson, E. A. (1982). Parent–child interaction training: Effects on family functioning. *Journal of Clinical Child Psychology, 11*, 130–137.
Fagan, J., & Barnett, M. (2003). The relationship between maternal gatekeeping, paternal competence, mother's attitudes about the father role, and father-child care involvement. *Journal of Family Issues, 24*(8), 1020–1043.
Fantuzzo, J., McWayne, C., Perry, M. A., & Childs, S. (2004). Multiple dimensions of family involvement and their relations to behavioral and learning competencies for urban, low-income children. *School Psychology Review, 33*(4), 467–480.
Fantuzzo, J., Tighe, E., & Childs, S. (2000). Family Involvement Questionnaire: A multivariate assessment of family participation in early childhood education. *Journal of Educational Psychology, 92*(2), 367–376.
Farruggia, S. P., Chen, C., Greenberger, E., Dmitrieva, J., & Macek, P. (2004). Adolescent self-esteem in cross-cultural perspective: Testing measurement equivalence and a mediation model. *Journal of Cross-Cultural Psychology, 35*(6), 719–733.
Feinberg, M. (2003). The internal structure and ecological context of coparenting: A framework for research and intervention. *Parenting: Science and Practice, 3*, 95–132.
Feldstein, S. W., & Miller, W. R. (2007). Does subtle screening for substance abuse work? A review of the Substance Abuse Subtle Screening Inventory (SASSI). *Addiction, 102*, 41–50.
First, M. B., Spitzer, R. L., Gibbon, M., & Williams, J. B. W. (1995). The structured clinical interview for DSM-III-R personality disorders (SCID-II). *Journal of Personality Disorders, 9*(2), 83–91.
Fitch, D. (2002). Unpublished data from doctoral dissertation, University of Texas-Clear Lake.
Foote, R. C. (2000). *The Dyadic Parent-child Interaction Coding System II (DPICS-II): Reliability and validity with father-child dyads*. Unpublished doctoral dissertation, University of Florida, Gainesville.
Forehand, R., & McMahon, R. J. (1981). *Helping the noncompliant child: A clinician's guide to parent training*. New York: Guilford Press.
Fredricks, J. A., & Eccles, J. S. (2005). Family socialization, gender, and sport motivation and involvement. *Journal of Sport & Exercise Psychology, 27*(1), 3–31.
French, D. C., & Waas, G. A. (1985). Behavior problems of peer-neglected and peer-rejected elementary-age children: Parent and teacher perspectives. *Child Development, 56*, 246–252.
Frick, P. J., Christian, R. E., & Wootton, J. (1999). Age trends in the association between parenting practices and conduct problems. *Behavior Modification, 23*, 106–128.
Frick, P. J., Kimonis, E. R., Dandreaux, D. M., & Farrell, J. (2003). The four-year stability of psychopathic traits in non-referred youth. *Behavioral Sciences and the Law, 21*, 713–736.
Fullerton, W. S. (1972). *Self-disclosure, self-esteem, and risk taking: A study of their convergent and discriminant validity in elementary school children*. Doctoral dissertation, University of California-Berkeley.
Furman, W., & Buhrmester, D. (1985). Children's perceptions of the qualities of sibling relationships. *Child Development, 56*, 448–461.
Furstenberg, F. F., Jr., Cook, T. D., Eccles, J., Elder, G. H., Jr., & Sameroff, A. (1999). *Managing to make it: Urban families and adolescent success*. Chicago: The University of Chicago Press.
Furstenberg, F. F., Nord, C. W., Peterson, J. L., & Zill, N. (1983). The life course of children of divorce. *American Sociological Review, 48*(5), 656–668.
Furstenberg, F. F., & Teitler, J. O. (1994). Reconsidering the effects of marital disruption: What happens to children of divorce in early childhood? *Journal of Family Issues, 15*(2), 173–190.
Galatzer-Levy, R., & Kraus, L. (Eds.). (1999). *The scientific basis of child custody decisions*. New York: Wiley.
Garmezy, N. (1973). Competence and adaptation in adult schizophrenic patients and children at risk. In S. R. Dean (Ed.), *Schizophrenia: The first ten Dean Award Lectures* (pp. 163–204). New York: MSS Information Corp.
Garmezy, N., & Devine, V. (1985). Project competence: The Minnesota studies of children vulnerable to psychopathology. In N. Watt, E. Anthony, L. Wynne, & J. Rolf (Eds.), *Children at risk for schizophrenia* (pp. 289–232). Cambridge: Cambridge University Press.

Garner, D. M. (1991). *Eating Disorders Inventory-2: Professional manual*. Odessa: Psychological Assessment Resources, Inc.

Gasper, J. A. F., Stolberg, A. L., Macie, K., & Williams, L. (2009). Co-parenting in intact and divorced families: Its impact on young adult adjustment. *Journal of Divorce and Remarriage, 49*(3/4), 114–127.

Gerard, A. B. (1994). *Parent-Child Relationship Inventory Manual*. Los Angeles: Western Psychological Services.

Gilligan, R. (2000). Adversity, resilience and young people: The protective value of positive school and spare time experiences. *Children and Society, 14*, 37–47.

Glover, R. J., & Steele, C. (1989). Comparing the effects on the child of post-divorce parenting arrangements. *Journal of Divorce, 12*(2/3), 185–201.

Gould, J. W. (1998). *Scientifically crafted child custody evaluations*. Thousand Oaks: Sage.

Gould, J. W. (2006). A guide for forensic mental health professionals. *Journal of Child Custody, 1*(1), 77–96.

Gourley, E. V., & Stolberg, A. L. (2000). An empirical investigation of psychologists' custody evaluation procedures. *Journal of Divorce and Remarriage, 33*(1/2), 1–29.

Graham, J. R., Ben-Porath, Y. S., & McNutly, J. L. (1999). *MMPI-2 Correlates for Outpatient Community Mental Health Settings*. Minnesota: University of Minnesota Press.

Grant, B. F. (2000). Estimates of U.S. children exposed to alcohol abuse and dependence in the family. *American Journal of Public Health, 90*(1), 112–115.

Green, B. A., Handel, R. W., & Archer, R. P. (2006). External correlates of the MMPI-2 content component scales in mental health inpatients. *Assessment, 13*, 80–97.

Griffiths, R. A., Beumont, P. J. V., Giannakopoulos, E., Russell, J., Schotte, D., Thornton, C., Touyz, S. W., & Varano, P. (1997). Measuring self-esteem in dieting disordered patients: The validity of the Rosenberg and the Coopersmith contrasted. *International Journal of Eating Disorders, 25*(2), 227–231.

Grisso, T. (1998). *Forensic evaluation of juveniles*. Sarasota, FL: Professional Resource Press.

Grisso, T. (2003). *Evaluating competencies: Forensic assessments and instruments* (2nd ed.). New York: Plenum.

Grothe, K. B., Dutton, G. R., Jones, G. N., Bodenlos, J., Ancona, M., & Brantley, P. J. (2005). Validation of the Beck Depression Inventory-II in a low-income African American sample of medical outpatients. *Psychological Assessment, 17*, 110–114.

Grove, W., & Meehl, P. (1996). Comparative efficacy of informal (subjective, impressionistic) and formal (mechanical, algorithmic) prediction procedures: The clinical-statistical controversy. *Psychology, Public Policy and Law, 2*, 293–323.

Grych, J., & Fincham, F. (2001). *Inter-parental conflict and child development*. New York: Cambridge University Press.

Grych, J. H., Seid, M., & Fincham, F. D. (1992). Assessing marital conflict from the child's perspective: The children's perception of interparental conflict scale. *Child Development, 63*, 558–572.

Guillon, M. S., Crocq, M. A., & Bailey, P. E. (2003). The relationship between self-esteem and psychiatric disorders in adolescents. *European Psychiatry, 18*(2), 59–62.

Gutman, L. M., & McLoyd, V. C. (2000). Parents' management of their children's education within the home, at school, and in the community: An examination of African American families living in poverty. *Urban Review, 32*, 1–24.

Gutman, L. M., Sameroff, A. S., & Eccles, J. S. (2002). The academic achievement of African American students during early adolescence: An examination of risk, promotive, and protective factors. *American Journal of Community Psychology, 30*(3), 376–399.

Guttman, J., Ben-Archer, C., & Lazar, A. (1999). Withdrawal threshold in interpersonal conflict among adolescents of divorced parents. *Educational Psychology: An International Journal of Experimental Educational Psychology, 19*(2), 181–190.

Hamilton, M. (1960). A rating scale for depression. *Journal of Neural Neurosurgery and Psychiatry, 23*, 56–61.

Hamilton, H. A., & Hango, D. W. (2008). Adolescent stigma towards drug addiction: Effects of age and drug use behaviour. *Addictive Behavior, 34*, 360–364.

Hammen, C., & Brennan, P. A. (2003). Severity, chronicity and timing of maternal depression and risk for adolescent offspring diagnoses in a community sample. *Archives of General Psychiatry, 60*, 253–258.

Hammen, C., Gordon, G., Burge, D., Adrian, C., Jaenicke, C., & Hiroto, G. (1987). Maternal affective disorder, illness and stress: Risk for children's psychopathology. *American Journal of Psychiatry, 144*, 736–741.

Hanf, C. (1969). *A two-stage program for modifying maternal controlling during mother–child (M–C) interaction.* Paper presented at the meeting of the Western Psychological Association, Vancouver, British Columbia.

Hansson, R. O., Jones, W. H., & Carpenter, B. N. (1984). Relational competence and social support. *Review of Personality and Social Psychology, 5*, 265–284.

Hare, R. D. (1991). *The Hare Psychopathy Checklist-Revised (PCL-R).* Toronto: Multi-Health Systems.

Harnett, P. H. (2007). A procedure for assessing a parent's capacity for change in child protection cases. *Children and Youth Services Review, 29*(9), 1179–1188.

Harper, S. E., & Fine, M. A. (2006). The effects of involved nonresidential fathers' distress, parenting behaviors, interparental conflict, and the quality of father-child relationships on children's well-being. *Fathering, 4*(3), 286–311.

Harris, C. A., & D'Eon, J. L. (2008). Psychometric properties of the beck depression inventory 2nd edition (BDI-II) in individuals with chronic pain. *Pain, 137*, 609–622.

Harter, S. (1985). *Manual for the social support scale for children.* Denver: University of Denver.

Hartup, W. W. (1999). Peer experience and its developmental significance. In M. Bennett (Ed.), *Developmental psychology: Achievements and prospects.* Philadelphia: Psychology Press.

Haskett, M. E., Ahern, L. S., Ward, C. S., & Allaire, J. C. (2006). Factor structure and validity of the Parenting Stress Index-Short Form. *Journal of Clinical Child and Adolescent Psychology, 35*(2), 302–312.

Hatcher, J., & Hall, L. A. (2009). Psychometric properties of the Rosenberg Self-Esteem Scale in African American single mothers. *Issues in Mental Health Nursing, 30*, 70–77.

Hathaway, S. R., & McKinley, J. C. (1989). *Minnesota Multiphasic Personality Inventory-2.* Minneapolis: University of Minnesota Press.

Hawes, D. J., & Dadds, M. R. (2006). Assessing parenting practices through parent-report and direct observation during parent-training. *Journal of Child and Family Studies, 15*(5), 555–568.

Haynes, S. N., & Horn, W. F. (1982). Reactivity in behavioral observation: A review. *Behavioral Assessment, 4*, 369–85.

Haz, A. M., & Ramirez, V. (1998). Preliminary validation of the Child Abuse Potential Inventory in Chile. *Child Abuse and Neglect, 22*(9), 869–879.

Heaton, T. B. (1990). Marital stability throughout the child-rearing years. *Demography, 27*, 55–63.

Heinze, M., & Grisso, T. (1996). Instruments used in child custody evaluations to assess parenting competencies. *Behavioral Sciences and the Law, 14*, 293–313.

Hellman, J. (1988). *A survey of the perceptions of judges, attorneys and mental health professionals with respect to child custody determinations.* Unpublished doctoral dissertation, University of Northern California, Greeley.

Hempel, C. (1965). *Aspects of scientific explanation and other essays in the philosophy of science.* New York: Collier-MacMillan Limited.

Herman, S. P., Duanne, J. E., Ayres, W., Arnold, V., Benedek, E., Benson, R. S., Bernet, W., Bernstein, G. A., Bryant, E., Licamele, W., McClellan, J., & Shaw, K. (1997). Practice parameters for child custody evaluation. *Journal of the American Academy of Child & Adolescent Psychiatry, 36*, 57S–69S.

Hess, R., & Camera, K. (1979). Post-divorce family relationships as mediating factors in the consequences of divorce for children. *Journal of Social Issues, 35*, 79–96.

Hetherington, E. M. (1990). Coping with family transitions: Winners, losers and survivors. *Annual Progress in Child Psychiatry & Child Development, 22*, 221–241.
Hetherington, E. M. (1999). Social capital and development of youth from nondivorced, divorced, and remarried families. In A. Collins & B. Laureen (Eds.), *Relationships as developmental contexts: The 29th Minnesota symposium on child psychology* (pp. 177–209). Hillsdale: Lawrence Erlbaum.
Hetherington, E. M., Bridges, M., & Insabella, G. M. (1998). What matters? What does not?: Five perspectives on the association between marital transitions and child adjustment. *American Psychologist, 53*(2), 167–184.
Hetherington, E. M., & Clingempeel, W. G. (1992). Coping with marital transitions: A family systems perspective. *Monographs of the Society for Research in Child Development, 57*(2/3), 1–242.
Hetherington, E. M., Cox, M., & Cox, R. (1982). Effects of divorce on parents and children. In M. Lamb (Ed.), *Nontraditional families*. Hillsdale: Erlbaum.
Hetherington, E. M., & Kelly, J. (2002). *For better or for worse: Divorce reconsidered*. New York: W.W. Norton & Company.
Hetherington, E. M., & Stanley-Hagan, M. (1999). The adjustment of children with divorced parents: A risk and resiliency perspective. *Journal of Child Psychology and Psychiatry, 40*, 129–140.
Hill, N. E., & Taylor, L. C. (2004). Parental school involvement and children's academic achievement: Pragmatics and issues. *Current Directions in Psychological Science, 13*(4), 161–164.
Hinshaw, S. P. (2002). Preadolescent girls with attention-deficit/hyperactivity disorder: I. Background characteristics, comorbidity, cognitive and social functioning, and parenting practices. *Journal of Consulting and Clinical Psychology, 70*, 1086–1098.
Horvath, L. S., Logan, T. K., & Walker, R. (2002). Child custody cases: A content analysis of evaluations in practice. *Professional Psychology: Research and Practice, 33*(6), 557–565.
Huebner, A. J., & Mancini, J. A. (2003). Shaping structured out-of-school time use among youth: The effects of self, family, and friend systems. *Journal of Youth and Adolescence, 32*, 453–463.
Hutchison, J. J., & Black, M. M. (1996). Psychometric properties of the Parenting Stress Index in a sample of low-income African American mothers of infants and toddlers. *Early Education and Development, 7*(4), 381–400.
Jacobo, M. C., Blais, M. A., Baity, M. R., & Harley, R. (2007). Concurrent validity of the personality assessment inventory borderline scales in patients seeking dialectical behavior therapy. *Journal of Personality Assessment, 88*(1), 74–80.
Jacobson, D. (1978). The impact of marital separation/divorce on children: 1. Parent-child separation and child adjustment. *Journal of Divorce, 1*(4), 341–360.
Jefferson, A. L., Powers, D. V., & Pope, M. (2000). Beck Depression Inventory II (BDI-II) and the Geriatric Depression Scale (GDS) in older women. *Clinical Gerontologist, 22*, 3–12.
Jenkins, J. M., Rasbash, J., & O'Connor, T. G. (2003). The role of the shared family context in differential parenting. *Developmental Psychology, 39*, 99–113.
Jenuwine, M. J., & Cohler, B. J. (1999). Major parental psychopathology and child custody. In R. M. Galatzer-Levy & L. Kraus (Eds.), *The scientific basis of child custody decisions* (pp. 285–318). New York: Wiley.
Johnson, B. W., Redfield, D. L., Miller, R. L., & Simpson, R. E. (1983). The Coopersmith Self-Esteem Inventory: A construct validation study. *Educational and Psychological Measurement, 43*, 907–913.
Johnston, D. (1995). Effects of parental incarceration. In K. Gabel & D. Johnson (Eds.), *Children of incarcerated parents* (pp. 59–88). New York: Lexington Books.
Johnston, J. R., Kline, M., & Tschann, J. (1989). Ongoing postdivorce conflict in families contesting custody: Effects on children of joint custody and frequent access. *American Journal of Orthopsychiatry, 59*, 576–592.
Jordan, W. J., & Nettles, S. M. (1999). *How students invest their time out of school: Effects on school engagement, perceptions of life chances, and achievement* (Report no. 29). Washington: Center for Research on Education of Students Placed At Risk.

Kamphaus, R. W., & Reynolds, C. R. (1992). *Behavioral and emotional screening system (BASC).*: Pearson Educations Inc.

Kamphaus, R. W., & Reynolds, C. R. (2006). *Parenting relationship questionnaire manual.* Minneapolis: NCS Pearson Inc.

Katz, L. F., & Gottman, J. M. (1997). Buffering children from marital conflict and dissolution. *Journal of Clinical Child Psychology, 26*, 157–171.

Kazarian, S. S., & McCabe, S. B. (1991). Dimensions of social support in the MSPSS: Factorial structure, reliability, and theoretical implications. *Journal of Community Psychology, 19*, 150–160.

Keilin, W. G., & Bloom, L. J. (1986). Child custody evaluation practices: A survey of experienced professionals. *Professional Psychology: Research and Practice, 17*, 338–346.

Kelly, J. B. (1988). Longer-term adjustment in children of divorce: Converging findings and implications for practice. *Journal of Family Psychology, 2*(2), 119–140.

Kelly, J. B., & Emery, R. E. (2003). Children's adjustment following divorce: Risk and resilience perspectives. *Family Relations, 52*, 352–362.

Kelly, J., & Lamb, M. (2000). Using child development research to make appropriate custody and access decisions for young children. *Family & Conciliation Courts Review, 38*(3), 297–311.

Kimball, O. M. (1973). *Development of norms for the Coopersmith Self-Esteem Inventories: Grade 4 through 8.* Unpublished doctoral dissertation, Northern Illinois University, DeKalb.

King, G., Law, M., King, S., Hurley, P., Hanna, S., Kertoy, M., et al. (2006). Measuring children's participation in recreation and leisure activities: Construct validation of the CAPE and PAC. *Child: Care, Health and Development, 33*, 28–39.

King, G., Law, M., King, S., Rosenbaum, P., Kertoy, M., & Young, N. L. (2004). *Children's Assessment of Participation and Enjoyment (CAPE) and Preferences for Activities in Children (PAC).* San Antonio: Harcourt Assessment.

King, G., Petrenchik, T., Law, M., & Hurley, P. (2009). The enjoyment of formal and informal recreation and leisure activities: A comparison of school-aged children with and without physical disabilities. *International Journal of Disability, Development and Education, 56*(2), 109–130.

Kirk, S. A., McCarthy, J. J., & Kirk, W. D. (1961). *Illinois Test of Psycholinguistic Abilities* (3rd ed.).: University of Illinois Press.

Kline, M., Tschann, J. M., Johnston, J. R., & Wallerstein, J. S. (1989). Children's adjustment in joint and sole physical custody families. *Developmental Psychology, 25*(3), 430–438.

Knickmeyer, N., Sexton, K., & Nishimura, N. (2002). The impact of same-sex friendships on the well-being of women: A review of the literature. *Women & Therapy, 25*(1), 37–59.

Knight, G. P., Virdin, L. M., Ocampo, K. A., & Roosa, M. (1994). An examination of the cross ethnic equivalence of measures of negative life events and mental health among Hispanic and Anglo-American children. *American Journal of Community Psychology, 22*(6), 767–783.

Kolko, D. J., Dorn, L. D., Bukstein, O., & Burke, J. D. (2008). Clinically referred ODD children with or without CD and healthy controls: Comparisons across contextual domains. *Journal of Child and Family Studies, 17*(5), 714–734.

Kot, L., & Shoemaker, H. M. (1999). Children of divorce: An investigation of the developmental effects from infancy through adulthood. *Journal of Divorce and Remarriage, 31*, 161–78.

Kovacs, M. (1981). Rating scales to assess depression in school-aged children. *Acta Paedopsychiatry, 46*, 305–315.

Kunin, C. C., Ebbesen, E. B., & Konecni, V. J. (1992). An archival study of decision-making in child custody disputes. *Journal of Clinical Psychology, 48*, 564–573.

Kurdek, L. A. (1987). Children's adjustment to parental divorce: An ecological perspective. In J. P. Vincent (Ed.), *Advances in family intervention and theory* (Vol. 4, p. 131). Greenwich: JAI Press.

Kurdek, L. A., & Berg, B. (1983). Correlates of children's adjustment to their parents' divorces. In L. A. Kurdek (Ed.), *Children and divorce* (pp. 47–60). San Francisco: Jossey-Bass.

Kurdek, L. A., & Blisk, D. (1983). Dimensions and correlates of mothers' divorce experiences. *Journal of Divorce, 6*, 1–24.

Kushner, M. A. (2006). Whose best interests: The ruling or the children? *Journal of Divorce and Remarriage, 44*(3/4), 17–29.

Ladd, G. W. (2006). Peer rejection, aggressive or withdrawn behavior and psychological maladjustment from ages 5 to 12: An examination of four predictive models. *Child Development, 77*, 822–846.

Ladd, G. W., Herald-Brown, S. L., & Andrews, R. K. (2009). The Child Behavior Scales (CBS) Revisited: A longitudinal evaluation of CBS with children, preadolescents and adolescents. *Psychological Assessment, 21*(3), 325–339.

Ladd, G. W., Kochenderfer, B. J., & Coleman, C. C. (1996). Friendship quality as a predictor of young children's early school adjustment. *Child Development, 67*(3), 1103–1118.

Ladd, G. W., & Profilet, S. M. (1996). The Child Behavior Scale: A teacher-report measure of young children's aggressive, withdrawn and prosocial behaviors. *Developmental Psychology, 32*, 1008–1024.

Lamb, M. E., Sternberg, K. J., & Thompson, R. A. (1997). The effects of divorce and custody arrangements on children's behavior, development, and adjustment. *Family and Conciliation Courts Review, 35*, 393–404.

Lamborn, S. D., Mounts, S., Steinberg, L., & Dornbusch, S. M. (1991). Patterns of competence and adjustment among adolescents from authoritative, authoritarian, indulgent, and neglectful families. *Child Development, 62*, 1049–1065.

Lane, G. G., White, A. E., & Henson, R. K. (2002). Expanding reliability generalization methods with KR-21 estimates: An RG study of the Coopersmith Self-Esteem Inventory. *Educational and Psychological Measurement, 62*(4), 685–711.

Larson, R. W. (2000). Toward a psychology of positive youth development. *American Psychologist, 55*(170), 183.

Laudan, L. (1977). *Progress and its problems: Towards a theory of scientific growth*. Berkeley and Los Angeles, CA: University of California Press.

Laux, J. M., Salyers, K. M., & Kotova, E. (2005). A psychometric evaluation of the SASSI-3 in a college sample. *Journal of College Counseling, 8*, 41–51.

Lazowski, L. E., Miller, F. G., Boye, M. W., & Miller, G. A. (1998). Efficacy of the Substance Abuse Subtle Screening Inventory-3 (SASSI-3) in identifying substance dependence disorders in clinical settings. *Journal of Personality Assessment, 71*, 114–128.

Lee, M. Y. (2002). A model of children's postdivorce behavioral adjustment in maternal- and dual-residence arrangements. *Journal of Family Issues, 23*(5), 672–697.

Lee, Y., & Enright, R. D. (2009). Father's forgiveness as a moderator between perceived unfair treatment by a family of origin member and anger with own children. *The Family Journal: Counseling and Therapy for Couples and Families, 17*(1), 22–31.

Lengua, L. J., Wolchik, S. A., & Braver, S. L. (1995). Understanding children's divorce adjustment from an ecological perspective. *Journal of Divorce and Remarriage, 22*, 25–53.

Lerner, R. M., & Lerner, J. V. (2006). Toward a new vision and vocabulary about adolescence: Theoretical, empirical, and applied bases of a "Positive Youth Development" perspective. In L. Balter & C. S. Tamis-LeMonda (Eds.), *Child psychology: A handbook of contemporary issues* (pp. 445–469). New York: Psychology Press.

LeVine, R. A. (1974). Parental goals: A cross-cultural view. *Teachers College Record, 76*, 226–239.

Linville, D., & Huebner, A. (2005). The analysis of extracurricular activities and their relationship to youth violence. *Journal of Youth and Adolescence, 34*(5), 483–492.

Litovsky, V. G., & Dusek, J. B. (1985). Perceptions of child rearing and self-concept development during the early adolescent years. *Journal of Youth and Adolescence, 14*, 373–387.

Lord, S. E., Eccles, J. S., & McCarthy, K. A. (1994). Surviving the junior high school transition: Family processes and self-perceptions as protective and risk factors. *Journal of Early Adolescence, 14*, 162–199.

Lovejoy, M. C., Weis, R., O'Hare, E., & Rubin, E. C. (1999). Development and initial validation of the Parenting Behavior Inventory. *Psychological Assessment, 11*(4), 534–545.

Lowery, C. R. (1981). Child custody decisions in divorce proceedings: A survey of judges. *Professional Psychology, 12*, 492–498.

Luepnitz, D. A. (1986). A comparison of maternal, paternal, and joint custody: Understanding the varieties of post-divorce family life. *Journal of Divorce, 9*(3), 1–12.

Lundahl, B. W., Nimer, J., & Parsons, B. (2006). Preventing child abuse: A meta-analysis of parent training programs. *Research on Social Work Practice, 16*, 251–262.

Luthar, S. S. (Ed.). (2003). *Resilience and vulnerability: Adaptation in the context of childhood adversities*. New York: Cambridge University Press.

Luthar, S., & Suchman, N. (2000). Relational psychotherapy mothers' group: A developmentally informed intervention for at-risk mothers. *Development and Psychopathology, 12*(2), 235–253.

Maccoby, E. E., & Martin, J. A. (1983). Socialization in the context of the family: Parent–child interaction. In P. H. Mussen (Ed.), & E. M. Hetherington (Vol. Ed.), *Handbook of child psychology: Vol. 4. Socialization, personality, and social development*. New York: Wiley.

Maccoby, E. E., & Mnookin, R. H. (1992). *Dividing the child: Social and legal dimensions of child custody*. Cambridge: Harvard University Press.

Macie, K. M. (2002). *Influence of co-parenting and marital status on young adult adjustment*. Unpublished doctoral dissertation, Virginia Commonwealth University.

MacKinnon, C. E. (1989). An observational investigation of sibling interactions in married and divorced families. *Developmental Psychology, 25*, 36–44.

MacPhee, D., Fritz, J., & Miller-Heyl, J. (1996). Ethnic variations in personal social networks and parenting. *Child Development, 67*, 3278–3295.

Maffei, C., Fossati, A., Agostoni, I., Barraco, A., Bagnato, M., Deborah, D., Namia, C., Novella, L., & Petrachi, M. (1997). Interrater reliability and internal consistency of the Structured Clinical Interview for DSM-IV Axis II personality disorders (SCID II) version 2. *Journal of Personality Disorders, 11*(3), 279–284.

Mahoney, J. L. (2000). School extracurricular activity participation as a moderator in the development of antisocial patterns. *Child Development, 71*(2), 502–516.

Mahoney, J. L., & Cairns, R. B. (1997). Do extracurricular activities protect against early school dropout? *Developmental Psychology, 33*(2), 241–253.

Mahoney, J. L., Cairns, B. D., & Farmer, T. W. (2003). Promoting interpersonal competence and educational success through extracurricular activity participation. *Journal of Educational Psychology, 95*, 409–418.

Mahoney, J. L., Lord, H., & Carryl, E. (2005a). An ecological analysis of after-school program participation and the development of academic performance and motivational attributes for disadvantaged children. *Child Development, 76*, 811–825.

Mahoney, J. L., Lord, H., & Carryl, E. (2005b). Afterschool program participation and the development of child obesity and peer acceptance. *Applied Developmental Science, 9*, 201–214.

Mann, B. J., & MacKenzie, E. P. (1996). Pathways among marital functioning, parental behaviors, and child behavior problems in school-age boys. *Journal of Clinical Child Psychology, 25*, 183–191.

Manz, P. H., Fantuzzo, J. W., & Power, T. J. (2004). Multidimensional assessment of family involvement among urban elementary students. *Journal of School Psychology, 42*(6), 461–475.

March, J. S., Parker, J. D., Sullivan, K., Stallings, P., & Connors, C. K. (1997). The Multidimensional Anxiety Scale for Children (MASC): Factor structure, reliability, and validity. *Journal of the American Academy of Child and Adolescent Psychiatry, 36*, 554–565.

Marcus, R. F., & Betzer, P. D. (1996). Attachment and antisocial behavior in early adolescence. *The Journal of Early Adolescence, 16*(2), 229–248.

Markham, M. S., Ganong, L. H., & Coleman, M. (2007). Coparental identity and mothers' cooperation in coparental relationships. *Family Relations, 56*, 369–377.

Marriage, K., & Cummins, R. A. (2004). Subjective quality of life and self-esteem in children: The role of primary and secondary control in coping with everyday stress. *Social Indicators Research, 66*, 107–122.

Marshall, N. L., Noonan, A. E., McCartney, K., Marx, F., & Keefe, N. (2001). It takes an urban village: Parenting networks of urban families. *Journal of Family Issues, 22*(2), 163–182.

Mart, E. G. (2007). *Issue focused forensic child custody assessment.* Sarasota: Professional Resource Press.

Mason, M. A., & Quirk, A. (1997). Are mothers losing custody? Read my lips: Trends in judicial decision-making in custody disputes – 1920, 1960, and 1995. *Family Law Quarterly, 31*, 215–236.

Masten, A. S., Best, K. M., & Garmezy, N. (1990). Resilience and development: Contributions from the study of children who overcome adversity. *Development and Psychopathology, 2*, 425–444.

Masten, A. S., & Coatsworth, J. D. (1995). Competence, resilience, & psychopathology. In D. Cicchetti & D. Cohen (Eds.), *Developmental psychopathology: Vol. 2. Risk, disorder, and adaptation* (pp. 715–752). New York: Wiley.

Masten, A. S., & Coatsworth, J. D. (1998). The development of competence in favorable and unfavorable environments: Lessons from research on successful children. *American Psychologist, 53*, 205–220.

Masten, A. S., & Garmezy, N. (1985). Risk, vulnerability and protective factors in developmental psychology. In B. B. Lahey & A. E. Kazdin (Eds.), *Advances in child clinical psychology* (pp. 1–52). New York: Plenum.

Masten, A. S., & Shaffer, A. (2006). How families matter in child development: Reflections from research on risk and resilience. In A. Clarke-Stewart & J. Dunn (Eds.), *Families count: Effects on child and adolescent development* (pp. 5–25). Cambridge: Cambridge University Press.

McCabe, K., Yeh, M., Lau, A., Argote, C. B., & Liang, J. (2010). Parent-child interactions among low-income Mexican American parents and preschoolers: Do clinic referred families differ from nonreferred families? *Behavior Therapy, 41*, 82–92.

McCormick, C. B., & Kennedy, J. H. (2000). Father-child separation, retrospective and current views of attachment relationships with father, and self-esteem in late adolescence. *Psychological Reports, 86*, 827–834.

McFarlane, A. H., Bellissimo, A., & Norman, G. R. (1995). Family structure, family functioning and adolescent well-being: The transcendent influence of parental style. *Journal of Child Psychology/Psychiatry, 36*, 847–864.

McHale, S. M., Crouter, A. C., & Tucker, C. J. (2001). Free-time activities in middle childhood: Links with adjustment in early adolescence. *Child Development, 72*, 1764–1778.

McLanahan, S. (1999). Father absence and the welfare of children. In M. Hetherington (Ed.), *Coping with divorce, single parenting, and remarriage: A risk and resiliency perspective* (pp. 117–145). Mahwah: Lawrence Erlbaum.

McLanahan, S., & Sandefur, G. (1994). *Growing up with a single parent: What hurts, what helps.* Cambridge: Harvard University Press.

McLoyd, V. C. (1998). Socioeconomic disadvantage and child development. *American Psychologist, 53*, 185–204.

McNally, S., Eisenberg, N., & Harris, J. D. (1991). Consistency and change in maternal child-rearing practices and values: A longitudinal study. *Child Development, 62*, 190–198.

McNeal, R. B. (1998). High school extracurricular activities: Closed structures and stratifying patterns of participation. *Journal of Educational Research, 91*(3), 183–191.

Meehl, P. E. (1954). *Clinical versus statistical prediction: A theoretical analysis and a review of the evidence.* Minneapolis: University of Minnesota Press.

Melton, G. B., & Limber, S. P. (1989). Psychologists' involvement in cases of child maltreatment: Limits of role and expertise. *American Psychologist, 44*, 1225–1233.

Melton, G. B., Petrila, J., Poythress, N. G., & Slobogin, C. (1997). *Psychological evaluations for the courts: A handbook for mental health professionals and lawyers* (2nd ed.). New York: Guilford Press.

Mendez, J. L. (2010). How can parents get involved in preschool? Barriers and engagement in education by ethnic minority parents of children attending Head Start. *Cultural Diversity and Ethnic Minority Psychology, 16*(1), 26–36.

Mendez, J. L., Carpenter, J. L., LaForett, D. R., & Cohen, J. S. (2009). Parental engagement and barriers to participation in a community-based preventive intervention. *American Journal of Community Psychology, 44*(1–2), 1–14.

Menning, C. L. (2002). Absent parents are more than money: The joint effect of activities and financial support on youths' educational attainment. *Journal of Family Issues, 23*(5), 648–671.

Miles, S. B., & Stipek, D. (2006). Contemporary and longitudinal associations between social behavior and literacy achievement in a sample of low-income elementary school children. *Child Development, 77*, 103–117.

Miller, F., & Lazowski, L. (1999). *Substance Abuse Subtle Screening Inventory-3*. Bloomington: Baugh Enterprises.

Miller, B. A., Smyth, N. J., & Mudar, P. J. (1999). Mother's alcohol and other drug problems and their punitiveness toward their children. *Journal of Studies of Alcohol, 60*, 21–34.

Millon, T., Millon, C., Davis, R., & Grossman, S. (2009). *MCMI-III Manual* (4th ed.). Minneapolis: NCS Pearson.

Milner, J. S. (1986). *The Child Abuse Potential Inventory: Manual* (2nd ed.). Webster: Psytec.

Milner, J. S., & Crouch, J. L. (1997). Impact and detection of response distortions on parenting measures used to assess risk for child physical abuse. *Journal of Personality Assessment, 69*(3), 633–650.

Milner, J. S., & Crouch, J. L. (1999). Child physical abuse: Theory and research. In R. L. Hampton (Ed.), *Family violence: Prevention and treatment* (pp. 33–65). Newbury Park: Sage.

Milner, J. S., Gold, R. G., Ayoub, C., & Jacewitz, M. M. (1984). Predictive validity of the Child Abuse Potential Inventory. *Journal of Consulting and Clinical Psychology, 52*(5), 879–884.

Minze, L. C., McDonald, R., Rosentraub, E. L., & Jouriles, E. N. (2010). Making sense of family conflict: Intimate partner violence and preschoolers' externalizing problems. *Journal of Family Psychology, 24*(1), 5–11.

Mnookin, M. (1975). Child custody adjudication: Judicial functions in the face of indeterminacy. *Law and Contemporary Problems, 39*, 226–293.

Morey, L. C. (1996). *An Interpretive Guide to the Personality Assessment Inventory (PAI)*. Odessa: Psychological Assessment Resources.

Morrell, J., & Murray, L. (2003). Postnatal depression and the development of conduct disorder and hyperactive symptoms in childhood: A prospective longitudinal study from 2 months to 8 years. *Journal of Child Psychology and Psychiatry, 44*(4), 489–508.

Mullis, R. L., Graf, S. C., & Mullis, A. K. (2009). Parental relationships, autonomy, and identity process of high school students. *The Journal of Genetic Psychology, 170*(4), 326–338.

Murray, L., Fiori-Cowley, A., Hooper, R., & Cooper, P. (1996). The impact of postnatal depression and associated adversity on early mother-infant interactions and later infant outcome. *Child Development, 67*(5), 2512–2526.

Murray, L., Woolgar, M., Cooper, P. J., & Hipwell, A. (2001). Cognitive vulnerability in five year old children of depressed mothers. *Journal of Child Psychology and Psychiatry, 42*(7), 891–899.

Myers, S. M. (1997). Marital uncertainty and childbearing. *Social Forces, 75*, 1271–1289.

National Center for Health Statistics (NCHS). (2008). *Births, marriages, divorces and deaths, provisional data for 2008*. Downloaded August 2008 at: http://www.cdc.gov/nchs/fastats/divorce.htm.

National Institute of Child Health and Human Development (NICHD) Early Child Care Research Network. (1999). Chronicity of maternal depressive symptoms, maternal sensitivity and child functioning at 36 months. *Developmental Psychology, 35*, 1297–1310.

Nealer, J. B. (1992). A multivariate study of intergenerational transmission of child abuse The Ohio State University. *Dissertation Abstracts International, 53*, 1848.

Noom, M. J., Dekovic, M., & Meeus, W. H. J. (1999). Autonomy, attachment and psychosocial adjustment during adolescence: A double-edged sword? *Journal of Adolescence, 22*, 771–783.

Noom, M. J., Dekovic, M., & Meeus, W. H. J. (2001). Conceptual analysis and measurement of adolescent autonomy. *Journal of Youth and Adolescence, 30*(5), 577–595.

Nord, C. W., Brimhall, D., & West, J. (1997). *Fathers' involvement in their children's schools (NCES 98-091)*. Washington: U.S. Department of Education, National Center for Education Statistics.

Novak, G. (1996). *Developmental psychology: Dynamic systems and behavior analysis*. Reno: Context Press.

O'Brien, E. J., & Epstein, S. (1988). *MSEI: The Multidimensional Self-Esteem Inventory*. Odessa: Consulting Psychologists Press.

O'Donnell, E. H., Moreau, M., Cardemil, E. V., & Pollastri, A. (2010). Interparental conflict, parenting, and childhood depression in a diverse urban population: The role of general cognitive style. *Journal of Youth and Adolescence, 39*, 12–22.

O'Donohue, W., Beitz, K., & Cummings, N. (2007). A model for constructs relevant to child custody evaluations. *Journal of Forensic Psychology Practice, 7*(4), 125–139.

O'Donohue, W. T., Beitz, K., & Tolle, L. W. (2008). Controversies in child custody evaluations. In J. Skeem & S. Lillenfeld (Eds.), *Psychological science in the courtroom*. Berkeley: Guilford Press.

O'Donohue, W. T., & Bradley, A. (1999). Conceptual and empirical issues in child custody evaluations. *Clinical Psychology: Science and Practice, 6*, 310–322.

O'Koon, J. (1997). Attachment to parents and peers in late adolescence and their relationship with self-image. *Adolescence, 32*, 471–483.

Orathinkal, J., Vansteenwegen, A., Enright, R. D., & Stroobants, R. (2007). Further validation of the Dutch version of the Enright Forgiveness Inventory. *Community Mental Health Journal, 43*(2), 109–128.

Orvaschel, H., Walsh-Allis, G., & Ye, W. J. (1988). Psychopathology in children of parents with recurrent depression. *Journal of Abnormal Child Psychology, 16*, 17–28.

Otto, R. K., & Edens, J. F. (2003). Parenting capacity. In T. Grisso (Ed.), *Evaluating competencies: Forensic assessments and instruments*. New York: Plenum.

Papp, L. M., Cummings, E. M., & Goeke-Morey, M. C. (2005). Parental psychological distress, parent-child relationship qualities, and child adjustment: Direct, mediating and reciprocal pathways. *Parenting: Science and Practice, 5*(3), 259–283.

Parker, J. G., & Asher, S. R. (1993). Friendship and friendship quality in middle childhood: Links with peer group acceptance and feelings of loneliness and dissatisfaction. *Developmental Psychology, 29*, 611–621.

Parker, G., Tupling, H., & Brown, L. B. (1979). A parental bonding instrument. *British Journal of Medical Psychology, 52*, 1–10.

Patterson, G. R., DeBaryshe, B. D., & Ramsey, E. (1989). A developmental perspective on antisocial behavior. *American Psychologist, 44*, 329–335.

Paul, G. L., & Bernstein, D. A. (1976). Anxiety and clinical problems. In Spencer, Carson, & Thibout (Eds.), *Behavioral approaches to therapy*. Morristown: General Learning Press.

Pearson, J., & Thoennes, N. (1990). Custody after divorce: Demographic and attitudinal patterns. *American Journal of Orthopsychiatry, 60*(2), 233–249.

Peters, E. R., Day, S., McKenna, J., & Orbach, G. (1999). The incidence of delusional ideation in religious and psychotic populations. *British Journal of Clinical Psychology, 38*, 83–96.

Peters, R. H., Greenbaum, P. E., Steinberg, M. L., Carter, C. R., Ortiz, M. M., Fry, B. C., et al. (2000). Effectiveness of screening instruments in detecting substance use disorders among prisoners. *Journal of Substance Abuse Treatment, 18*, 349–358.

Peters, E. R., Joseph, S. A., & Garety, P. A. (1999). Measurement of delusional ideation in the normal population: Introducing the PDI (Peters et al. Delusions Inventory). *Schizophrenia Bulletin, 25*(3), 553–576.

Phillips, J., Charles, M., Sharpe, L., & Matthey, S. (2009). Validation of the subscales of the Edinburgh Postnatal Depression Scale in a sample of women with unsettled infants. *Journal of Affective Disorders, 118*(1–3), 101–112.

Pilowsky, D. J., Zybert, P. A., & Vlahov, D. (2005). Resilient children of injection drug users. *Journal of the American Academy of Child and Adolescent Psychiatry, 43*(11), 1372–1379.

Pong, S., & Ju, D. (2000). The effects of change in family structure and income on dropping out of middle and high school. *Journal of Family Issues, 21*(2), 147–169.

Popliger, M., Toste, J. R., & Heath, N. L. (2009). Perceived social support and domain-specific adjustment of children with emotional and behavioral difficulties. *Emotional & Behavioral Difficulties, 14*(3), 195–213.

Porter, B., & O'Leary, K. D. (1980). Marital discord and childhood behavior problems. *Journal of Abnormal Child Psychology, 8*, 287–295.

Powell, D. (2003) Divorce-on-demand: Forget about gay marriage – what about the state of regular marriage? *National Review, 55*(i20).

Powell, B., & Downey, D. B. (1997). Living in single-parent households: An investigation of the same-sex hypothesis. *American Sociological Review, 62*(4), 521–540.

Preuss, U. W., Watzke, A. B., Zimmermann, J., Wong, J. W. M., & Schmidt, C. O. (2010). Cannabis withdrawal severity and short-term course among cannabis-dependent adolescent and young adult inpatients. *Drug and Alcohol Dependence, 106*(2–3), 133–141.

Prinstein, M. J., & La Greca, A. M. (2004). Childhood rejection, aggression, and depression and predictors of adolescent girls' externalizing and health risk behaviors: A six-year longitudinal study. *Journal of Consulting and Clinical Psychology, 72*, 103–112.

Pruett, M. K., Williams, T. Y., Insabella, G., & Little, T. D. (2003). Family and legal indicators of child adjustment to divorce among families with young children. *Journal of Family Psychology, 17*(2), 169–180.

Ramey, S. L. (2002). The science and art of parenting. In J. G. Borkowski, S. L. Ramey, & M. Bristol-Power (Eds.), *Parenting and the child's world: Influences of academic, intellectual, and social-emotional development* (pp. 47–71). Mahwah: Erlbaum.

Rareshide, M., & Kern, R. (1991). Social interest: The haves and have nots. *Individual Psychology, 47*, 464–476.

Reidy, T. J., Silver, R. M., & Carlson, A. (1989). Child custody decisions: A survey of judges. *Family Law Quarterly, 13*, 75–87.

Reitman, D., Rhode, P. C., Hupp, S. D. A., & Altobello, C. (2002). Development and validation of the Parental Authority Questionnaire-Revised. *Journal of Psychopathology and Behavioral Assessment, 24*, 119–127.

Repetti, R. L., Taylor, S. E., & Seeman, T. E. (2002). Risky families: Family social environments and the mental and physical health of offspring. *Psychological Bulletin, 128*, 330–366.

Resnick, M. D., Bearman, P. S., Blum, R., Bauman, K. E., Harris, K. M., Jones, J., Tabor, J., Beuhring, T., Sieving, R. E., Shew, M., Ireland, M., Bearinger, L. H., & Udry, J. R. (1997). Protecting adolescents from harm, findings from the national longitudinal study on adolescent health. *Journal of the American Medical Association, 278*(10), 823–832.

Reynolds, C. R., & Kamphaus, R. W. (1992). *Behavioral Assessment Scale for Children*. Circle Pines: American Guidance Service.

Robins, D. L., Fein, D., Barton, M. L., & Green, J. A. (2001). The Modified Checklist for Autism in Toddlers: An initial study investigating the early detection of Autism and Pervasive Developmental Disorders. *Journal of Autism and Developmental Disabilities, 31*, 131–144.

Rockhill, C. M., Stoep, A. V., McCauley, E., & Katon, W. J. (2009). Social competence and social support as mediators between comorbid depressive and conduct problems and functional outcomes in middle school. *Journal of Adolescence, 32*(3), 535–553.

Rohrbaugh, J. B. (2008). *Comprehensive guide to child custody evaluations: Mental health and legal perspectives*. New York: Harvard Medical School/Springer.

Rolf, J., & Johnson, J. (1990). Protected and vulnerable: The challenge of AIDS to developmental psychopathology. In J. Rolf, A. S. Masten, K. Cicchetti, K. H. Nuechterlein, & S. Weinstraub (Eds.), *Risk and protective factors in the development of psychopathology* (pp. 384–404). Cambridge: Cambridge University Press.

Romano, L. J., Hubbard, J. A., McAuliffe, M. D., & Morrow, M. T. (2009). Connections between parents' friendships and children's peer relationships. *Journal of Social and Personal Relationships, 26*, 327–339.

Rosenberg, M. (1965). *Society and the adolescent self-image*. Princeton: Princeton University Press.

Rosenberg, M. (1979). *Conceiving the self.* New York: Basic.

Rossman, R. B., Hughes, H. M., & Rosenberg, M. S. (2000). *Children and interparental violence: The impact of exposure.* New York: Psychology Press.

Rossman, B., & Rea, J. (2005). The relation of parenting styles and inconsistencies to adaptive functioning for children in conflictual and violent families. *Journal of Family Violence, 20*(5), 261–277.

Rothbaum, F., & Weisz, J. (1994). Parental converging and child externalizing behavior in non-clinical samples: A meta-analysis. *Psychological Bulletin, 116*, 55–74.

Rounsaville, B. J., Carroll, K. M., & Onken, L. S. (2001). *NIDA's stage model of behavioral therapies research: Getting started and moving on from Stage I Clinical Psychology: Science & Practice, 8*, 133–142.

Rutter, M. (1990). Psychosocial resilience and protective mechanisms. In J. Rolf, A. S. Masten, D. Cicchetti, K. H. Nuechterlein, & S. Weintraub (Eds.), *Risk and protective factors in the development of psychopathology* (pp. 181–214). Cambridge: Cambridge University Press.

Rutter, M. (1999). Resilience concepts and findings: Implications for family therapy. *Journal of Family Therapy, 21*, 119–144.

Rutter, M. (2000). Resilience reconsidered: Conceptual considerations, empirical findings, and policy implications. In J. P. Shonkoff & S. J. Meisels (Eds.), *Handbook of early childhood intervention* (2nd ed., pp. 651–682). New York: Cambridge University Press.

Rutter, M. (2006). *Genes and behavior: Nature-nurture interplay explained.* Oxford: Blackwell.

Rutter, M., Maughan, B., Mortimore, P., Ouston, J., & Smith, A. (1979). *Fifteen thousand hours.* Cambridge: Harvard University.

Sameroff, A. J., Bartko, W. T., Baldwin, A., Baldwin, C., & Seifer, R. (1999). Family and social influences on the development of child competence. In M. Lewis & C. Feiring (Eds.), *Families, risk, and competence* (pp. 161–186). Mahwah: Lawrence Erlbaum.

Sameroff, A. J., Seifer, R., Baldwin, A., & Baldwin, C. (1993). Stability of intelligence from preschool to adolescence: The influence of social and family risk factors. *Child Development, 64*, 80–97.

Sameroff, A. J., Seifer, B., Barocas, M., Zax, M., & Greenspan, S. (1987). IQ scores of 4-years old children: Social environmental risk factors. *Pediatrics, 79*, 343–350.

Sanchez-Villegas, A., Schlatter, J., Ortuno, F., Lahortiga, F., Pla, J., Benito, S., & Martinez-Gonzalez, M. A. (2008). Validity of a self-reported diagnosis of depression among participants in a cohort study using the structured clinical interview for DSM-IV (SCID-I). *BMC Psychiatry, 8*(43), 1–18.

Saunders, J. B., Aasland, O. G., Babor, T. F., de la Fuente, J. R., & Grant, M. (1993). Development of the Alcohol Use Disorders Identification Test (AUDIT): WHO collaborative project on early detection of persons with harmful alcohol consumption. II. *Addiction, 88*, 791–804.

Scarborough, H. S. (1998). Early identification of children at risk for reading disabilities: Phonological awareness and some other promising predictors. In B. K. Shapiro, P. J. Accardo, & A. J. Capute (Eds.), *Specific reading disability: A view of the spectrum* (pp. 75–119). Timonium: York Press.

Scarborough, H. S., & Dobrich, W. (1994). On the efficacy of reading to preschoolers. *Developmental Review, 14*, 245–302.

Schludermann, E., & Schludermann, S. (1970). Replicability of factors in children's report of parent behavior (CRPBI). *The Journal of Psychology, 96*, 15–23.

Schneider, B. H., & Younger, A. (1996). Adolescent-parent attachment and adolescents' relations with their peers: A closer look. *Youth and Society, 28*, 95–108.

Schofield, G., & Beek, M. (2005). Providing a secure base: Parenting children in long-term foster family care. *Attachment and Human Development, 7*(1), 3–25.

Schutz, B. M., Dixon, E. B., Lindenberger, J. C., & Ruther, N. J. (1989). *Solomon's sword: A practical guide to conducting child custody evaluations.* San Francisco: Jossey-Bass.

Segal, D. L., Coolidge, F. L., Cahill, B. S., & O'Riley, A. A. (2008). Psychometric properties of the Beck Depression Inventory-II (BDI-II) among community-dwelling older adults. *Behavior Modification, 32*, 3–20.

Seginer, R., & Vermulst, A. (2002). Family environment, educational aspirations, and academic achievement in two cultural setting. *Journal of Cross-Cultural Psychology, 33*, 540–558.

Seifer, R., Sameroff, A. J., & Jones, F. H. (1981). Adaptive behavior in young children of emotionally disturbed women. *Journal of Applied Developmental Psychology, 1*, 251–276.

Seignourel, P. J., Green, C., & Schmitz, J. M. (2008). Factor structure and diagnostic efficiency of the BDI-II in treatment-seeking substance users. *Drug and Alcohol Dependence, 93*, 271–278.

Selzer, M. L. (1971). The Michigan Alcoholism Screening Test: The quest for a new diagnostic instrument. *American Journal of Psychiatry, 127*, 1653–1658.

Serretti, A., Olgiati, P., & Colombo, C. (2005). Components of self-esteem in affective patients and non-psychiatric controls. *Journal of Affective Disorders, 88*(1), 93–98.

Shaffer, H. R. (1996). *Social development*. Oxford: Blackwell.

Shear, M. K., Greeno, C., Kang, J., Ludewig, D., Frank, E., Swartz, H. A. et al. (2000). Diagnosis of nonpsychotic patients in community clinics. *American Journal of Psychiatry, 157*, 581–587.

Shelton, K. K., Frick, P. J., & Wootton, J. (1996). The assessment of parenting practices in families of elementary school-aged children. *Journal of Clinical Child Psychology, 25*, 317–327.

Sher, K. J., Walitzer, K. S., Wood, P., & Brent, E. E. (1991). Characteristics of children of alcoholics: Putative risk factors, substance use and abuse, and psychopathology. *Journal of Abnormal Psychology, 100*, 427–448.

Sherer, M., Maddux, J. E., Mercandante, B., Prentice-Dunn, S., Jacobs, B., & Rogers, R. W. (1982). The Self-Efficacy Scale: Construction and validation. *Psychological Reports, 51*, 663–671.

Shonkoff, J., & Phillips (2000). *From neurons to neighborhoods: The science of early childhood development*. Washington: National Academy Press.

Shumow, L., & Miller, J. D. (2001). Parents' at-home and at-school academic involvement with young adolescents. *The Journal of Early Adolescence, 21*, 68–91.

Silber, E., & Tippet, J. S. (1965). Self-esteem: Clinical assessment and measurement validation. *Psychological Reports, 16*, 1017–1071.

Silverman, W. K., & Ollendick, T. H. (2005). Evidence-based assessment of anxiety and its disorders in children and adolescents. *Journal of Clinical Child and Adolescent Psychology, 34*(3), 380–411.

Simpkins, S. D., & Parke, R. D. (2002). Do friends and nonfriends behave differently? A social relations analysis of children's behavior. *Merrill-Palmer Quarterly, 48*(3), 263–283.

Skafte, D. (1985). *Child custody evaluations: A practical guide*. New York: Sage.

Skopp, N. A., McDonald, R., Jouriles, E. N., & Rosenfield, D. (2007). Partner aggression and children's externalizing problems: Maternal and partner warmth as protective factors. *Journal of Family Psychology, 21*(3), 459–467.

Solis, M. L., & Abidin, R. R. (1991). The Spanish version Parenting Stress Index: A psychometric study. *Journal of Clinical Child Psychology, 20*, 372–37.

Sorenson, E., Goldman, J., Sheeber, L., Albanese, I., Ward, M., Williamson, L., & McDanal, C. (1997). Judges' reliance on psychological, sociological, and legal variables in contested custody decisions. *Journal of Divorce and Remarriage, 27*(1/2), 1–24.

Spatz, K. C., & Johnston, J. O. (1973). Internal consistency of the Coopersmith Self- Esteem Inventory. *Educational and Psychological Measurement, 33*, 875–876.

Spitzer, R. L., Williams, J. B., Gibbon, M., & First, M. B. (1992). The structured clinical interview for DSM-III-R (SCID) I: History, rationale, and description. *Archives of General Psychiatry, 49*(8), 624–629.

Squires, J., Bricker, D., & Twombly, E. (2002). *The ASQ:SE User's Guide: For the Ages and Stages Questionnaire: Social-emotional*. Baltimore: Paul H. Brookes Publishing.

Squires, J., Potter, L., & Bricker, D. (1995). *The ASQ user's guide for the Ages and Stages Questionnaires: A parent-completed child monitoring system*. Baltimore: Paul H. Brookes Publishing.

Sroufe, L. A. (1997). Psychopathology as an outcome of development. *Development and Psychopathology, 9*, 251–268.

Stahl, P. (2010). Conducting child custody evaluations. New York: Sage.
Stahl, P. M. (1994). *Conducting child custody evaluations: A comprehensive guide*. Newbury: Sage.
Stamps, L. E., Kunen, S., & Rock-Faucheux, A. (1997). Judges' beliefs dealing with child custody decisions. *Journal of Divorce & Remarriage, 28*(1–2), 3–16.
Stanger, C., Dumenci, L., Kamon, J., & Burstein, M. (2004). Parenting and children's externalizing problems in substance-abusing families. *Journal of Clinical Child and Adolescent Psychology, 33*, 590–600.
Steinberg, L. (2001). We know some things: Parent-adolescent relationships in retrospect and prospect. *Journal of Research on Adolescence, 11*, 1–19.
Steinberg, L., Elmen, J., & Mounts, N. (1989). Authoritative parenting, psychosocial maturity, and academic success among adolescents. *Child Development, 60*, 1424–1436.
Steinberg, L., Lamborn, S. D., Dornbusch, S. M., & Darling, N. (1992). Impact of parenting practices on adolescent achievement: Authoritative parenting, school involvement, and encouragement to succeed. *Child Development, 63*, 1266–1281.
Storch, E. A., Roberti, J. W., & Roth, D. A. (2004). Factor structure, concurrent validity, and internal consistency of the Beck Depression Inventory – Second Edition in a sample of college students. *Depression and Anxiety, 19*, 187–189.
Straus, M. A. (1979). Measuring intrafamily conflict and violence: The conflict tactics scales. *Journal of Marriage and the Family, 41*, 75–88.
Straus, M. A. (2004). *Cross cultural reliability and validity of the multidimensonal neglectful behavior scale adult recall short form*. New York: Federal Child Neglect Research Consortium.
Straus, M. A., Hamby, S. L., Boney-McCoy, L., & Sugarman, D. B. (1996). The revised Conflict Tactics Scales (CTS2): Development and preliminary psychometric data. *Journal of Family Issues, 17*, 283–316.
Subkoviak, M. J., Enright, R. D., Wu, C. R., Gassin, E. A., Freedman, S., Olson, L. M., et al. (1995). Measuring interpersonal forgiveness in late adolescence and middle adulthood. *Journal of Adolescence, 18*, 641–655.
Sun, Y. (2001). Family environment and adolescents' well-being before and after parents' marital disruption: A longitudinal analysis. *Journal of Marriage and Family, 63*, 697–713.
Suomi, S. J. (2000). A biobehavioral perspective on developmental psychopathology: Excessive aggression and serotonergic dysfunction in monkeys. In A. J. Sameroff, M. Lewis, & S. Miller (Eds.), *Handbook of developmental psychopathology* (pp. 237–256). New York: Plenum.
Svanum, S., & McGrew, J. (1995). Prospective screening of substance dependence: The advantages of directness. *Addictive Behaviors, 20*, 205–213.
Taub, D. (1997). Autonomy and parental attachment in traditional-age undergraduate women. *Journal of College Student Development, 38*(6), 645–653.
Thomson, E., Hanson, H. L., & McLanahan, S. S. (1994). Family structure and child well-being: Economic resources vs. parental behaviors. *Social Forces, 73*(1), 221–242.
Thornton, A. (1985). Changing attitudes toward separation and divorce: Causes and consequences. *American Journal of Sociology, 90*, 856–872.
Tschann, J. M., Flores, E., Pasch, L. A., & Marin, B. (1999). Assessing interparental conflict: Reports of parents and adolescents in European American and Mexican American families. *Journal of Marriage and the Family, 61*, 269–283.
Ullrich, S., Deasey, D., Smith, J., Johnson, B., Clarke, M., Broughton, N., & Coid, J. (2008). Detecting personality disorders in the prison population of England and Wales: Comparing case identification using the using the SCID-II screen and the SCID-II clinical interview. *The Journal of Forensic Psychiatry and Psychology, 19*(3), 301–322.
Uniform Marriage and Divorce Act. (1979). *9A Uniform Laws Annotated Sec. 316*.
Urquiza, A. J., & McNeil, C. B. (1996). Parent–child interaction therapy: An intensive dyadic intervention for physically abusive families. *Child Maltreatment, 1*, 134–144.
US Census Bureau. (1998). *Marital status and living arrangement*. March 1998 (Updated) Downloaded August 2008 at: http://www.census.gov/prod/99pubs/p20-514.pdf.
Vega, E. M., & O'Leary, K. D. (2007). Test-retest reliability of the revised conflict tactics scale (CTS2). *Journal of Family Violence, 22*, 703–708.

Walker, H. M., Stieber, S., Ramsey, E., & O'Neill, R. E. (1991). Longitudinal prediction of the school achievement, adjustment, and delinquency of antisocial versus at-risk boys. *Remedial and Special Education, 12*(4), 43–51.

Wallace, S. R., & Koerner, S. S. (2003). Influence of child and family factors on judicial decisions in contested custody cases. *Family Relations, 52*, 180–188.

Waller, E. M., & Daniel, A. E. (2004). Purpose and utility of child custody evaluations: From perspective of judges. *The Journal of Psychiatry and Law, 32*, 5–27.

Waller, E. M., & Daniel, A. E. (2005). Purpose and utility of child custody evaluations: The attorney's perspective. *Journal of the American Academy of Psychiatry Law, 33*(2), 199–207.

Wallerstein, J. S., & Kelly, J. B. (1980). Effects of divorce on the visiting father-child relationship. *American Journal of Psychiatry, 137*(12), 1534–1539.

Wallerstein, J. S., & Lewis, J. M. (2004). The unexpected legacy of divorce: Report of a 25-year study. *Psychoanalytic Psychology, 21*(3), 353–370.

Warshak, R. A. (2007). The approximation rule, child development research, and children's best interests after divorce. *Child Development Perspectives, 1*(2), 119–125.

Weissman, M. M., Warner, V., Wickramaratne, P., Moreau, D., & Olfson, M. (1997). Offspring of depressed parents 10 years later. *Archives of General Psychiatry, 54*, 932–940.

Weissman, M. M., Wickramaratne, P., Nomura, Y., Warner, V., Pilowsky, D., & Verdeli, H. (2006). Offspring of depressed parents: 20 years later. *American Journal of Psychiatry, 163*, 1001–1008.

Wesley, Y. (2003). Desire for children among black women with and without HIV infection. *Journal of Nursing Scholarship, 35*(1), 37–43.

White, W. W., & Mika, K. (1983). Family divorce and separation: Theory and research. In H. McCubbin, M. Sussman, & J. Patterson (Eds.), *Social stress and the family: Advances and developments in family stress theory and research* (pp. 175–193). New York: Haworth Press.

Whiteside, M. F., & Becker, B. J. (2000). Parental factors and the young child's postdivorce adjustment: A meta-analysis with implications for parenting arrangements. *Journal of Family Psychology, 14*(1), 5–26.

Willats, B. D. (1993). *Breaking up is easy to do*. Michigan: Michigan Family Forum.

Williams, J. B. W., Gibbon, M., First, M. B., Spitzer, R. L., Davis, M., Borus, J., Howes, M. J., Kane, J., Pope, H. G., Rounsaville, B., & Wittchen, H. (1992). The Structured Clinical Interview for DSM-III-R (SCID) II. Multi-site test-retest reliability. *Archives of General Psychiatry, 49*, 630–636.

Wittgenstein, L. (Ed.). (2009). *Philosophical investigations* (Rev. 4th ed.). Chichester, West Philosophical Investigations. Sussex: Wiley-Blackwell

Wolchik, S. A., Braver, S. L., & Sandler, I. N. (1985). Maternal versus joint custody: Children's postseparation experiences and adjustment. *Journal of Clinical Child Psychology, 14*(1), 5–10.

Wolraich, M. L., Feurer, I., Hannah, J. N., Pinnock, T. Y., & Baumgaertel, A. (1998). Obtaining systematic teacher reports of disruptive behavior disorders utilizing DSM-IV. *Journal of Abnormal Child Psychology, 26*, 141–152.

Wolraich, M. L., Hannah, J. N., Baumgaertel, A., & Feurer, I. (1998). Examination of DSM-V criteria for attention deficit/hyperactivity disorder in a county-wide sample. *Journal of Developmental and Behavioral Pediatrics, 19*, 162–168.

Wood, J. J., Repetti, R. L., & Roesch, S. C. (2004). Divorce and children's adjustment problems at home and school: The role of depressive/withdrawn parenting. *Child Psychiatry and Human Development, 35*(2), 121–142.

Wright, M. O., & Masten, A. S. (2005). Resilience in development: Fostering positive adaptation in the context of adversity. In S. Goldstein & R. B. Brooks (Eds.), *Handbook of resilience in children* (pp. 17–37). New York: Springer.

Xu, Y., Farver, J. M., Chang, L., Zhang, Z., & Yu, L. (2007). Moving away or fitting in? Understanding shyness in Chinese children. *Merrill-Palmer Quarterly, 53*, 527–556.

Zanarini, M. C., & Frankenburg, F. R. (2001). Attainment and maintenance of reliability of axis I and axis II disorders over the course of a longitudinal study. *Comprehensive Psychology, 42*(5), 369–374.

Zanarini, M. C., Skodol, A. E., Bender, D., Dolan, R., Sanislow, C., Schaefer, E., Morey, L. C., Grilo, C. M., Shea, M. T., McGlashan, T. H., & Gunderson, J. G. (2000). The Collaborative Longitudinal Personality Disorders Study: Reliability of axis I and II diagnoses. *Journal of Personality Disorders, 14*(4), 291–9.

Zarrett, N., Lerner, R. M., Carrano, J., Fay, K., Peltz, J. S., & Li, Y. (2008). Variations in adolescent engagement in sports and its influence on positive youth development. In N. L. Holt (Ed.), *Positive youth development through sport* (pp. 9–23). Oxford: Routledge.

Zaslow, M., Weinfield, N. S., Gallagher, M., Hair, E., Ogawa, J., Egeland, B., Tabors, P., & DeTemple, J. (2006). Longitudinal prediction to child outcomes from differing measures of parenting in a low income sample. *Developmental Psychology, 42*, 27–37.

Zimet, G. D., Dahlem, N. W., Zimet, S. G., & Farley, G. K. (1988). The Multidimensional Scale of Perceived Social Support. *Journal of Personality Assessment, 52*, 30–41.

Zimet, G. D., Powell, S. S., Farley, G. K., Werkman, S., & Berkoff, K. A. (1990). Psychometric characteristics of the Multidimensional Scale of Perceived Social Support. *Journal of Personality Assessment, 55*, 610–617.

Zubrick, S., Smith, G., Nicholson, J., Sanson, A. & Jackiewicz, T. (2008). *Social policy research paper number 34, parenting and families in Australia.* Curtin University of Technology, Centre for Developmental Health, Curtin Research Centre.

Index

DOI 10.1007/978-1-4614-3405-4,

MIX
Papier aus verantwortungsvollen Quellen
Paper from responsible sources
FSC® C105338

If you have any concerns about our products,
you can contact us on
ProductSafety@springernature.com

In case Publisher is established outside the EU,
the EU authorized representative is:
Springer Nature Customer Service Center GmbH
Europaplatz 3, 69115 Heidelberg, Germany

Printed by Libri Plureos GmbH
in Hamburg, Germany